Johann Wolfgang von Goethe

Titles in the series Critical Lives present the work of leading cultural figures of the modern period. Each book explores the life of the artist, writer, philosopher or architect in question and relates it to their major works.

In the same series

Johann Wolfgang von Goethe

Jeremy Adler

REAKTION BOOKS

For Katharina Mommsen
Mentor and Friend

Published by
REAKTION BOOKS LTD
Unit 32, Waterside
44–48 Wharf Road
London N1 7UX, UK

www.reaktionbooks.co.uk

First published 2020
Copyright © Jeremy Adler 2020

Printed and bound in India by Replika Press Pvt. Ltd

A catalogue record for this book is available from the British Library

ISBN 978 1 78914 198 6

Contents

Abbreviations

Citations from Goethe's works are provided in the text by references to the following editions. All translations of these works are my own unless otherwise indicated.

Adam	Pierre Loti, *Lettres de Pierre Loti à Madame Juliette Adam, 1880–1922* (Paris, 1924)
CE	*Conversations of Goethe with Eckermann and Soret*, trans. John Oxenford, revd edn (London, 1901)
CW	*Collected Works*, 12 vols (Princeton, NJ, 1995)
FA	*Sämtliche Werke, Frankfurter Ausgabe*, 40 vols (Frankfurt, 1985–2013)
GA	*Werke, Briefe und Gespräche, Gedenkausgabe*, 24 vols (Zurich, 1948–60)
GHB	*Goethe Handbuch*, 4 vols in 5 (Stuttgart, 1996–8)
GLTT	*Goethes Leben von Tag zu Tag*, 6 vols (Zurich, 1982–96)
HA	*Werke, Hamburger Ausgabe*, 14 vols (Munich, 1982)
HAB	*Briefe, Hamburger Ausgabe*, 5 vols (Munich, 1988)
LA	*Die Schriften zur Naturwissenschaft, Leopoldina Ausgabe* (Weimar, 1947–2005)
MA	*Sämtliche Werke, Münchener Ausgabe*, 21 vols in 33 (Munich, 2006)
SP	*Selected Poems*, trans. John Whaley (London, 1998)
WA	*Werke, Weimarer Ausgabe*, 133 vols in 143 (Weimar, 1887–1919)
WED	*West-Eastern Divan*, trans. Martin Bidney (Albany, NY, 2010)

Introduction

Every great culture appears to have one supreme literary exponent. For Greece, this is Homer; for Italy, Dante; for Spain, Cervantes; for England, Shakespeare; for France, Molière; for Russia, Pushkin; and for Germany, Goethe. Though the idea is perhaps not very fashionable today, these are *national* writers: figures who grasp an entire culture and express it in manifold ways. Even among these writers, there is something special about Goethe. Indeed, he so far outshines the majority of his peers in depth and range that he bids to be considered one of the finest artists of all time – along with Michelangelo and Mozart. These figures reimagine human identity. For although it has been argued that Shakespeare invented the human,[1] it would be fairer to say that each of the great national writers created a new way of being human. Their work became the template for the future. Contemporaries regarded them with wonder, as Haydn did Mozart, and for generations mankind has looked back on their accomplishments in gratitude and amazement. Marcel Proust (1871–1922) singled Goethe out as 'the greatest intelligence that ever existed' and his achievement led Friedrich Nietzsche (1844–1900) to call Goethe an 'entire culture'.[2] In recognition of his role, even his epoch has been named after him, the Age of Goethe, to enthrone him like an emperor as its most representative figure. No wonder that Napoleon made a point of meeting him during the Conference of Erfurt in 1808, greeting him with the words 'Voilà, un homme!' Goethe's artistic renown probably equalled the emperor's political prestige.[3] Such a major writer does not just shape his own age. Thomas Mann (1875–1955) praised him as the representative figure of the whole bourgeois era, and never ceased to revisit Goethe's creations.[4]

German politics also looks back to Goethe. The country's first successful democracy, the so-called Weimar Republic, was convened at Weimar after the First World War on 11 August 1919. The place was largely chosen because of its practical location, but also perhaps in honour of Goethe and Schiller. Goethe was closely associated with the ideals of the Republic. Brave intellectuals such as Wolfgang Frommel (1902–1986), Ernst Robert Curtius (1886–1956)[5] and Thomas Mann[6] invoked him in the struggle against Nazism. Taking up their views, at the festivities for the anniversary of the Constitution on 11 August 1932 (shortly before the centenary of Goethe's death), the journalist Werner Thormann (1894–1947) held a combative speech in which he recalled how Goethe's ethos had actually inspired the founding document of the Weimar Constitution.[7] Although it was once thought that the Nazis had little use for Goethe, it now seems that the Third Reich did indeed try to pervert his views for political ends, if not on a grand scale.[8] After the Second World War, however, leading public intellectuals, such as the philosopher Karl Jaspers (1883–1969),[9] the classicist Wolfgang Schadewaldt (1900–1974) and the politician Carlo Schmid (1896–1974),[10] rejected this misappropriation outright and returned to Goethe's authentic views. They sought to implement his beliefs – one thinks of liberty and self-culture, tolerance and sociality – in order to overcome the ideology of the Third Reich. His religion of humanity served to lend a positive direction to the new German polity, not least by helping to shape the German Basic Law.[11] Although he himself was politically conservative – even reactionary – there can be little doubt about the contribution of Goethe's cosmopolitan humanism to the modern liberal state.

Modernity defines its modes of thinking and feeling in relation to his innovations. Vasari's claim for Michelangelo might well have been made for Goethe: that here was a 'genius universal in each art . . . endowed . . . with true moral philosophy and a sweet poetic spirit'.[12] Although such eulogies have often been bestowed on Goethe, as soon as one tries to define his qualities, especially to a native English speaker, they seem to melt away.

Goethe's language, so vital to his achievement, is hard to translate; his ideas, for all their originality, seem to vanish in the air; his literary gifts, so apparent in his own words, seem to reject transplantation; and his scientific ideas, so new and brilliant, appear wrong-headed to the English temper. Even his wisdom – and there is much – often strikes an English sensibility as trite. Nonetheless, the list of English writers who admired Goethe is considerable. William Makepeace Thackeray (1811–1863) visited him in Weimar and Thomas Carlyle (1795–1881) befriended the ageing master; among the Romantics, both Wordsworth (1770–1850) and Coleridge (1772–1834), Byron (1788–1824) and Shelley (1792–1822) paid homage to him; in the great tradition of novelists from Charles Dickens (1812–1870) and George Eliot (1819–1880) to Henry James (1844–1916) and D. H. Lawrence (1885–1930), Goethe's role proved pivotal, not least as the author of the pre-eminent *Bildungsroman*; and James Joyce's *Finnegans Wake* (1939) recognizes his place among the giants with 'Daunty, Gouty and Shopkeeper' – a series of puns on the names of Dante, Goethe and Shakespeare. Goethe's autobiography and the book it inspired, G. H. Lewes's *The Life of Goethe* (1855), shaped the new genre of biography as we know it today, combining history with empathy, and facticity with imaginative recreation. Literary criticism also imbibed his principles, from Matthew Arnold (1822–1888) and Walter Pater (1839–1894) to F. R. Leavis (1895–1978) – who neither knew nor cared about his debt to Goethe – and implemented his aesthetic programme, notably his valuation of 'life'.

Few have risked so much. None has achieved such a range. True, one English poet harped on Goethe's 'perilous multiplicity', but this seems to me misguided.[13] If ever a writer extended his talent with ease, it was Goethe, who could occupy himself with many different fields in a single day, including administration and science, or poetry and philosophy. Goethe knew how to live and how to love, how to maximize life, but also – as only few have done, among them Confucius and Montaigne – how to transmit wisdom. He belongs to that select band who not only invite admiration but instil adulation.

Among the accolades was that by Arnold:

> Goethe is the greatest poet of modern times, not because he
> is one of the half-dozen human beings who in the history
> of our race have shown the most signal gift for poetry,
> but because, having a very considerable gift for poetry, he
> was at the same time, in the width, depth, and richness of
> his criticism of life, by far our greatest modern man.[14]

Goethe conducted his labours in a constant dialogue with other figures – poets, artists, philosophers, sages and statesmen. He wished that Mozart had set his *Faust* to music. The Homeric epics prompted him to write his own more modest poem, the bourgeois epic *Hermann and Dorothea* (*Hermann und Dorothea*; 1797). The Latin love poets suggested his *Roman Elegies* (*Erotica Romana*; 1795). The Persian poet Hafiz (1315–1390) inspired his *West-Eastern Divan* (*West-Östlicher Divan*; 1819). Plotinus taught him how to imagine perception. Spinoza constituted his lodestar, from the early writings to his late, reflective poetry: apart from his pantheism, Goethe respected Spinoza's humanity and uprightness, his selflessness (*GHB*, 4/2, 1,001ff.). Leonardo showed him how a multifaceted genius might operate. Likewise Michelangelo. On viewing the Sistine Chapel, Goethe achieved a sense of what 'one man' could accomplish, and henceforth the Florentine master provided a model for his own productivity. And Rembrandt preoccupied him throughout his career. Among the scientists, he owed most to Linnaeus, whom he places straight after Shakespeare and Spinoza in his pantheon (*LA*, 1/9, 16). But it was Immanuel Kant (1724–1804) who taught him how to think: to read Kant, he once told Arthur Schopenhauer (1788–1860), is like entering a brightly lit room.[15]

Yet if there was one figure who accompanied him throughout his career, from his beginnings as a dramatist into mature old age, it was Shakespeare. In his early manifesto, the effusive speech that he wrote following Garrick's Jubilee celebrations of 1769, *On Shakespeare's Birthday* (*Zum Shakespeares-Tag*; 1771), Goethe celebrates the Swan of Avon. He calls his theatre a 'cabinet of curiosities' (*Raritätenkasten*) in which 'the history of the world wanders past our eyes dancing on invisible threads' (*HA*, XII, 224ff.). This vision of plenitude certainly captures Shakespeare's creativity. Goethe's appreciation of Shakespeare recalls David Hume's definition of the mind as 'a kind of theatre': for Goethe, the English dramatist depicts both the empirical outer world and an inner, psychological reality.[16] The view infused Goethe's first drama and opened the way to his *Faust*, which leads 'from Heaven through the World to Hell' in a spectacular trajectory. To honour Shakespeare, the interlocutor in Goethe's first novel *The Sorrows of Young Werther* (*Die Leiden des jungen Werthers*; 1774) is called Wilhelm. Similarly, the hero of his second novel is called Wilhelm Meister. This homage offers just a hint of the goal to which Goethe aspires. Then, over forty years after the first, spirited speech, the reflective 'Shakespeare Without End' ('Shakespeare und kein Ende'; 1813–16) gives a more philosophical summation of Shakespeare's art. Here Goethe offers a mirror of his own self:

> The highest point to which a human being may ascend is the consciousness of his own opinions and ideas, the knowledge

of himself, which provides him with the insight to know other kinds of spirit most intimately. Now, there are people who are born with this natural ability and who know how to educate others by means of experience for practical ends. By this means the ability emerges to acquire something in a higher sense from the world and one's activities. The poet is also born with this talent, but with the difference that he does not develop it for this immediate, earthly purpose, but for a higher, spiritual, general purpose. Now if we call Shakespeare one of the greatest poets, we also recognize at one and the same time that no-one will easily perceive the world as he did, and that no-one who expresses his inner vision transports the reader into a consciousness of the world to a higher degree. It becomes completely transparent for us . . . (*HA*, XII, 287–8)

Goethe's mature response to Shakespeare both places him among the immortal writers and elevates him to the rank of the sages.

Goethe also frequently revisits the wisdom of the ancients, notably the motto 'know thyself' (*gnothi seauton*) on the Temple of Apollo at Delphi. The maxim appears in several of Plato's dialogues, including the *Phaedrus*, where Socrates uses it to repudiate obscurities: 'I have no leisure for them at all; and the reason, my friend, is this: I am not yet able, as the Delphic inscription has it, to know myself; so it seems to me ridiculous, when I do not yet know that, to investigate irrelevant things' (*Phaedrus*, 229E). Goethe repeatedly worries at this apothegm. He rejects its teaching in favour of outer reality: 'I must confess that I have long been suspicious of the grand and pompous maxim to "know thyself". The human being only knows himself insofar as he knows the world.' (*CW*, XII, 39) By reversing the ancient dictum Goethe tacitly establishes a new motto for the Enlightenment (*CW*, XII, 39). This could be formulated as 'know the world'. The maxim is more pragmatic, more attainable, than Kant's motto for the age, 'sapere aude' – dare to know.[17]

By pursuing science and experimentation in relation to the observer, and not some abstract principle, Goethe validates Western humanity: art and science form part of a single whole. With thinkers such as John Stuart Mill (1806–1873) and A. N. Whitehead (1861–1947) this holism entered the intellectual mainstream. Goethe's organic view of life entails the development, or *Bildung*, of the individual. The quiddity of things is integral to this vision. Nature is his watchword – often to the exclusion of social norms. Thus even as an establishment figure, Goethe remained a nonconformist and never ceased to scandalize his contemporaries. He embraced contradiction. Now an idealist; now a rationalist; now an empiricist (*FA*, 1/10, 754, 760); he grasped at totality. An almost pre-Socratic directness shapes his sensibility, lending it a lofty, timeless quality; and the fusion of poetry with philosophy, the linking of disciplines, enriches his vision with a manifold and practical intelligence. When, for instance, he discusses Giambattista Vico (1668–1774), the father of the philosophy of history,[18] he fuses sagacity with factuality; and when he summarizes his own wisdom in the poem 'Primal Words, Orphic' ('Urworte. Orphisch'; 1817) (*SP*, 122), he delves into the origins of philosophy, recapitulating its most obscure doctrines. Thus he enunciates the laws that govern life. His vision culminates in 'Hope': 'She lifts us up, to soar on wings elated.' (*SP*, 125) In this way Goethe refines his sensibility in the best humanistic tradition.

Simply to list Goethe's activities invites admiration, even awe. It seems, with hindsight, as if he had set out to master every field, except mathematics, which never appealed to him. In each he sought perfection. Given the systematic nature of his explorations, it looks as if his encyclopaedism was planned. In each area, we find completion. In the drama, he variously wrote in the crude style of the reformation poet Hans Sachs (1494–1576), in a Shakespearean manner, or that of the Greeks. What could be called Goethe's progressive assimilation of the world is most obvious in his poetry.

He delved into various cultures from as far afield as Persia (now Iran) and China for his models and assimilated examples from every historical epoch – from antiquity to the middle ages and the Baroque. In so doing he employed almost every known form from the epigram to the epic, but also developed a signal innovation: the 'poetry of experience' or *Erlebnislyrik*. The individual is the measure of all things: his knowledge is grounded in the 'heart'. It is this vibrant subjectivism that centres Goethe's fecundity.

The list of his roles is dizzying. They include poet, dramatist, novelist, short-story writer, essayist, aphorist, literary critic, art critic, cultural critic, biographer, autobiographical writer, diarist, letter writer, translator, editor, philosopher, scientist, artist, collector, theatre director, administrator and statesman. Individual roles also comprise a multitude: as administrator, for example, Goethe served as an inspector of mines and oversaw the roads and waterways in Weimar, but he also supervised cultural institutions like the University of Jena, and helped to make this one of the most vital contemporary seats of learning. As a scientist, he did basic research in mineralogy, geology, botany, anatomy – that is, all three kingdoms of nature as classically conceived – as well as colour theory. As a draughtsman he produced some excellent drawings and watercolours. In his assignment as Theatre Director of Weimar for many years he himself acted, selected the repertoire, directed the plays and rehearsed the actors. Finally, as an administrator, he sat on the Privy Council, took decisions in all the multifarious matters of state, and eventually crowned his political career by becoming a minister. Even such a summary confirms Goethe's status as a polymath.

It comes as no surprise that Goethe is known wistfully as the last Renaissance Man. As with these artists, his restless curiosity infuses his works with a unique depth, but updates their views by a more modern concern with nature and society, such as political liberty and cosmopolitanism. Yet perhaps a word of qualification is in order to quell this hero-worship. Heinrich Heine (1797–1856) seasoned his praise of Goethe as a mirror of nature with a damning portmanteau word, calling him a *Zeitablehnungsgenie* – a genius who denies his epoch.[19] Other major writers were also sceptical. Franz Kafka (1883–1924), who adored him, wryly planned an essay on 'Goethe's Terrible Nature'.[20] And in a scintillating review, Bernard Levin (1928–2004), our last all-round journalist, somewhat mischievously observed: 'I can think of only one other man who could match Goethe in so enormously successful an exercise in self-making' – Voltaire; and 'I am by no means sure that Goethe would have been pleased' by the comparison.[21] Levin intimates that Goethe's self-creation may have been a tad cynical. Yet such criticisms do not seem to touch him. Indeed, even today, a spirited but sceptical British writer such as Ferdinand Mount treats Goethe as a kind of literary superman.[22]

In this connection it is worth quoting from the historian Jacob Burckhardt (1818–1897), who first fully defined the historical epoch of the Renaissance. Goethe is a perfect example of Burckhardt's 'Renaissance man',[23] displaying a 'harmonious development' and thereby becoming 'all-sided' – 'l'uomo universale'. Such a figure possesses 'encyclopaedic knowledge'. Although today we would regard this as a definition of Goethe, Burkhardt's example is Dante. If we look at the *Divine Comedy*, 'we find that in the whole spiritual or physical world there is hardly an important subject which the poet has not fathomed'.[24] The view also defines Goethe's *Faust*. Burkhardt's characterization of Renaissance man counts as the key modern definition of that epoch. Yet almost a century before, Goethe anticipated his thesis. It is fair to say that Goethe invented the modern concept of the Renaissance. This is typical of the way he creates tradition.

Exactly how the Renaissance style impacted on Goethe would be a complex matter to analyse: his experience of court life, his voracious reading, his reception of humanist culture, his immersion in fine art and above all his extended trip to Italy, all played a part in fashioning a world-view in which the rounded human being perceives him or herself as living at the centre of creation. He or she both mirrors, imitates and perfects the world. In presenting this view at the height of the German Enlightenment, Goethe laid the foundations for modern German literature – with an influence that extended up to Kafka, Mann and Grass – and also for the use of the German language. It was Martin Luther whose Bible translation at the beginning of the Reformation first shaped the modern German language. Goethe gave it a new flexibility and polish.

It is this multifaceted individual, as practical as he was visionary, as sensual as he was spiritual, as earthy as he was elevated and as homespun as he was sophisticated, that this book seeks to understand. Since he was first and foremost a poet, Goethe's poetry will provide what Goethe himself would have called a 'red thread' through the narrative, as we range far and wide through his ideas. Lest we take matters too seriously, it is worth recalling that he had a wicked sense of humour, too, with an occasional penchant for self-mockery. Take this piece of light verse:

> *Vom Vater hab' ich die Statur,*
> *Des Lebens ernstes Führen,*
> *Von Mütterchen die Frohnatur*
> *Und Lust zu fabulieren.*
> *Urahnherr war der Schönsten hold,*
> *Das spukt so hin und wieder,*
> *Urahnfrau liebte Schmuck und Gold,*
> *Das zuckt wohl durch die Glieder.*
> *Sind nun die Elemente nicht*
> *Aus dem Komplex zu trennen,*
> *Was ist denn an dem ganzen Wicht*
> *Original zu nennen?* (*FA*, 1/2, 682)

16

The poem has been charmingly translated by the late John Whaley:

My stature is my Father's part,
Life's earnest from the cradle;
From Mother I've my sunny heart
And fancy for a fable.
Great-grandpa had an eye for girls,
At times in me it itches;
Great-grandma fancied gold and pearls,
An urge all through for riches.
These parts make up a man like me
And can't be separated,
So where's originality
In what a chap's created? (*SP*, 119)

Goethe's poetry exhibits a unique fluidity, as here, where the phrasing, the syntax, the rhythms and the rhymes lull the reader into genial appreciation. He is, incidentally, a master of minute imperfections which always creates a spark of authenticity. Every line becomes a surprise. He does not just sing. He inspires. To read his poetry is to be invigorated. To become more alive. That is his magic: his capacity to communicate feelings and ideas in a tactile, sensuous way, and so to actively educate his public just as much as he informs with his vision. By absorbing the world as he experienced it, Goethe became a world poet, and in later years found the unique formula for this attainment: 'world literature'.

Throughout my introduction I have been arguing for Goethe's originality, and this was certainly not a point he despised; but in the little poem on his ancestry he mocks the very idea. As ever with Goethe, just when you believe that you have grasped him, or pigeon-holed an opinion, the opposite viewpoint rears up and refutes one's tidy beliefs. Loftiest of poets, he can at a venture descend into the absurd. Along with Keats, he is a 'chameleon poet'; he even pre-empted this tag of Keats's, having used it of himself in a letter at the age of fourteen.[25] Goethe, then, is not to be grasped. He is as changeable as the elements, now erupting like fire, now wafting like the evening air, now like the rippling waves, now thoroughly down-to-earth. As a critical biographer, one can accordingly at best assay the land; attempt again what others have done before; build on the best studies; and whenever possible try to offer new readings. In this spirit, I will consider Goethe's best-known poem in the light of Hinduism; examine his second major play, *Egmont* (1789), on the dawn of the Dutch Golden Age in light of Spinoza and Rembrandt; argue that his much-maligned colour theory is in fact correct, having been confirmed experimentally by Edwin Land (1909–1991); show the reflections of the Industrial Revolution in his last novel, *Wilhelm Meister's Travels* (*Wilhelm Meisters Wanderjahre*), which converges with the views of Robert Owen (1771–1858); and touch on the importance of Adam Smith's (1723–1790) political economy for *Faust II*.

Just as Goethe absorbed influences from every sphere, he had a ramified impact on countless areas. Throughout this book I have taken pains to show the effect of Goethe's thinking in many of these different fields. Even in psychology, Goethe was influential: Sigmund Freud (1856–1939) regarded him as seminal for his development.[26] In the life sciences he influenced not only Darwin's idea of evolution but Agnes Arber's (1879–1960) botanical theories and, more surprisingly, Alan Turing's (1912–1954) concept of morphogenesis. German-speaking physicists from Ludwig Boltzmann (1844–1906) and Ernst Mach (1838–1916) to Werner Heisenberg (1901–1976) studied Goethe's works, too, but his most significant role was in the thought of Albert Einstein (1879–1955).[27] The importance of German culture for Einstein's thought has only recently become apparent. He owned two editions of Goethe's collected works as well as a separate edition of the colour theory, and kept a bust of the poet in his study in

Princeton: indeed, it has been argued that Goethe's monism had a profound impact on Einstein's own, Faustian, quest for the 'unity' of nature.

In philosophy, Goethe proved especially influential for thinkers such as Nietzsche and Ludwig Wittgenstein (1889–1951) as well as for the modern revaluation of feeling as a mode of thought, notably in the work of Susanne Langer (1895–1985), Susan Sontag (1933–2004) and Martha Nussbaum (1947–). Then, to pick out just one more field, he was equally inspiring for the classical sociologists Herbert Spencer (1820–1903), Émile Durkheim (1858–1917), Georg Simmel (1858–1918) and Max Weber (1864–1920). He adumbrated Spencer's concept of an organic society, Weber's idea of an 'ideal type' (which derives from Goethe's 'archetypal phenomenon' (*Urphänomen*) and Simmel's schema of 'social circles'. No less striking was his importance for Durkheim's 'social morphology'. If Durkheim's method departed from Goethe, major facets of the latter's project can still be noted in the great French tradition of 'social morphology' represented by the pioneering thinkers Marcel Mauss (1872–1950) and Maurice Halbwachs (1877–1945).[28] If one were to single out a further feature – setting aside his view of nature and of the individual subject – to pinpoint the quintessence of his achievement, one might say that the Goethean turn is chiefly defined by the rejection of allegory and the introduction of symbolism. By this means Goethe accomplished an epochal change. His view became widespread, initially via the German Romantics and its adoption in poetry by Charles Baudelaire (1821–1867), yet no less significantly, if rather later, in Ernst Cassirer's (1874–1945) 'philosophy of symbolic forms':[29] the world is filled with inter-reflecting symbols; every existing being reflects and illuminates every other. By this theory Goethe expands G. W. Leibniz's (1646–1716) view of the 'monad' (a kind of atom mirroring the world) to include every natural or artistically created body. Typically, when he summed up his wisdom at the end of *Faust II*, it was to maintain that 'Everything that transpires/ Is but a symbol' (*HA*, I, 364).

A centrepiece of this book is the rehabilitation of the colour theory. Goethe believed that this was his most important work. As he told Eckermann on 19 February 1829: 'I don't take a pride in everything that I have achieved as a poet . . . But that I am the only person in my century who saw the truth in the difficult science of colour is a fact that fills me with satisfaction.' (*GHB*, IV, 740) It is customary to ridicule this statement as delusionary; but it is the job of scholarship to understand, not to mock. I shall therefore try to understand Goethe's position in relation to his times as well as to modern science. He does indeed create a new, non-mathematical, human science, whose urgency cannot be gainsaid, leastwise in this age of technological overkill and the natural destruction of species – perhaps including our own. As with so much of his work, Goethe's science is an exercise in danger limitation. It is a matter for celebration that building on Hippocrates (*c*. 460–370 BCE) and Aristotle (*c*. 384–322 BCE), Paracelsus (1493/4–1541) and Francis Bacon (1561–1626), he founded an innovative, humanistic science.

As can be seen, the richness and variety of Goethe's thought – especially his organicism – has inspired followers in very different areas, who transposed his ideas into their spheres, and thereby achieved an innovative cultural transfer. His morphology proved especially influential. Thus, for example, his work in this area may even have furnished a model for Karl Marx (1818–1883), one of his most devoted readers,[30] who in all likelihood introduced Goethe's scientific notion of 'metamorphosis' to economics in the first volume of *Capital* (1867): it is mirrored here as the 'transformation of capital into surplus-value'. What makes Goethe's work so very useful are his first-order concepts: unifying terms like 'polarity' or 'morphology', 'metamorphosis' or the 'archetypal phenomenon', which he either invented or reformulated, are not limited to a single specialism but can be implemented in any field. Hence if Goethe was not a professional philosopher, scientist or sociologist, let alone a political economist, his use of new foundational concepts, usually in the form of generative ideas, lends his findings an exceptional interest. Innumerable writers and thinkers have been touched by this achievement. His impact can still be felt across the disciplines, not least in linguistics: the philologist August Schleicher, who was steeped in German culture, created the concept of 'linguistic morphology' in 1869, and it is now a central field in linguistics.[31] Indeed, the humanities in general as well as musicology and art history in particular continue to adapt this Goethean model;[32] and one of the great texts of Russian formalism, Vladimir Propp's *Morphology of the Folktale* (1928), adapted Goethe's paradigm in order to re-orientate poetics.[33] Goethe's idea of genetic form subsequently became key for Structuralism, notably through the writings of Propp's brilliant French admirers, Claude Lévi-Strauss (1908–2009) and Roland Barthes (1915–1980). From literature to politics, and from philosophy to science, Goethe has left a profound mark on today's world. Through his impact on such makers of modernity as Nietzsche and Freud, Darwin and Weber, or Marx and Einstein, his innovations have evolved into countless new forms and taken root in various different circles and cultures. Indeed, it is fair to say that Goethe has gone global: yet if his place in world literature is well-attested, it has not, I think, been sufficiently recognized how decisively he helped to shape the course of modern civilization.

I have included an exceptionally large number of references in the text in the hope that readers will be able to follow up any aspect of my argument and find a ready access to the critical literature. Wherever possible, I have tried to give sources written in English, as there are a very large number of English-language critical works, to which I am grateful, and happily acknowledge my debt.

If this short book can serve to shed a little light on some aspects of Goethe's achievements, to win him new friends, to encourage others to engage with his works – since to read Goethe is always to be invited to think and feel anew – it will have served its purpose as a cultural biography of Europe's supreme polymath.

1

The Birth of a Poet

Johann Wolfgang Goethe was born in the prosperous city of
Frankfurt on 28 August 1749. With its population of about 36,000,
Frankfurt was a thriving commercial centre on the River Main.
It was ruled by patricians and enjoyed a flourishing cultural
scene. Apart from the predominant Lutherans, there were also
substantial Catholic and Calvinist minorities, and a small Jewish
ghetto containing two hundred houses and a synagogue, which
the young Goethe visited with particular interest. The walls,
bastions and watchtowers preserved the medieval spirit; four
major churches, one cathedral and a host of timber-framed houses
lent it an antiquarian style. Its profitable trades included banking
and textiles, wine – from the local vineyards – metal, dye-stuffs
and porcelain.[1] This wealthy polity boasted eight millionaires.
The citizens were outward looking and cosmopolitan, an attitude
Goethe himself epitomized. It was a Free Imperial City of the Holy
Roman Empire, which gave it quasi-republican status. It also had
the symbolic honour of providing the seat where the Holy Roman
Emperor was crowned prior to his official coronation at Aachen.
Just before Goethe's birth, the emperor Charles vii had used it as
his official residence, and in 1764 Joseph ii was formally elected
and crowned in Frankfurt, an event witnessed by the fourteen-
year-old Goethe. He describes the ceremony in his autobiography,
Poetry and Truth (*Dichtung und Wahrheit*; 1811–33). Among the city's
commercial activities, the book trade occupied an important place.

The art of printing invented in nearby Mainz had migrated here. Frankfurt had hosted the most important German book fair in the sixteenth and seventeenth centuries but ceded this role to Leipzig in 1750; yet it remained a major focus for printing and publishing. Above all, though, it was as a banking centre, positioned at the crossroads of several major trading routes, that Frankfurt enjoyed a privileged place in Europe. Such was its wealth that in 1779 it even made a vast loan to the emperor.

Goethe was born at the height of the German Enlightenment.[2] Its ideas were formed by the polymath Leibniz,[3] who established the rationalist philosophy in Germany in his *New Essays on Human Understanding* (1704). Here he rebuts Locke's empiricism. Leibniz grounded the optimism of the age in his *Theodicy* (1710), which seeks to vindicate God's existence in light of the problem of evil.[4] The argument hinges on Leibniz's belief in 'the best of all possible worlds', which does not, as it is often taken to mean, claim that this was the best of all worlds, but that out of all the worlds that were theoretically possible – and that includes some truly dreadful ones – God chose the best. These views were popularized by the prolific Christian Wolff (1679–1754), who gave the final stamp to German rationalism. The best-known redaction of optimism, Alexander Pope's *Essay on Man* (1734), also appeared in German in 1756. It formed part of Goethe's early reading. Here Pope explains the character of the world order. This is composed of infinite interlocking parts, which establish a universal harmony:

> The general ORDER, since the whole began,
> Is kept in Nature, and is kept in Man.
> . . .
> All are but parts of one stupendous whole,
> Whose body Nature is, and God the soul;
> . . .

Anton Johann Kern, *Johann Wolfgang Goethe*, 1765, oil painting.

All nature is but Art, unknown to thee;
All Chance, Direction, which thou canst not see;
All Discord, Harmony, not understood;
All partial Evil, universal Good:
And, spite of Pride, in erring Reason's spite,
One truth is clear, 'Whatever is, is RIGHT.'[5]

Pope's chiastic apothegm, so frequently cited, proved to be the motto for the era. Only a catastrophe of huge dimensions, such as erupted years later, could shake this intellectual premise: for it was as noble as a credo as it was effective as an explanation. This positive temper provided the context for Goethe's belief in a well-ordered universe, and underwrote his poetry, his science and indeed his entire *Weltanschauung* of a man-centred world.

One of Goethe's first biographers, the founder of modern literary biography G. H. Lewes, remarks how 'in the soft round lineaments of childhood we trace the features which after years will develop into more decided forms.'[6] This holds especially for Goethe's immersion in all aspects of culture. His autobiography recalls his childhood discovery of the traditional chap-books, such as *Fortunatus* (1509) and *Till Eulenspiegel* (1515), which he acquired for a few kreutzers. Most emphatically, however, it applies to his encounter with Mozart. On 18 August 1763 he attended a concert where the seven-year-old composer performed with his elder sister, Nannerl, at which the celebrated *Wunderkind*'s 'extraordinary talent' became apparent. Mozart's father has left us a brief account of the series of concerts in Frankfurt: 'our concert . . . *was good* . . . Everyone was amazed! May God give us the grace, praises be to God, to remain healthy, and to be admired everywhere. Wolfgang is quite extraordinarily jolly, but also naughty.'[7] Mozart played the piano and the violin and improvised on the organ. Years later, Goethe still recalled the event: 'I saw Mozart as a seven year old boy . . . I was fourteen years old, and I can clearly remember the little man in his wig and with a sword.' (*CE*, 3 February 1830, 431) Thus we can imagine the curious near-encounter of the two most notable artists German culture has produced. To form an opinion of the playing, one might listen to Mozart's allegro in C major for keyboard K. 9a/5a composed that summer. Although Goethe himself learned music, too, studying the piano and later the cello, he never attained proficiency and rated himself a poor musician.

In later years he praised the power of Mozart's Singspiel, *The Abduction from the Seraglio* (*Die Entführung aus dem Serail*; 1782), and even wrote a fragmentary libretto to *The Second Part of the Magic Flute* (*The Magic Flute, Der Zauberflöte zweiter Teil*; 1802–7). So high was Goethe's esteem for Mozart that he regarded him as the only possible composer for his *Faust*. Despite his own poor playing, music remained essential to Goethe's life. In 1820, in conversation with Joseph Pleyer, he remarked: 'Whoever does not love music is not a human being, whoever only loves it, is half a human being, but whoever pursues it is a complete human being.' (*GA*, III/1, 560) It is perhaps not coincidental that Goethe formed one of his closest friendships with a musician, the composer Carl Friedrich Zelter (1758–1832); their absorbing correspondence touches on many themes, and most especially on points of music theory.

Goethe's father, Johann Caspar Goethe (1710–1782), was a lawyer. After practising for a while he travelled in Italy and wrote a book, *Viaggio per l'Italia* (A Journey Through Italy, *c*. 1765). The episode proved of lasting importance for Goethe, who later followed in his father's footsteps. Prevented from pursuing a political career in the town council for personal reasons, Johann Caspar purchased an honorific title, 'True Imperial Councillor', and, being able to live from his investments, retired from public life. On 28 August 1748 he married Catharina Elisabeth Textor (1731–1808). Goethe was to enjoy a particularly close relationship to his mother, who was ever a shrewd and affectionate parent to him. A year after Goethe's birth his sister, Cornelia, was born on 7 December 1750. Johann Caspar devoted himself to collecting books and works of art and educating his children. After the death of his mother on 1 April 1754, Goethe's father rebuilt his two houses on the Großer Hirschgraben into an imposing building on four floors with twenty rooms and an impressive staircase. Though the house did not survive the Second World War, it was faithfully rebuilt, and today serves as a fine museum. A new Museum of Romanticism has recently been erected

Goethe's father, 1767.   Goethe's mother, 1767.

next door. For anyone wishing to recapture the atmosphere of
Goethe's era, these museums have much to commend them. But
privilege for the young Goethe did not necessarily mean security.
In 1759, during the Seven Years War, the French commandant
François de Théas, comte de Thorenc was billeted in the family
home. This was not only stressful for the family, but dangerous. On
one occasion Johann Caspar roundly cursed the French troops. His
misconduct almost landed him in prison.

The event that most affected the young Goethe, if we are to
believe *Poetry and Truth*, was the Lisbon earthquake of 1 November
1755.[8] Between 10,000 and 100,000 people lost their lives.[9] This
horrific event changed the intellectual climate of the age. The
earthquake was seen to constitute absolute evil. The chief issue it
raised was the question of God's existence. Voltaire's 'Poème sur
le désastre de Lisbonne' (A Poem on the Lisbon Disaster; or, An
Enquiry into the Axiom 'All is Well'; 1755) rebukes Pope's optimistic
dictum 'whatever is, is right' and claims 'Nature is silent, we appeal
to her in vain – only a god can speak to humanity.'[10] Jean-Jacques
Rousseau responded to Voltaire by asserting Nature's innocence,[11]

to which Voltaire then replied scathingly in *Candide* (1759).[12] The disaster continued to trouble thinkers down to the twentieth century. Among the modern critics to have been preoccupied with the event is Walter Benjamin.[13] As Theodor Adorno later argued in his celebrated chapter 'After Auschwitz' in *Negative Dialectics* (1966), the Lisbon earthquake affected the epoch much as the Holocaust shaped our own self-understanding: 'Our metaphysical faculty is paralyzed because actual events have shattered the basis on which speculative thought could be reconciled with experience.'[14] The earthquake destroyed the certainties of the Enlightenment, undermined its optimism and introduced the philosophical pessimism of the modern age. In *Poetry and Truth*, basing himself on contemporary accounts, Goethe represents himself aged just six as a witness of the catastrophe:

> [my] tranquillity of mind was deeply shaken for the first time by an extraordinary event. On first November, 1755 occurred the great earthquake of Lisbon, spreading enormous terror to a world accustomed to peace and quiet. A large, splendid city, both a port and a trade centre, is hit without warning by the most fearful calamity. The earth quivers and rocks, the sea rages, ships collide, houses collapse, churches and towers fall on top of them, the royal palace is partly swallowed up by the sea, and the severed earth seems to spit flames, for everywhere the ruins start to smoke and burn. Sixty thousand human beings, who were calm and content just a moment before, perish together, and the happiest man among them is he who had no time to feel or consider his misfortune. The flames rage on, and with them rages a mob of criminals, now coming out into the open, or perhaps set free by the disaster. The unfortunate survivors are exposed to robbery, murder, and every possible mistreatment; and so nature on every hand asserts her arbitrary will. (*CW*, IV, 35)

Goethe's vivid description, which is historically correct down to such events as the tsunami, reveals the mastery he later attained as a writer, here employed in the service of a childhood impression. Benjamin believes that the disaster prompted Kant's interest in seismology, and it may be that it also contributed to Goethe's preoccupation with the earth, in which he takes a line compatible with Leibniz's geology in his *Protogaea*, written between 1691 and 1693, and first published in 1749.[15] Leibniz does not believe that 'there is chaos' at work when, for example, 'Vesuvius erupts', but that 'anyone who had sense organs penetrating enough to perceive the smallest part of things would find everything organized.'[16] In the spirit of Leibniz Goethe later adopted a meaningful, non-catastrophic theory of the earth, marked by a gradualist, continuous genesis. The terrible interaction between the natural disaster and the human sphere fills out his narration of the earthquake and details the most fearful consequences – the collapse of the human order. Indeed, at the top of the Great Chain of Being, even the metaphysical order appears to disintegrate under the impact.[17] As Goethe writes in *Poetry and Truth*:

> Hereupon God-fearing persons were moved to wise observations, philosophers offered consoling arguments, and clergymen preached fiery sermons. So much happening at once drew the world's attention for a while to this one spot . . .
>
> I was more than a little disconcerted . . . in my boyish mind. God, the Creator and Preserver of heaven and earth, who had been represented to me as so very wise and merciful in the first article of the Creed, had shown Himself by no means fatherly when He abandoned both the just and the unjust to the same destruction. My young mind tried in vain to resist these impressions, and it was not made any easier for me by the philosophers and scholars when they themselves could not agree on the way to view such a phenomenon. (*cw*, IV, 35)

Whether or not Goethe actually experienced these feelings as a child does not matter; what counts is his subsequent self-alignment with the thinking of the age. He positions himself as a spiritual victim of the cataclysm. His faith is tested as he sets himself between the two extremes: Voltaire's scepticism and Rousseau's optimistic rejoinder. Torn between these views, he achieves adulthood, as he is liberated intellectually. This intimates that already as a child he acquired individual freedom, that noblest of qualities, by which to judge, to act and to learn.[18] In portraying himself as a doubter, moreover, he anticipates his re-making as a free-thinker who will one day invent his own protean religion.

Time and again, Goethe positions himself at the centre of his age, to depict himself as its intellectual leader. Speaking to Johann Peter Eckermann, who recorded his conversations, Goethe remarked on this centrality:

> I had the great advantage of being born at a time that was ripe for earth-shaking events which continued throughout my long life, so that I witnessed the Seven Years War, then the separation of the American colonies from Britain, the French Revolution, and finally the whole Napoleonic Era down to the defeat of the hero. As a result I have attained completely different insights and conclusions than will ever be possible for people who are born now. (*CE*, 25 February 1824, 64)

Thus Goethe views himself as the archetype of his era. Not least because of this identification, by which he turned himself into the representative man of modernity, as I observed earlier, the epoch in which he lived came to be known as the Age of Goethe – an honorific usually accorded to kings rather than poets. In this he somewhat resembles the Hobbesian ruler: 'He that is to govern a whole Nation, must read in himself, not this, or that particular man, but Mankind.'[19] A genius imbues his life with the events and ideas of his times, focuses them, enriches them, transcends them and lends them form. He hereby preserves their transient essence for posterity. Goethe theorizes this symbiosis of a man and his age in his essay on the founder of modern art history, Johann Joachim Winckelmann (1717–1768),[20] in which he observes the correlation between childhood and greatness. His analysis of Winckelmann matches his own case:

> The memory of remarkable men, no less than the presence of remarkable works of art, causes us from time to time to reflect. Both represent a legacy for every generation, the former by virtue of immortal deeds, the latter as ineffable but tangible presences. The perceptive person knows full well that only contemplating their uniqueness is of real value; yet, we keep on trying to deepen our understanding through thought and words. . . .
>
> Nature presents human beings at birth with a precious gift: the strong urge to take hold of the world and experience it, find a place in it and become a harmonious part of it. Some excellent minds, on the other hand, tend to shy away from real life, withdraw into themselves, create a special world within and achieve excellence which is inwardly directed. However, if a highly gifted human being is capable of combining both tendencies, that is, if he seeks to complement his inward abilities with corresponding experiences in the outer world and hence develop his gifts to their utmost potential, then we can be assured that his existence will delight his contemporaries and generations to come.[21]

Such a man was Goethe, who educated himself by means of his discoveries. Few writers have been such avid readers (he is supposed to have read a book a day in later life), such ready learners in conversation. His early formal education fell largely to his father, who had a 'pedagogic nature',[22] as well as to private tutors, who instructed him in Latin and Greek as well as in French, English and Italian. This was followed by Hebrew, in which Goethe never attained mastery. As a ten-year-old he read Aesop, Homer, Virgil and Ovid. Among the other books he read were *The Arabian Nights*, which was to have a lasting impact, and *Robinson Crusoe*. His religious education was of particular importance. He read the Bible every day and so became what the Germans call *bibelfest* – 'secure in the Bible' (WA, I/7, 129). Of particular significance were his early studies in natural history:

> From my earliest years I had felt the urge to examine natural things. Sometimes it is interpreted as a tendency to cruelty when children, after having played for a while with such objects, handling them this way and that, end by mangling, dismembering, and mutilating them. Yet this is also how curiosity is manifested, that is, the desire to find out how such things are constructed and how they look inside. I remember that I, as a child, picked flowers apart to see how the petals fit into the calyx, and that I plucked birds to observe how the feathers are attached to the wings. (CW, IV, 97)

Here Goethe locates the origin for his pursuit of the natural sciences, uncovering the child's natural 'curiosity', a term much theorized in philosophy, from Aristotle's cryptic statement 'all men by nature desire to know' to Hobbes, who records the desire to see 'why and how'.[23] By pinpointing his childhood 'curiosity', the mature Goethe effectively locates himself in a tradition that reaches back to antiquity and defines the rise of the sciences accomplished by Galileo, Copernicus and Kepler. They too were characterized by a similar curiosity.[24] At the very start of *The Two New Sciences* (1638), Galileo apostrophizes curiosity as a virtue.[25] In contrast to these empiricists, Goethe's favourite philosopher, Benedict de Spinoza

(1632–1677), formed the notion that the world is a single substance comprising God and nature.[26] As the world only consists of a single substance, cognition, according to Spinoza, depends upon a reciprocal action between subject and object. This philosophy contributed to Goethe's ontology and his epistemology.[27] The development of these ideas can be seen throughout his mature works, as in the following epistemological reflections in 'The Collector and his Circle' ('Der Sammler und die Seinigen'; 1778–89):

> I: Each experience needs the appropriate organ.
> Guest: Some special organ I suppose?
> I: No, not a special one, but it must have a specific quality.
> Guest: And what might that be?
> I: It must be able to produce.
> Guest: Produce what?
> I: Experience! There is no experience that is not produced, brought forth, created. (*CW*, III, 146; *HA*, XII, 85)

Throughout, Goethe's vision is organic, creative, Spinozistic. As he writes elsewhere, every object calls forth, when contemplated, a new inner organ. The organ of perception is at the same time an organ of creation.[28] Thus he rewrites the Delphic maxim 'know thyself' by intertwining self-knowledge with the world: 'The human being knows himself only insofar as he knows the world; he perceives the world only in himself, and himself only in the world. Every new object, clearly seen, opens up a new organ of perception in us.' (*MA*, XII, 306–10) Just as Goethe links the individual to the world, he fuses epistemology with ontology, so that knowing and acting, being and thinking become unified. This is a vital, organic philosophy, and the human being as Goethe conceives it experiences continuous change and growth.

The text that meant most to Goethe as a child was Friedrich Gottlieb Klopstock's (1724–1803) epic poem *Der Messias* (The

Messiah). The first books were published in 1748. Klopstock designed the poem as a national epic in the style of Milton's *Paradise Lost*. Just as Milton had written of the Fall of Man, Christ and Salvation were the theme of Klopstock's poem. The brilliant opening books had an enormous impact in Germany, especially on the younger generation. They encouraged a cult of religious feeling and helped to lay the foundations for a new verse form, the German hexameter, of which Goethe became a major exponent. Before Klopstock, metre depended largely on alternating rhythms; but he opened up a panoply of new possibilities. Adapting Homer's verse for German poetry, he founded a style used by Goethe, Voss, Schiller and Hölderlin, captivating his readers with his evocative and mellifluous lines, as in the opening: 'Sing, immortal soul, of sinful mankind's redemption'.[29] Klopstock's poetic revolution inspired Goethe. He learned long passages of *Der Messias* by heart, reciting them to visitors, whom he apparently moved to tears (*cw*, IV, 70f.). Klopstock's poetry was fundamental in launching the poetry of the *Sturm und Drang* (Storm and Stress).

Goethe's juvenilia include a vivid poem on Jesus' descent to Hell, 'Poetic Thoughts on Jesus Christ's Journey to Hell' ('Poetische Gedancken über die Höllenfahrt Jesu Christi'; 1764–5), based on Psalm 15:9 and 1 Peter 3:18, according to which Jesus travelled to the underworld between his death on the cross and his resurrection. Goethe's poem was much influenced by Baroque poetry, with its powerful imagery: 'Hell sees the victor approach/ And feels his power broach.' (*FA*, I, 17) Aspects of the Baroque mode – comparable to English metaphysical verse – endured into the poetry and drama of Goethe and Schiller. Its urgent vocabulary, strong visual quality and strict metrical form remained a feature of German writing until around 1800. Only by grasping such links can one fully appreciate Goethe's pivotal role, inasmuch as he both recalled the Baroque past and pre-empted the Romantic future. Indeed, the grand manner favoured by the German Baroque poets finds an echo in Goethe's *Faust* as well as in Schiller's grandiloquent 'An die Freude' (Ode to Joy; 1785), best known today from Beethoven's Ninth 'Choral' Symphony. As a sample of Goethe's talent, one may consider an English poem, written when he was not yet seventeen, in May 1766, with some idiosyncratic spelling:

'A Song over the Unconfidence
Towards Myself'

Thou knowst how heappily they Friend
Walks upon florid Ways:
Thou knowst how heaven's bounteous hand
Leads him to golden days.

But hah! A cruel enemy
Destroies all that Bless;
In moments of Melancholy
Flies all my Happiness.

Then fogs of doubt do fill my mind
With deep obscurity;
I search my self, and cannot find
A spark of Worth in me.

When tender friends, to tender kiss,
Run up with open arms;
I think I merit not that bliss,
That like a kiss me warmeth.

Hah! When my child, 'I love thee', sayd
And gave the kiss I sought;
Then I – forgive me tender maid –
'She is a false one', thought.

She cannot love a peevish boy,
She with her godlike face.
Oh, could I, friend, that tought destroy,
It leads the golden days.

An other tought is misfortune,
Is death and night to me:
I hum no supportable tune,
I can no poet be.

When to the Altar of the Nine
A triste incense I bring;
I beg 'let poetry be mine
O Sistres let me sing.'

But when they then my prayer not hear,
I break my whispering lire;
Then from my eyes runs down a tear,
Extinguish th' incensed fire.

Then curse I, Friend, the fated sky,
And from th'altar I fly;
And to my Friends aloud I cry,
'Be happier than I' (*MA*, I/1, 88–90)[30]

The imperfections notwithstanding, this little poem is an exquisite performance. Its theme of melancholy was widespread at the time. Ever since Dürer's etching *Melencolia I* (1514) had popularized the idea that geniuses suffer from melancholy, because they depend on imagination rather than on reason, poets have stressed the link between melancholy and creativity.[31] Goethe inclined to the common view that melancholy is caused by social factors,[32] as can be seen in two of his finest works: his first novel,

The Sorrows of Young Werther, and his drama, *Faust.* Today this perception has been replaced by a more complex view, and the link between melancholy and creativity has been largely forgotten.[33] It appears that Goethe suffered from violent mood swings in his youth, but he learned to master them as he matured, and – to an unusual degree – his later work is largely based on a faith in happiness.[34]

Goethe arrived in Leipzig to study law, at his father's insistence, on 3 October 1765, and remained for almost three years. The episode had a profound effect on his development, albeit chiefly because of his extra-curricular activities. Leipzig was a fashionable town; it was known as 'Little Paris'. Courtly, smart and culturally alert, its artistic life was presided over by the Wolffian philosopher, critic, poet and dramatist Johann Christoph Gottsched (1700–1766). Gottsched represented the old school, the Neoclassicism that the younger generation wished to displace. Goethe is unsparing in his criticism of the shallow and insipid 'trash' which he believed that Gottsched promoted (*cw,* iv, 194). A new direction was being taken by men like the artist Adam Friedrich Oeser (1717–1799). Oeser instructed Goethe in drawing and had a decisive impact on his aesthetics: 'His lessons will have consequences for my entire life,' Goethe wrote. 'He taught me that the ideal of beauty is simplicity and quietness.' (*ghb,* iv/2, 806) This was the image of Oeser's most celebrated pupil, Johann Joachim Winckelmann, whom Goethe now read avidly, acquiring insight into his ideal of *edle Einfalt und stille Größe* (noble simplicity and quiet grandeur).[35] Goethe probably read such works of his as the *Thoughts on the Imitation of Greek Works* (1755) and the *History of Ancient Art* (1764). From these he would have learned to view art in context and to grasp it as shaped by a historical process comprising its rise, its flourishing and its decline. Winckelmann's ideal of beauty served as a model for Goethe's own concept of form:

The wise, who have pondered the origins (or causes) of beauty, exploring its occurrence in the objects of creation, and seeking to reach the source of the highest beauty, have located it in the perfect harmony of a being with its purposes, and its parts among one another, and with its entirety.[36]

Adapting Pope's adage, 'The proper study of mankind is man,' Winckelmann taught that 'The highest aim of art for thinking people is man.'[37] Goethe's planned meeting with Winckelmann never came about, however, being prevented by the latter's tragic murder in Italy.

Perhaps the key literary event for Goethe in Leipzig was the performance of G. E. Lessing's play *Minna von Barnhelm* (1767):

One work, however, the most genuine offspring of the Seven Years' War, with consummate North German national content, must receive the most honourable mention of all. As the first theatrical product based on important events in real life, with definite contemporary content, it had an incalculable effect: *Minna von Barnhelm* . . . It is easily seen that the play in question was begotten of war and peace, of hatred and affection. This was the work that succeeded in opening our view into a higher, more significant world (*cw*, IV, 213)

Lessing's 'sentimental comedy' is Germany's paramount political drama. It invites reconciliation between the formerly warring parties Prussia and Saxony, an event symbolized by the difficult courtship but ultimate marriage of the two main characters. For this topical event Lessing introduces the modern form of prose drama to German literature. Goethe adopted the same form in his first major play, *Götz von Berlichingen with the Iron Hand* (1771), and it was later used by Georg Büchner in his own social drama *Woyzeck* (1836). For the young Goethe, Lessing's play heralded a new national literature, a style created for the German nation concerning 'contemporary' issues.

Goethe's creativity generally relies less heavily on politics than on the experience of love. Love poetry is one of his great themes, from his early Anacreontic verse of the late 1760s through the poetry of the *Sturm und Drang* in the mid-1770s, the *Roman Elegies* of 1788, the *West-Eastern Divan* of 1814 and the 'Marienbad Elegy' ('Die Marienbader Elegie') of 1823. He first tapped into this vein at an early stage, when, according to *Poetry and Truth*, he fell in love with a girl he calls Gretchen. His retrospective account evokes young love in a stilted way when he writes of 'the first durable effect that a person of the feminine sex had ever made on me' (*CW*, IV, 132ff.). In this somewhat self-regarding account he refers to both the tenderness and the confusions of love. The earliest lover of Goethe's we know by name is the daughter of a Leipzig innkeeper, Anna Katharina Schönkopf (1746–1810). In this early romance we note a pattern which characterizes many of Goethe's subsequent amours: an intense passion that inspires him to write poetry; a period of doubt marked by mood swings; and finally, a flight from commitment.[38] Although Goethe destroyed most of his Leipzig poems, seventeen love poems survive (*MA*, I/1, 98–121). They reveal considerable facility, albeit they are chiefly characterized by the artificial imagery typical of Rococo eroticism. But around this time his own aesthetic began to form. He discarded traditional poetics as exemplified by Gottsched, set aside contemporary verse (*MA*, I/1, 799), and turned to first-hand experience:

> I found my greatest pleasure in giving poetic form to what I perceived in myself, in others, and in nature. My facility at this increased constantly because I was led by instinct and had not yet been confused by any criticism. Even if I did not have complete confidence in my productions, I viewed them as merely imperfect rather than as worthless. (*CW*, IV, 184f.)

Goethe rejects rules and rhetoric. Instead he invokes intuition and immediate experience. This new poetics raced ahead of his ability, but the attitude was eventually to launch a poetic revolution, and ultimately formed a template of Romanticism. He locates the emergence of his genius at the moment when he transfers his affections from Gretchen, a colourless figure, to Anna, whom we recognize as a real human being:

> And so began the tendency which throughout my life I have never overcome, namely to transform whatever gladdened or tormented me, or otherwise occupied my mind, into an image, a poem, and to come to terms with myself by doing this, so that I could both refine my conceptions of external things and calm myself inwardly in regard to them. It is likely that no one needed this talent more than I, since my nature kept propelling me from one extreme to the other. Therefore all my published works are but fragments of one great confession . . . (*CW*, IV, 234)

This latter statement is one of the most oft-quoted sentences in Goethe's work. It serves to illustrate the autobiographical character of his writing. More deeply, it indicates its confessional quality – a mode that looks ahead to John Berryman (1914–1972) and Robert Lowell (1917–1977) – as well as testifying to the authenticity of his art. Casting aside book-learning and poetic imitation, Goethe grounds poetry in the direct experience of a unique individual. This tenet intimates his writing's claim to an inner unity. Some years later he defined his need for spontaneity with exceptional radicalism: 'Every form, even one that we feel the most, is in some way untrue.' Goethe always maintained a capacity to deconstruct conventional wisdom. (*WA*, 1/37, 314)

If the academic results of the Leipzig stay were meagre, the store of knowledge and experience he gained from it helped to shape Goethe's life. His studies were cut short by a mysterious illness, perhaps occasioned by excessive mood swings, as recorded in *Poetry and Truth*, and manifesting itself in what appeared to be a tubercular infection. He left Leipzig on his birthday, 28 August 1768, to begin a long period of convalescence at the family home in Frankfurt. This introduced a different turn to his preoccupations, notably a new, religious direction. Goethe gravitated towards a circle of Pietists, whose spiritualism he recorded in *Wilhelm Meister's Apprenticeship* (*Wilhelm Meisters Lehrjahre*; 1795). One of the Pietists' chief contributions was to instil in him a belief in holism, a trust in the harmony of mind and body (*cw*, IV, 254f.). His spiritual guide in this development was a cousin of his mother, Susanne von Klettenberg (1723–1774), who followed the teachings of the religious social reformer Nicolaus von Zinzendorf (1700–1760).[39] Even in his later life Frau von Klettenberg continued to offer Goethe guidance: 'she was usually able to indicate the right path precisely because she looked down into the labyrinth from above and was not entrapped in it herself.' (*HA*, X, 57) Zinzendorf belonged to the Moravian Brethren, a body which originated in the Hussite movement, and advocated living in a free community like the Apostolic Church. Particular ideals of the Moravian Brethren include truthfulness, piety, spirituality, freedom and ecumenicalism. The fact that Goethe's first religious experience depended on nonconformism no doubt contributed to his subsequent iconoclasm.

No less significant than this encounter with a religious life that relied on meditation, inwardness and the aspiration towards moral goodness, was the discovery of occultism. Contrary to the prevailing rationalist trend of the Enlightenment, the Pietists cultivated mysticism and Kabbala, alchemy and hermetic lore. This was the stuff from which Goethe concocted his own creed, as he later records:

Goethe's study in his parental home, Frankfurt. Probably a self-portrait, after 1770, pencil drawing.

My friend [Susanne von Klettenberg] had already studied Welling's Opus *mago cabbalisticum* in secret . . . Only a slight stimulus was necessary for me to become inoculated with the same disease. I procured the work, which, like all writings of the kind, could trace its genealogy back in a straight line to the Neo-Platonic school . . . We now turned, trying to understand and apply them, to the works of Theophrastus Paracelsus and Basilius Valentinus, but also to Helmont, Starkey, and others whose teachings and precepts were based more or less on nature or imagination. I was especially drawn to the *Aurea Catena Homeri* [by Anton Josef Kirchweger], which represents nature in a beautiful, though perhaps fantastic, synthesis. (*cw*, IV, 254f.)

Goethe's early studies of alchemy, mysticism and other occult matters afforded an irrational balance to rationalism.[40] In revealing an alternative *Weltanschauung* – or world-view – the occult grounded Goethe in an older method, rooted in the Renaissance, which depended on magic. The material proved particularly helpful when he came to formulate the view of the world in works such as *Urfaust* (1772–5) and *The Fairy Tale* (*Das Märchen*; 1795). It engaged not just the mind, with its quest for empirical data and laws, but the spirit too, with all its aspirations for intuitive contemplation. The view finds its best expression in Goethe's private religion:

I was fully minded to posit a deity that reproduces itself, by itself, from eternity. Since, however, reproduction cannot possibly be imagined without diversity, the only immediate result could be the appearance of a second entity, which we acknowledge under the name of the Son. These two had to continue the act of reproduction and they reappeared to themselves in the third entity, which was just as consistently alive and eternal as the others. That closed the circle of divinity. (*cw*, IV, 261–3)

This entire narrative, which culminates in the emergence of Lucifer, bears witness to Goethe's mythopoeic imagination – a faculty not normally associated with the rationalist Enlightenment. Thus his experience of very different circles in his early life afforded him an exceptionally rich and complex if iconoclastic world-view. Even in his youth, and before his first works appeared, he was proving to be a somewhat unusual fellow.

2

Sturm und Drang

Goethe's removal to Strasbourg to resume his studies around Easter 1770 not only marked a new phase in his life, it heralded a new epoch in German literature, the so-called *Sturm und Drang* (Storm and Stress).[1] Landscape and town, reading and education, friendship and romance all combined to affect a striking metamorphosis in Goethe's thought. Contrary to the prevailing rationalism, the watchwords now were 'nature' and 'feeling', 'genius' and 'freedom'. The presiding spirit was Jean-Jacques Rousseau.[2] Works like Rousseau's novel *The New Heloise* (*La nouvelle Heloïse*; 1761), and his treatise *Discourse on Inequality* (*Discourse sur l'inégalité*; 1754) provided a justification for nature as the foundation for society. His *The Social Contract* (*Du Contrat sociale*; 1762), which begins with the famous declaration 'Man was born free, and he is everywhere in chains' provided the motto for the age:

> So long as a people is constrained to obey, and obeys, it does
> well; but as soon as it can shake off the yoke, it does better;
> for since it regains its freedom by the same right as that
> which removed it, a people is either justified in taking back its
> freedom, or there is no justifying those who took it away.[3]

Goethe's attitude to Rousseau was ambivalent; he recoiled from the streak in Rousseau's thought which, as here, promoted revolution, but in a late appraisal he celebrates him, with reservations, as 'honoured in the highest sense' (*WA*, ii/6, 110). In his first play, *Götz von Berlichingen with the Iron Hand* (1771), the hero dies with the word 'liberty' on his lips: 'Freedom! Freedom!' he cries (*CW*, vii, 82). This was also the watchword for Goethe's close friend, Friedrich Schiller (1759–1805), who is celebrated above all others as the poet of freedom. In a famous couplet, Schiller varied Rousseau's dictum. For Schiller, liberty came to mean a spiritual birthright, an inalienable quality: 'Man is created free, and is free,/ Although he is born in chains.'[4] The *Sturm und Drang* movement, which strove for political freedom, lasted approximately from Goethe's *Götz* (1773) to Schiller's *Kabale und Liebe* (Love and Intrigue; 1784). Both plays, like several others from the same period, demanded socio-political renewal. The world historical event at the centre of this activity, although not linked to the movement, was the American Declaration of Independence, and the aspirations of the young German writers broadly conformed to the ideals espoused by the Founding Fathers. *Sturm und Drang* shared the key ideals of the American Revolution:

> We hold these truths to be self-evident, that all men are
> created equal, that they are endowed by their Creator
> with certain unalienable Rights that among these
> are Life, Liberty and the pursuit of Happiness.[5]

The young Goethe subscribed to these ideals, but chiefly to 'life' and 'happiness'; his view of liberty was more sceptical. In *On Shakespeare's Birthday* he apostrophizes the collision between 'freedom' and 'the world' (*CW*, iii, 165). In *Poetry and Truth*, however, he recalls the excitement of the War of Independence: 'We wished the Americans good luck, and the names of Franklin and Washington shone and sparkled in the political heavens.' (*WA*, i/29, 68f.) America remained for Goethe a kind of El Dorado:

Amerika, du hast es besser
Als unser Kontinent, das alte,
Hast keine verfallene Schlösser
Und keine Basalte. (*FA*, II, 719)

America, you are better off
Than our ancient continent.
You have no tumbledown castles
And no basalt deposits.[6]

Even when he did not actually participate in world events, Goethe
knew how to relate to them, so that he appears to shine in their
reflection. When it comes to the *Sturm und Drang*, therefore,
it seems fair to note a concordance between the aesthetic and
the political, by virtue of which Goethe may be regarded as an
exemplary figure of the age, a participant in world historical events.

The key moment in Goethe's early development lay in his
meeting in Strasbourg with Johann Gottfried Herder (1744–1803).[7]
A detailed record of their acquaintance features in *Poetry and Truth*
(*CW*, IV, 298ff.). Goethe vividly records his friend's appearance:
his round face, impressive forehead, slightly upturned nose,
kindly mouth, coal black eyes and personal magnetism (*CW*,
IV, 299). Herder, having from 1762 to 1764 studied with Kant,[8]
made his mark as a critic with his *Fragmente* (Fragments; 1767).
It seems fair to infer that Kant helped Herder to overcome the
prevailing rationalism. Herder instilled a grasp in Goethe of the
chthonic forces and powers that still operate in the civilized world.
Around 1770 Kant introduced the concept of 'sensibility' into
epistemology, by which he aligned not just the mind but the senses
with knowledge.[9] This contributed to the philosophical ground
of the *Sturm und Drang* as advanced by Herder, its theoretician: a
standpoint in which the apprehension of reality through the senses
came to the fore. In a bold offensive against the Enlightenment,

Anton Graff, *Johann Gottfried Herder*, 1785, oil painting.

the *Sturm und Drang* prioritized 'feeling'. As Goethe's Faust put it: 'Feeling is all.' (*HA*, III, 110)

Herder was a man of immense learning and resources. It has been said that he helped to found several disciplines, from the philosophy of language to biblical criticism, from aesthetics to the philosophy of history and from folklore to anthropology.[10] Several new ideas entered the mainstream thanks to his advocacy, among them the trust in origins, organic growth, world history, cultural relativism and – more problematically – nationalism. Goethe praised Herder's 'fine and noble qualities, his manifold knowledge and his profound insights' (*WA*, 1/27, 307). It was in his prize essay *Abhandlung über den Ursprung der Sprache* (Treatise on the Origins of Language; 1772), which he discussed with Goethe, that Herder coined the concept of 'nationalism', and in his *Fragmente* he called for a 'national poet'.[11] The meeting of Goethe with Herder was to prove an event of supreme significance that brought together the future national poet with the first prophet of the nation state. The key to literary revival, according to Herder, lay in a new style, whereby the poet effects a congruence between 'feeling', 'idea' and 'expression': the very truthfulness that Goethe espoused.[12] He learned from Herder that poetry 'is a gift for the world and for the nation' (*WA*, 1/27, 313). Under this tutelage, therefore, Goethe began to learn how to take on the role of Germany's national poet.

Goethe rightly called the new movement Herder inspired 'a German literary revolution' (*WA*, 1/27, 68). Above all, Herder directed the younger generation towards 'nature' as an overarching formula through which to order experience and to guide creativity. In talks which sometimes lasted all day, he stimulated new views in Goethe – daily, and even hourly (*CW*, IV, 300). Through Herder Goethe suddenly became acquainted with 'all the new ventures and all the new directions' on the cultural scene (*CW*, IV, 301).

Herder's theories developed gradually, but their seed can be found in his *Journal of my Journey* (*Journal meiner Reise*; 1769). The text evokes his explosive inspiration, as he effervesces with knowledge, showering the reader with new ideas:

> How much we still have to search and discover! . . . The origins of Greece from Egypt or Phoenicia, Etruria from Egypt or Phoenicia or Greece? – Now the origins of the North, from Asia or India, or Aboriginals? And the new Arabians? From Tartary

or China! And the nature and form of them all! And then the future forms of American-African literature, religion, customs and laws – What a study of the Human Race! The culture of the earth! Every space! Epoch! People! Force! Mixture! Form! Asiatic religions and chronology and policy and philosophy! Phoenician arithmetic and language and luxury! Greek all! Roman all! Nordic religion, law, customs, war, honour! Papal epoch, monks, erudition! Nordic-Asiatic crusaders, pilgrims, knights! Christian, heathen awakening of erudition! Century of France! English, Dutch, German form! Chinese, Japanese politics! Natural history of a new world! American customs etc. – Big topic: The human race will not pass away, until everything takes place! Until the genius of illumination has gone through the earth! Universal history of the formation of the world![13]

The exclamations reveal Herder's enthusiasm. It as if he were speaking in a primal language. He proposes a holistic approach to history, comparative studies, anthropology and the history of ideas, culminating in a vision of 'universal history'. This was an idea which he borrowed from his teacher, Kant, but he took it much further than Kant did by including the sciences in his vision.[14] What he proposes is a history of every nation, every custom, every political event, every item of learning and every geological and biological event. Herder's organic vision, his holistic view of the world, provided Goethe with his first direct contact with the living encyclopaedism he made his own.

Goethe adopted the 'different angle' on poetry that Herder provided, which had 'great appeal' (CW, IV, 303). The themes that most directly impacted on him include the belief that poetry constitutes mankind's first language; that all cultures are relative; that languages and cultures follow their own patterns of growth, fruition and decay; that the most authentic culture has its roots in the people, or *Volk*; and that folk poetry expresses the essence of a

Johann Daniel Bager, *Goethe Aged 24*, miniature oil painting.

culture. Consistent with this conception, at Herder's suggestion, Goethe collected local folksongs in the Alsace. One of the poems he recorded, 'Rose on the Heath' ('Heidenröslein'), found its way into Goethe's oeuvre. The poem was first printed in Herder's seminal collection of *Volkslieder* (Folk Songs; 1778–9), and has since reached a wide audience through Schubert's setting, D 257:

Heidenröslein

Sah ein Knab' ein Röslein stehn,
Röslein auf der Heiden,
War so jung und morgenschön,
Lief er schnell es nah zu sehn,
Sah's mit vielen Freuden.
Röslein, Röslein, Röslein rot,
Röslein auf der Heiden.

Knabe sprach: Ich breche dich,
Röslein auf der Heiden.
Röslein sprach: Ich steche dich,
Daß du ewig denkst an mich,
Und ich will's nicht leiden.
Röslein, Röslein, Röslein rot,
Röslein auf der Heiden.

Und der wilde Knabe brach's
Röslein auf der Heiden;
Röslein wehrte sich und stach,
Half ihm doch kein Weh und Ach,
Mußt' es eben leiden.
Röslein, Röslein, Röslein rot,
Röslein auf der Heiden. (*FA*, 1, 124)

'Rose on the Heath'

Young boy saw a rose – a dear
Rosebud in the heather.
Fresh as dawn and morning-clear;
Ran up quick and stooped to peer,
Took his fill of pleasure,
Rosebud, rosebud, rosebud red,
Rosebud in the heather.

Young boy blurts: 'I'll pick you, though,
Rosebud in the heather!'
Rosebud: 'Then I'll prick you so
That there's no forgetting, no!'
I'll not stand it, ever!'
Rosebud, rosebud, rosebud red,
Rosebud in the heather.

But the wild young fellow's torn
Rosebud from the heather.
Rose, she pricks him with her thorn;
Should she plead, or cry forlorn?
Makes no difference whether.
Rosebud, rosebud, rosebud red,
Rosebud in the heather.

With a simplicity that parallels that of Robert Burns's 'A Red, Red Rose' (1794), written sixteen years later, Goethe depicts not eternal love but a seduction. The symbol of the red rose epitomizes both the love and the joy, the pain and the distress, experienced by the abandoned girl.

In total, Goethe collected a creditable twelve such lyrics for what was to be the first anthology of European 'folksongs' – a concept that Herder coined himself.[15] Herder provided a detailed range of terms to characterize the form in his essay *Briefwechsel über Ossian und die Lieder alter Völker* (Correspondence on Ossian and the Songs of Ancient Peoples; 1773), and we can assume that Goethe would have become familiar with its tenets, which he followed while in Strasbourg: these include vividness, symbolic imagery, brevity, sensuality, liveliness, rhythmicality, imaginativeness and musicality, as well as what Herder calls 'leaps and bounds.' Hitherto, verse had been based on rhetoric and poetics. Herder did away with this classical heritage. Criticism provided the key. This enabled the poetic revolution.[16] Herder dismissed civilization, artificiality and politics and replaced them with primitivism, which involved roughness, simplicity, magic, awe and inspirational profundity. It was not just the style of poetry that he altered, but a whole sensibility. This brought about a paradigm shift. Whereas previously poetry had revolved around the epic, such as the *Odyssey*, Herder re-centred it to focus on song: the lyric poem became the national form. Moreover, Herder understood

Homer not so much as an epic poet but as a folk poet. For Herder, folk poetry exhibited 'the flower of the particularity of a people, its language and its land, its business and its judgement, its passions and presumptions, its music and its soul.'[17] Goethe's output follows this general plan and includes no pivotal epic, but largely comprises a succession of shorter lyrics.

Yet one should not exaggerate Herder's importance for Goethe, who was already an advocate of spontaneity, as an early letter indicates: 'Just write as you would speak, and you will write a good letter.' (*HA*, Briefe, I, 17ff.) This confessional stance, which recalls Sir Philip Sidney's famous line 'Look in thy heart and write', provided Goethe with the starting point for his poetry.[18] From an early age poetic authenticity had constituted his cardinal literary virtue. His epistolary verses written in 1765–6 already exhibit this immediacy (*FA*, I, 27–33), and he never deviated from the precept. Years later he lent it a definitive formulation: 'All my poems are occasional poems.' (*CE*, 18 September 1823, 18) The poetry he began to write in Strasbourg and continued to create into his old age has come to be known as *Erlebnislyrik* – the poetry of experience. True poetry originates in intimate illumination. It is the spontaneous expression of a unique moment.

Goethe's intellectual reorientation coincided with his love for Friederike Brion. He first met her at her family home in Sesenheim, a month after he encountered Herder, on 15 October 1770. The romance inspired his first major phase – his *Sturm und Drang* poetry. A single surviving letter to her on the day of their meeting documents their relationship (*WA*, IV/1, 251). He calls her his 'new girl' and speaks of love 'at first sight'. The romance is memorably treated in *Poetry and Truth* (*CW*, IV, 319ff.). The poems inspired by his love for Friederike revel in love and the glorious springtime. Few in number, amounting to about eleven texts, this florilegium changed the course of German literature. 'Mailied' (May Song), originally entitled 'Maifest' (May Celebration), which was set to music by Beethoven in his Opus 52, No. 4, was written in spring 1771, and has come to be regarded as the signature poem of the age. It begins as follows:

Mailied

Wie herrlich leuchtet
Mir die Natur!
Wie glänzt die Sonne
Wie lacht die Flur!

Es dringen Blüten
Aus jedem Zweig,
Und tausend Stimmen
Aus dem Gesträuch.

Und Freud' und Wonne
Aus jeder Brust.
O Erd'! o Sonne!
O Glück! o Lust! (*FA*, 1, 287f.)

The poem has been charmingly rendered by John Whaley. Here is the opening:

'May Song'

How splendid nature
Shines all for me!
The sun, it sparkles
Fields laugh with glee!

From all the branches
The blossoms push,

A thousand voices
From every bush

And joy and rapture
From every breast.
O earth! o sunshine!
O bliss! o zest! (*CP*, 2f.)

No other poet burst upon the scene with such immediacy. Pindar
is more complex, Petrarch more reflective, Ronsard more splendid
and Donne more cerebral. Only Goethe treats spontaneity as the
measure of perfection. He speaks with directness and simplicity,
with exuberance and delight, inasmuch as he knows how to
intimate his union with his lover and the world by the most direct
means. Conforming to Herder's belief that language originated
in interjections, the basic utterances, Goethe structures his poem
as a series of exclamations. Yet the enthusiasm assumes a perfect
form. The symmetries of nature and self, sun and earth, lover and
beloved, are replicated in the poem's formal parallels, which are
arranged around the 'world' in the central stanza. The poem reads
as if Herder's prize essay on language had served as a manifesto,
and Goethe had transmuted its theory into verse. It treats the most
basic linguistic units – sounds and cries – as verbal artefacts. He
could say with Herder, 'Let your feelings sing!'[19] Thus the primal
cry of 'glee' arises as a semantic chime to the poet's emotion. The
vowel sounds in the original, so bright and vivid, create a phonic
cascade, redolent of the first utterances of Herder's original man.
Poems such as this changed the course of modern poetry. An echo
of the poem's joy enters English verse in Wordsworth's 'My Heart
Leaps up . . .';[20] and Wordsworth's vision of poetry in the 'Preface'
to the *Lyrical Ballads*, which defines lyric verse as 'the spontaneous
overflow of powerful feelings', is a precise recollection of Goethe's
ideals.[21]

Among the various writers to whom Herder introduced Goethe was the critic Johann Georg Hamann (1730–1784), who was an early anti-Enlightenment prophet of the irrational, and the proponent of the idea that 'poetry is the mother tongue of the human race.'[22] Various such ideas of Hamann also fed into 'May Song', such as a schema in his *Aesthetics in a Nutshell* (*Aesthetica in Nuce*; 1762), linking imagery, feeling, nature, happiness and light – some of the very ideas celebrated in Goethe's poem:

> The senses and passions speak and understand nothing but images. The entire treasure of human understanding and happiness consists of images. The first outburst of creation and the first impression of its historian – the first manifestations and the first enjoyment of nature in a word: Let there be light! Herein originates the feeling of the presence of all things.[23]

Into this stream of interconnected ideas, Goethe inserts the all-important feature of the human subject, the voice of a person in love. Insofar as he relies on theory, Goethe modifies it, revivifies it and lends it form. He will have been especially attracted to Hamann's *Aesthetics in a Nutshell* as it advertises itself as 'A Rhapsody in Kabbalistic Prose'. Ever since his Frankfurt convalescence, he had maintained an interest in the occult, and in a letter from Strasbourg of 26 August 1770 he confirms: 'chemistry [that is, alchemy] is still my secret lover' (*HA*, Briefe, I, 116). But this would not have appealed to Herder. In *Poetry and Truth* Goethe admits:

> I took great care to conceal from [Herder] my interest in certain subjects which had rooted themselves in me and seemed to be developing gradually into poetic form . . . But most of all however I hid . . . my mystical-cabbalistic chemistry. (*CW*, IV, 306f.)

'May Song' belongs to the works that contain an occult motif, but this remains hidden, unobtrusive.[24] For Hamann had taught how to sublimate an ancient doctrine into a living form. The conception at the heart of 'May Song' is a mystical commonplace: it comprises the underlying identity of God and sun, light and love. The means by which these phenomena are connected is 'sympathy',[25] a quality that links each individual body into a single, analogical chain. One of the most distinctive expressions of this doctrine appears in the writings of Jakob Böhme (1575–1624),[26] who had an impact on literature and philosophy from the Romantics to the modernists: Novalis and Jorge Luis Borges, Schelling and Hegel, Blake and Coleridge all absorbed his teachings. If Goethe barely mentions him, he certainly knew his work, which systematizes ancient hermetic lore in a form suitable for the Renaissance.[27] Böhme's doctrine clearly prefigures the ideas that lie behind 'May Song': the Creator imbues the sun with His essence; the sun illuminates the world; it endows all creatures with life; plants and flowers come alive; and every mortal being experiences joy.[28] Goethe presents these hermetic ideas as a lived experience – as if untouched by theory. The same ideas appear in the opening words of *The Golden Chain of Homer* (*Aurea Catena Homeri*; 1723). This book, compiled by Anton Kirchweger, proposes an alchemico-mystical 'history of the origin of nature and the natural world'. It was widely studied by the Pietists and Goethe read it with Frau von Klettenberg:

Nature comprehends the visible and invisible creatures of the whole universe. What we call nature especially, is the universal fire of Anima Mundi, filling the whole system of the universe, and therefore is a universal agent, omnipresent, and endowed with an unerring instinct, and manifests itself in fire and light. It is the first creature of Divine omnipotence.[29]

While adopting this arcane law, Goethe transforms it into a sensual experience, intuited by a human subject. A new mode can be noted here: Goethe's symbolism. Whereas allegory denotes an unequivocal meaning, the symbolic works like 'May Song', are imbued with subtle ideas which shine forth with a suggestive, tantalizing plurality.

One may further note a synchronicity in viewpoint between the symbolic mode and the new philosophy that was in the making in the 1770s. While Goethe was discovering subjectivity, Herder's teacher, Kant, had embarked on a similar enterprise. Starting around 1770 he developed a new philosophy that culminated in *The Critique of Pure Reason* (*Kritik der reinen Vernunft*; 1783).[30] Just as the speaker in 'May Song' generates his own world, Kant construes the rules by which we may know nature; and just as Goethe's 'I' reflects the world of nature in the mind's eye, Kant's transcendental subject projects the laws of space and time onto the natural world. In this way, both Goethe and Kant invent forms of idealism, by means of which to overcome the dualism that had dominated the history of philosophy since Descartes. Indeed Kant, like Goethe, placed symbolism into the centre of modern discourse.[31] This approach was adopted by several philosophers down to the neo-Kantian Ernst Cassirer.[32] In each case the point of the symbolism is to mediate between nature and experience. Thus the debate between empiricism and rationalism, between Locke and Leibniz, concluded with a new synthesis. It can be seen, then, that the young man whose love is reflected in the mirror of nature in 'May Song' proved to be the harbinger of a vital, holistic philosophy. This subjectivity paved the way for the next generation – the European Romantics.

The rhythm of the palpitating heart now entered poetry, as did perception as a bodily experience. Incorporating the skills of the ballad into his art – its narrative, its symbolism, its leaps and bounds – Goethe invented a form with which to incorporate the essence of an experience, and to present it as a drama. The nocturnal rides to Sesenheim, the horse, the woods, the meetings, the emotion, produced one of the most affecting of all of his poems. The poem has been masterfully set to music by Schubert, Opus 56/1.

Willkomm und Abschied

Es schlug mein Herz, geschwind zu Pferde!
Es war getan fast eh' gedacht,
Der Abend wiegte schon die Erde,
Und an den Bergen hing die Nacht:
Schon stand im Nebelkleid die Eiche,
Ein aufgetürmter Riese, da,
Wo Finsternis aus dem Gesträuche
Mit hundert schwarzen Augen sah.

Der Mond von einem Wolkenhügel
Sah kläglich aus dem Duft hervor,
Die Winde schlangen leise Flügel,
Umsaus'ten schauerlich mein Ohr;
Die Nacht schuf tausend Ungeheuer;
Doch frisch und fröhlich war mein Mut:
In meinen Adern welches Feuer!
In meinem Herzen welche Glut!

Dich sah ich, und die milde Freude
Floß von dem süßen Blick auf mich,
Ganz war mein Herz an deiner Seite,
Und jeder Atemzug für dich.

Ein rosenfarbnes Frühlingswetter
Lag auf dem lieblichen Gesicht
Und Zärtlichkeit für mich, ihr Götter,
Ich hofft' es, ich verdient' es nicht.

Der Abschied, wie bedrängt, wie trübe!
Aus deinen Blicken sprach dein Herz.
In deinen Küssen welche Liebe,
O welche Wonne, welcher Schmerz!
Du gingst, ich stund und sah zur Erden
Und sah dir nach mit nassem Blick.
Und doch, welch Glück, geliebt zu werden,
Und lieben, Götter, welch ein Glück!

John Whaley has succeeded in translating the visionary passion of
Goethe's original into a vibrant English poem.

'Meeting and Parting'

My heart beat wild. And off, like lightning!
I rode as if to meet the foe.
In evening cradled earth was quietening
And on the hills the night hung low.
In cloak of mist the oak tree towered
Rising like a giant there
Where darkness from the bushes glowered
With all a hundred eyes' black stare.

On high banked clouds the moon was peering
From out the haze with sleepy eyes,
The winds on quiet wings were veering
And passed me by with awesome sighs,
Though night spawned monstrous thousands lowering
A thousandfold more bold I stood,
My spirit was a flame devouring
And all my heart a burning flood.

I saw you, and the gentling sweetness
Flowed over me with each look from you.
Whole was my heart, you brought completeness,
For you was every breath I drew.
A rosy hue of springtime's season
Coloured that dearest lovely face
And tenderness for me, beyond reason,
Ye gods, I'd hoped, not earned such grace.

The parting, how oppressed, how troubled!
Your look spoke all your heart again.
In all your kisses love redoubled!
How great the bliss, how great the pain!
You went, downcast I stook unmoving
And followed you with moistening eyes.
And yet, what prize to win such loving,
To love, oh gods, oh what a prize! (*SP*, 5)

The speaker adopts the posture of a medieval knight and, in
tune with that role, evokes the ethos of the troubadours. Goethe
admired the medieval poets (*MA*, XVI, 510). He specifically recalls
a verse by an early medieval love poet Der von Kürenberg (*fl c.*
1150–70), in which the speaker calls for his horse in order to visit
his beloved.[33] The use of an ancient model answers Herder's call
for poets to return to their roots, an attitude continued by Ezra
Pound's medievalism.[34] The avant-garde often looks back to find
the way ahead. In this vein, progressive German writers around
1750 started a revival of medieval verse, regarding it as 'authentic',
realistic and filled with 'emotive ideas' (*Gemüthsgedanken*).[35] But
Goethe captures the quiddity of the occasion and enlarges the
archetype with vital images: the pulsating ride, omnipresent
nature, the forest, the hint of the supernatural, the night, the times
of day, the meeting, the parting, the overwhelming feelings and the

subject – the poet himself – who exudes the thrill of youthful love. The poem seems grounded in experience. The girl is natural, not a phantom, and fully shares his joy. The kisses are sensuous, effusive and tender. The oxymoron of bliss and pain here signifies a genuine high.[36] Most other great love poets, such as Petrarch, bewail their unrequited love, but Goethe belongs to the few who depict the fulfilment of mutual passion. The girl lives by the same right as the man and shares his capacity to enjoy her body. Love is a reciprocal joy. Finally, the divinity that lies behind the earthly events appears almost casually in the demotic invocation, 'To love, oh gods, oh what a prize!' The departure, so innocent yet cruel, has come to emblematize the desertion of Friederike, as narrated in *Poetry and Truth*: 'here I became guilty for the first time; I had wounded the loveliest heart in its depths, and so the era of a profound regret became unbearable' (*HA*, IX, 520). Goethe, endowed with an almost superhuman capacity to feel, was slowly beginning to come to terms with what he later called his inner 'demon'. He abruptly ceased the courtship on 6 August 1771. She never married.

The *Sturm und Drang* manifesto, *Of German Style and Art* (1773),[37] contains essays by several hands, including Herder on Ossian and Goethe on the Strasbourg Minster. The book is a monument to the cultural atavism of the avant-garde. Whereas the Gothic had been a matter of derision for Voltaire, who berated its 'fantastic compound of rudeness and filigree', the young Goethe and his friends elevated it to an ideal.[38] In this regard they adopted the sensibility for the Gothic that originated in England that had received such an impetus from the antiquarian Horace Walpole (1717–1797). The tradition of the Gothic revival is well-known: it led from Sulpiz (1783–1854) and Melchior Boisserée (1786–1851) to Eugène Viollet-le-Duc (1814–1879) and A.W.N. Pugin (1812–1852) down to John Ruskin (1819–1900).[39] Goethe gives voice to wonderment at the Gothic cathedral:

But what unexpected emotions seized me when I stood
before the edifice! My soul was suffused with a feeling of
immense grandeur, which, because it consisted of thousands
of harmonizing details, I was able to savour and enjoy, but
by no means understand and explain. They say it is thus
with the joys of Heaven, and how often I returned to savour
such joys on earth, to embrace the gigantic spirit expressed
in the work of our brothers of yore! How often I returned
to view its dignity and magnificence from all sides, from
every distance, at different times of day! (*cw*, III, 6)

Goethe's effusion provides a fine instance of affective criticism. He
grasps the linking of architecture and man, of stone and spirit, and
of earth and heaven, that makes the gothic style so 'sublime'. Proust
admired Goethe's essay and wrote a plea to restore the French
cathedrals.[40] He regarded them as a form of book, calling them
'a Bible in stone'.[41] Both Goethe and Proust understood how the
cathedral may constitute a model for the writer bent on grandeur:
Goethe's will to build a structure of superhuman proportions in
Faust, which originated in the *Sturm und Drang*, and the earliest
scenes of which take place in a Gothic room, may well have taken
shape in contemplating Strasbourg Minster. From this early age,
Goethe attuned his sensibility to adopt the insights acquired from
one medium and apply them to another, and thereby expanded his
artistic range.

   The aesthetic event that meant most to the young Goethe,
however, was his discovery of Shakespeare. This began in
Leipzig with his reading of William Dodd's *The Beauties of
Shakespeare* (1757), and reached its first climax with a celebration
of Shakespeare's birthday held in 1771, when Goethe declaimed a
speech, that pullulates with excitement:

Shakespeare's theatre is a rarity cabinet where the history of the world passes before our eyes on the invisible thread of time. The structure of his plays, in the accepted sense of the word, is no structure at all. Yet each revolves around an invisible point which no philosopher has discovered or defined and where the characteristic quality of our being, our presumed free will, collides with the inevitable course of the whole . . . I cry Nature! Nature! Nothing is so like Nature as Shakespeare's figures. (*CW*, III, 164f.)

Goethe did not start the European craze for Shakespeare but joined the growing adulation that had climaxed in the Jubilee at Stratford in 1769.[42] This had international reverberations. It was mounted by the actor David Garrick (1717–1779) and Garrick's terms reappear in Goethe: 'nature', 'passion' and 'truth'. Likewise Garrick's enthusiasm, apparent in the exclamation 'Shakespeare! Shakespeare! Shakespeare!' also figures in Goethe. It is known that Garrick's celebration inspired him.[43] In his speech, Goethe seeks to compress the plays' essence into just a few words: the form, the structure, the content, the characters and the tragic clashes. Henceforth Shakespeare represented the supreme genius for Goethe. He was like the ancients, quite simply 'the star of the greatest heights' (*WA*, I/3, 45). He reverts to him in 'Shakespeare and No End' (1815; *CW*, III, 166–74) and never ceased to praise him.

Nothing amid the rage for Shakespeare prepared the German public for the dash and dazzle of Goethe's first major play, *Götz von Berlichingen with the Iron Hand* (1771).[44] Herder was less impressed. 'Shakespeare has spoiled you completely' (*HA*, Briefe, I, 132–3f.), he sniped regarding this sprawling monster. But Goethe took this in good part, and publicly Herder praised him ecstatically: 'Your work will last!'[45] Imitators tend to exaggerate, and *Götz* is no exception. The play rejects the conventional unities of time, place and action, which Goethe regarded as a 'prison' (*CW*, III, 164), and created his new

Cover of Goethe's
Ironhand, adapted by
John Arden (1967).

IRONHAND
Adapted by JOHN ARDEN
from GOETHE'S
Goetz von Berlichingen

and subversive aesthetic: world theatre. The action covers a number
of years. It includes several parallel plots. There are an astonishing 59
scenes in five acts including locations at a castle, an inn, a woodland
lodge, a dining hall, a tower, a village, a wood, a garden, a suitably
Gothic vault and open fields.

Memorable figures populate the drama. There are more than
thirty characters: notably Götz himself, the archetypal baron;
Lerse, his faithful knight; Georg, his squire; Elisabeth, his wife;
Carl, their son; Martin, the monk, a portrait of young Luther;
Weislingen, the weak but scheming antagonist; Olearius, a lawyer;
Adelheid, the *femme fatale*; and numerous Gypsies, courtiers, ladies,
judges, knights and soldiers. The language also flouts convention,
as in its exclamation, 'Leck mich am Arsch!' (Kiss my arse) – used

by Mozart for his canon in B-flat major for six voices, K. 231 (K. 382c). A wide range of feelings and attitudes encompassing tenderness and lust, loyalty and betrayal, honour and dishonesty, naivety and sophistication, belligerence and peacefulness, and optimism and resignation, lend the play exceptional depth. Crucially, it presents the ideal of 'the whole human being' (CW, VII, 5–8) through the celebration of man as both a spiritual and a sexual being, and the symbolic linking of the *vita activa* with the *vita contemplativa* – a contrast between the 'active' and the 'contemplative' life that has played a leading role in philosophy from Augustine (354–430) to Hannah Arendt (1906–1975). It might be thought a pageant but for the historical analysis, the political thrust and the tragic conflict, which combine to lend this exhilarating debut such lasting significance.

The play is set in the sixteenth century, at the turn of the Middle Ages, the supposed era of German greatness, which produced heroic figures such as the emperor Maximilian I (1459–1519), the painter Albrecht Dürer (1471–1528), the religious reformer Martin Luther (1483–1546) and the physician and alchemist Paracelsus. According to Herder this was the most important epoch since the Romans, and the most significant for the constitution of the West.[46] The underlying political theory of Goethe's play owes much to Justus Möser (1720–1795), another contributor to *Of German Style and Art*, who defended the medieval *Faustrecht* – literally the 'right to feud' – that was banned in 1492, but which more generally signified individual self-defence. Goethe followed Möser: 'The age of the *Faustrecht* in Germany appears to me to have been the one in which our nation had the greatest sense of honour, the noblest virtue, and its own national greatness.'[47] Following Möser, Goethe privileges the climax of German history in his play by examining the opposing forces of a medieval right to self-determination and the legalism of the modern state. It is, in his view, a world-historical moment (MA, XVI, 815). As the play reveals, the dilemmas that entrapped Germany on its path to modernity admit no easy resolution; but if he did not find an answer, by focusing on this epoch Goethe illuminates a defining moment – the origins of modernity. This was the cusp of history that Karl Marx and Friedrich Engels later analysed.[48] Goethe presents the transition from feudalism to capitalism: Götz upholds the feudal world and his antagonist, Weislingen, epitomizes the money economy, by living off the income from his estate, a capitalistic 'ocean of largesse' (cw, vii, 26). By analysing this epoch, Goethe created the first truly national history play.

Goethe himself maintained that his play depicted a 'turning point' (ma, xvi, 815) – the clash between two epochs, two ideas of law, two forms of society and two visions of the world. What is at stake, ultimately, is modernity, and the way to construct society. Faced with a moribund social order in Germany, like the radical followers of Rousseau in France who opted for revolution, the young German writers of the 1770s were seeking a form of liberty. Yet they eschew Rousseau's right to revolution and animadvert to the past. Götz's dying call for 'freedom' can only evoke a lost ideal. On this the play is clear: henceforth the world will be governed by a new, repressive order – the legal state based on Roman law that lasted into the Enlightenment. There can be no workable alternative; Rousseau's politics had no real German purchase, nor did Herder's determinism envisage fundamental change. So the play offers a threnody for a lost ideal. In the end, however, its freedom, its life and its thrusting nature lie beyond politics. They concern the individual. The stuff of humanity. Its eternal dreams. Thus the play's conclusion focuses on the art of the possible, and here we detect the origins of the theatre of resignation, an internalization of catharsis, which is Goethe's chief contribution to tragic drama.

At a stroke, Goethe gained acceptance as the major German writer of his day, dividing the critics between traditionalists, such as Lessing, and revolutionaries, such as the poet Gottfried August

Bürger (1747–1794). By its open form, its medievalism, its social criticism and its humane vision, the play altered the theatre forever, from Friedrich Schiller (1759–1805) to Georg Büchner (1813–1837) and Bertolt Brecht (1898–1956), but also to the early modernists Anton Chekhov (1860–1904) and Henrik Ibsen (1828–1906). It is not difficult to recognize in *Götz* the pattern of *The Master Builder*. The end of Ibsen's play recalls the end of Götz: 'At last! At last! Now I see him great and free again!'[49] This widespread impact vindicates Proust's view that Goethe was the finest dramatist of the nineteenth century.[50]

If he achieved success at home with *Götz*, his novel *The Sorrows of Young Werther* brought Goethe international acclaim.[51] The story is based on a love triangle that Goethe himself had become entangled in at the town of Wetzlar. This was the seat of the Imperial Court, where he began work after completing his degree. Two of the main characters are easily recognizable as Charlotte Buff (1753–1828) and Johann Christian Kestner (1741–1800), while the figure of Werther recalls the fate of their friend Karl Wilhelm Jerusalem, who committed suicide in 1772 at the age of 25. For the form of his book, Goethe adapted the epistolary novel used by Samuel Richardson in *Pamela* (1740) and *Clarissa* (1748), and by Rousseau in *Julie; or, The New Heloise* (*Julie, ou la nouvelle Héloïse*; 1761).[52] However, Goethe omits the letters by the hero's interlocutor and so creates a work that, by virtue of its single viewpoint, resembles an intimate journal – the first confessional novel. The mood fuses the sentimentalism of the 1760s found in Rousseau and Klopstock with a new, robust assault on society and its conventions typical of the *Sturm und Drang* in the 1770s. There is a realistic context; a sensitive, highly strung hero; a tender if inscrutable heroine; a violent passion; a fatal love-triangle; and a vivid scenery mirroring the action. This intensifies the narrative voice and generates a lyricism more familiar in poetry. In his springtime letter Werther overwhelms the reader with his enthusiasm:

D. Chodowiecki, engraving from *The Sorrows of Young Werther* (1774).

A wonderful serenity has taken possession of my entire soul, like these sweet spring mornings which I enjoy with all my heart. I am alone and feel the joy of life in this spot, which was created for souls like mine. I am so happy, my dear friend, so absorbed in the exquisite sense of tranquil existence, that I neglect my art. I could not draw at all now, not a single line, and yet I feel that I was never a greater painter than in such moments as these. When the lovely valleys teem with mist around me, and the high sun strikes the impenetrable foliage of my trees, and but a few rays steal in to the inner sanctuary, I lie in the tall grass by the trickling stream and notice a thousand familiar things; when I hear the humming of the little world among the stalks, and am near the countless indescribable forms of the worms and the insects, then I feel the presence of the Almighty Who Created us in His own image, and the breath of that universal love that sustains us, as we float in the eternity of bliss; and then, my friend, when the world goes dim before my eyes and earth and sky seem to dwell in my soul and absorb its power, like the form of a beloved – then I often think with longing: O, if only I could express it, could breathe onto paper all that lives so warm and full within me, that it might become the mirror of my soul, as my soul is the mirror of the infinite God! O my friend – but it will destroy me – I shall perish under the splendour of these visions! (*cw*, xi, 6)

Underlying the lived experience of nature, Goethe creates a scenery of topoi, fusing together some of the most vital tropes in Western art and literature. In the sense defined by Ernst Robert Curtius (1886–1956), he treats Europe not just as a physical place, but as a historical space.[53] He gives Werther the eye of a painter, and as such he recalls the German artist Albrecht Dürer. One work in particular stands out as a model – 'Piece of Grass' ('Das große Rasenstück'; 1503).[54] At the same time, Werther rehearses the heliocentric philosophy of Goethe's poetry, but it also follows the scheme of the three kingdoms of nature: as Werther's eye descends from the peaks into the valley, it also rises through these realms, represented by mountains (mineral), trees and grass (vegetable), insects and worms (animal) to mankind and the Creator. To complete this literary palimpsest, the scene also recalls a *locus amoenus*,[55] being a shady spot with pleasant grass, and a burbling brook. But two essentials are missing: the birds with their song and the colourful flowers to please the eye. The absence of these details suggests a pathological streak: it signals Werther's melancholia in the midst of nature. His love, not yet manifest, appears latent; and his ultimate destruction seems implicit in the fiery conclusion. I am not suggesting that the reader should recognize these patterns – presumably they will have become second nature to Goethe – but what I do suggest is that, as T. S. Eliot argues,[56] tradition informs the individual sensibility. Even at a relatively early age, Goethe had learned how to marshal such various modes of seeing in order to create a work of striking originality.

Werther's feelings mirror nature in terms of the 'pathetic fallacy', and his life echoes the changing seasons as he wanders through the landscape – with its fields, woods, streams, hills and mountains – and passes from spring to summer, and through autumn and winter, towards death. Although the action spans eighteen months, by a clever design the story's unseen narrator makes it appear as if it lasts just nine, whereby the trajectory from ecstasy to anguish gains a terrible, tragic velocity.

Werther's name signifies 'value' and 'worthiness'; this guides the reader to an appreciative judgement, and in this single person Goethe has created, by means of multiple narrative allusions, a uniquely complex figure: inter alia one who recalls Ulysses as a wanderer; Christ in his suffering; Cato for his suicide; Tristan by his love triangle; Petrarch in his tortured passion; Dürer as the artist of melancholy; St Preux, in Rousseau's novel, for his uprightness; the painter Conti, in Lessing's play, for his artistic impotence; Goethe's friend Jerusalem, a contemporary suicide; and Goethe himself, through insightful introspection. This richness of allusion lends Werther a signal depth. Moreover, he differs from all of these in his gentle worthiness and hypersensitivity, through which the overall viewpoint – largely Werther's own – attains a symbolic power. By focusing so exclusively on his perspective, we are led to empathize with him, and to participate in his agony. To read this book, then, is to 'share' its feelings, to 'take comfort from [its] suffering' as from a sacred text (*CW*, XI, 7, 3).

The plot, as indicated, is a fatal love triangle. Werther falls in love with Lotte, although he already knows she is engaged to Albert. He is ensnared from the start. This dilemma is embedded into a social nexus – an idyll reminiscent of Oliver Goldsmith's *The*

Vicar of Wakefield (1766) – and into a modern bourgeois society, with whose customs and rules he cannot accommodate. Thus he is imprisoned in multiple ways as a lost soul in the material world; as a pathological case; as a lover; as an artistic outsider; and as a social misfit. His anguish knows no bounds: 'Ah! The void – the fearful void within me!' (*cw*, xi, 58) Werther is both a rebel, a wanderer (*cw*, xi, 20) and a religious nonconformist, who succumbs to the *tedium vitae*. The positive, organic vision of nature intimated by the changing seasons undergoes a reversal in Werther's progressive disintegration, when his life passes inexorably to winter. As the unknown narrator observes:

> Sorrow and discontent had taken deep root in Werther's soul and gradually penetrated his whole being. His mind became completely deranged; perpetual excitement and mental irritation, which weakened his natural powers, produced the saddest effects upon him and rendered him at length the victim of a weariness against which he struggled with even greater effort than he had displayed in his other misfortunes. The anguish of his heart consumed his good qualities, his vivaciousness and his keen mind; he was soon a gloomy companion – increasingly unhappy, and the more unjust in his ideas, the more unhappy he became. (*cw*, xi, 65f.)

For Werther, suicide represents a heroic deed, like the liberation of a people, or a single act of bravery. (*cw*, xi, 34).

Upon its publication, the impact of the novel was overwhelming. From adulation and imitation to shock, condemnation and proscription, the book had the full range of reactions, including the 1892 opera by Jules Massenet (1842–1912), first performed with a rather overweight Werther. There were also frequent parodies, such as a poem by the novelist William Makepeace Thackeray:

WERTHER had a love for Charlotte
Such as words could never utter;
Would you know how first he met her?
She was cutting bread and butter.

Charlotte was a married lady,
And a moral man was Werther
And for all the wealth of Indies
Would do nothing for to hurt her.

So he sigh'd and pin'd and ogled,
And his passion boiled and bubbled,
Till he blew his silly brains out,
And no more was by it troubled.

Charlotte having seen his body
Borne before her on a shutter,
Like a well conducted person
Went on cutting bread and butter.[57]

The novel, with its stark (albeit distanced) view of suicide, changed the face of European literature. Most chillingly, it appears that several copycat suicides occurred because of the so-called 'Werther effect'.[58] Its portrayal of *angst* contributed to the emergence of existentialism, as is most evident in the title of Søren Kierkegaard's work *Sickness unto Death* (1849), which derives from John 11:14 but stems more directly from Goethe.[59] The book inaugurated three novelistic genres: the novel of interiority, the novel of the outsider and the suicide novel.[60] These genres differ greatly in form and character but share the motive of self-harm: Gustave Flaubert's portrait of French bourgeois life, *Madame Bovary* (1856); Fyodor Dostoyevsky's political novel lambasting the spiritual conditions in Russia, *The Devils* (1871–2);[61] and Leo Tolstoy's *Anna Karenina*

(1873–7). For all their differences, these books share a clear debt to Goethe's *Werther*, as does the oeuvre of Albert Camus (1913–1960), which grapples with 'philosophical suicide'.[62] Like Flaubert, each of these authors might well have said, 'I can understand Werther.'[63]

But there was also another heritage. This is the exploration of interiority from Novalis's fragmentary novel *The Novices of Saïs* (*Die Lehrlinge zu Sais*; 1787–9) to Proust's *Remembrance of Things Past* (*À la recherche du temps perdu*; 1913–27) – a novel that follows *Werther* by using lyrical prose to explore the inner world of a character in all its intricate detail.[64] At the very climax of his novel, Proust concludes with a reminiscence of Werther's *Angst*: 'A feeling of vertigo overwhelmed me as I looked down beneath me, yet within me, as though from a height, which was my own height, of many leagues, at the long series of years.' Werther's inner void was installed into the fabric of modernity.

3

First Years in Weimar

Having conquered the literary scene, Goethe set his sights on
the political arena and, in a career move that has puzzled his
aficionados ever since, removed himself to a small and out-of-the-
way centre of power in Thuringia, the Duchy of Weimar, where
he found employ as an administrator and statesman. Combining
this role with his poetic mission, he here began a long and arduous
trajectory that eventually brought him into contact with some of
the greatest world leaders – including the Prussian king, Frederick
William III; the Austrian Chancellor of State, Prince Clemens
von Metternich; and even the supreme hero of the age, Emperor
Napoleon. In this way Goethe transformed his vocation from
national writer into what the Germans call the 'prince of poets'.
Whereas most authors remain content to snipe from the sidelines, a
small few, such as Dante and Goethe, accept the responsibility their
views entail, and, to ameliorate the lot of their age, engage full time
in political action.

The arena Goethe entered comprised one small territorial
unit in the Holy Roman Empire.[1] This consisted of a patchwork
of approximately three hundred states. It therefore lacked the
cohesion, the power or the hegemony that defined Britain or
France. In his *Xenien* (1796), Goethe mocks the nation's political
ineffectiveness:

The German Reich
Germany? But where does it lie? I can't find the land,
　　Where the idea begins, and the political ends. (*FA*, I, 507)

His hard-won experience had taught him that union could not be achieved:

German National Character
You hope to form yourselves into a nation, you Germans, in vain,
　　But as a result, you can, all the better, become men. (*FA*, I, 507)

Had Germany adopted the policy proposed by its national poet and pursued self-improvement rather than adventurism, it might have averted the European cataclysm.

Weimar, according to the French intellectual Madame de Staël (1766–1816), resembled a 'chateau' rather than a 'town'.[2] It was the capital of a tiny sovereign state, the Duchy of Saxe-Weimar-Eisenach, with a mere 106,000 inhabitants. This was ruled by the widowed duchess consort Anna Amalia (1739–1807) who, upon his maturity, was succeeded by her son the grand duke Karl August (1758–1815). One likely reason for Goethe's attraction to Weimar lay in Anna Amalia's cultivation of the arts. She was herself a talented composer and had engaged no less a figure than the writer Christoph Martin Wieland (1733–1813) as a tutor to her sons. This laid the foundations for the so-called 'Court of the Muses' that flourished with the residency of Goethe, Herder and others, not to mention Schiller in nearby Jena. All of this briefly transformed this minuscule state into the cultural capital of the world:

Weimar and Jena
Your greatness, Berlin, is praised by every stranger;
　　But if his path brings him to us, he's amazed
　　　　to see us so small. (*FA*, I, 587)

Jens Juel, *Carl August, Grand Duke of Saxon-Weimar, c.* 1784, oil painting.

As Goethe later reflected, 'everything pointed to a brisk and lively literary and artistic life' (*HA*, X, 174).

Wieland has left a comical account of Goethe's arrival: 'In a juddering old carriage through un-swept snow . . . fog . . . frost . . . There we sat, we two great spirits! Wrapped up in furs as if we were a pair of bears . . . and yawning at each other in unison.' (*GLTT*, II, 14) Goethe later lamented that he produced nothing of value during his first ten years in Weimer, when his 'poetic talent' had been 'in conflict with reality' (*CE*, 10 February 1829, 363), albeit this had been for his own 'higher advantage'. Sacrificing the world of poetry to his mission as a politician was the precondition for his later greatness. His chief function was as a Privy Councillor. The Council dealt with taxation, military matters, legal issues, foreign policy, roads, the fire service, education and so on. Goethe was involved in more than 11,000 different items over a period of ten years. This entailed him in studying and preparing documents, fact-finding missions and trips abroad. Among his memoranda there is one on the measures against nationalistic student clubs, one on the installation of a chemical laboratory, others on the military, taxation, and on water, roads, mines and factories.[3] He served on various bodies, notably as the theatre director (from 1791), with his most arduous duties being on the Mining Directorate, which he joined in 1796, and which occupied itself for 36 years with attempting to restore the Ilmenau mine (*MA*, 11/2, 715–70). It was hoped this would provide some much-needed revenue for the state, by reopening the defunct silver and copper mines – as in the nearby Harz Mountains, the former being a source of wealth for Saxony – but it proved a complete fiasco. Goethe's functions here ranged from overseeing the mine and dealing with the miners to appeasing the disgruntled shareholders. It took eight and a half years to reach the seam. From pumping difficulties to the collapse of a gallery that almost drowned the miners, the enterprise was bedevilled by problems. But no significant ore was found and the project had to be abandoned. The shareholders lost every penny; the Weimar treasury likewise. Goethe himself nonetheless was promoted to a higher office. Among his many roles, in 1782 he became Finance Minister, in 1804 Privy Councillor and in 1813 he finally achieved the rank of Minister of State. His efforts cost him dearly. Though he hoped to accomplish his work with 'calm and uprightness' and in moral 'purity', he records his failures vis-à-vis his 'loathsome situation' (*MA*, 11/2, 778). Yet if this was a thankless task in a duodecimo state, it nonetheless furnished him with all-round experience, and this both sharpened his vision and endowed his works with a unique stamp of realism. If he was going to address the nation, at the very least he would understand its mechanics.

Goethe's appointment had another quite-fortuitous result. As he later observed: 'I came to Weimar highly ignorant in all natural studies, and only the need to give the Duke advice in many undertakings, buildings, and installations drove me to the study of nature.'[4] Goethe's duties at the mine prompted an interest in geology and this developed into a lifelong fascination with natural science, encompassing each kingdom of nature: meteorology, mineralogy, botany, comparative anatomy, and optics. There is a system in these interests by which Goethe structures his knowledge to represent the full range of approaches to the natural world. These studies, originating in part in his administrative work, also fused with his literary activity, such that every aspect of his life was mutually enhanced. Above all, his imaginative world now embraced empirical data and so his sensibility attuned itself to specific realities – from botany and anatomy to the study of clouds. His geological writings include documents of every kind (*LA*, I–III): notes, schemes, analyses, reports, memoranda, aides-memoires, diary entries, minutes, conversations, essays and even drawings and poems. Goethe produced no single overarching geological study, and did not make an important contribution to the field, but his doctrines can be delineated with some certainty.[5] Indeed, although his geological achievements remained slight, often contradicting the more advanced views of his day, he did make some positive observations, which have been accepted as valid. His stratigraphy is so precise that it still retains its value for researchers today. Over the years, moreover, he amassed a huge collection of 18,000 paleontological, mineralogical and geological curiosities, including 718 fossils.[6] In recognition of his achievements the mineral Goethite was named after him in 1808.

This was the formative period of modern geology, when James Hutton (1726–1797) and Abraham Gottlob Werner (1749–1817), with whom Goethe enjoyed close contact, laid the foundations for the modern science.[7] On the central issue of the Earth's origins they

Goethe, 'Granite Formation in the Fichtelgebirge', 1785, drawing.

held opposite views: Hutton believed that the centre of the Earth was hot, and that its heat gave rise to geological formations, while Werner maintained such formations arose from water. Hence Hutton and his followers were known as Plutonists, and Werner and his adherents, such as Goethe, were the Neptunists. Goethe rejected any theory of violent change, believing that, despite some exceptions such as earthquakes, nature acts gradually, gently and incrementally, according to a principle of continuity. He reverts to this debate in *Faust II* (1832), where he attributes the argument to the pre-Socratic philosophers Anaxagoras and Thales:

> ANAXAGORAS That cliff is here because of fire vapours.
> THALES All living things evolved in water.
> HOMUNCULUS (*hovering between them*) Please
>   let me come along beside you –
>   I'm eager to evolve myself.
> ANAXAGORAS Did you, oh Thales, in a single night
>   ever produce from mud a mountain such as this?

THALES Nature, and Nature's living fluxes,
    have never counted days and nights and hours.
    She fashions forms according to set rules,
    and even when they're huge, there is no violence.
ANAXAGORAS This time there was! A fierce Plutonic fire,
    tremendous outbursts of Aeolian gas,
    Broke through the ancient level crust of earth,
    creating instantly a recent mountain.
THALES But is this part of any lasting process?
    Your mountain's there, so let it be.
    This controversy is a waste of time,
    and only bores a patient audience. (*CW*, II, 200)

Goethe places the contemporary debate into the mouths of the
ancients – accurately in the case of Thales, less so in Anaxagoras'
case – to reveal the timelessness of scientific argument, and
concludes with an ironic dismissal, evoking the vanity of all
intellectual endeavour.[8] In this way he fuses science with poetry.

The various strands of Goethe's experience, including his
personal life, official duties, scientific research, and fine art and
literary pursuits, became increasingly entwined, leading to a
distinct refinement of his sensorium. On the occasion of his 82nd
birthday he recalled his three journeys to the Harz Mountains,
the highest in northern Germany, and above all his ascent of
their tallest peak, the Brocken, with an elevation of 1,140 metres
(3,740 ft), which revealed to him nature's 'infinite variety' (*GLTT*,
II, 135). For centuries there had been lucrative mines in the Harz
Mountains for lead, copper, silver and iron, among them in the
so-called Samson Pit, the deepest in the world. Karl August hoped
that these lucrative mines would prove to be a model for the mine
at Ilmenau. Goethe's first exploration took place from 29 November
to 14 December 1777. We are well informed about the trip thanks
to Goethe's letters and diary entries; the former are written to his

mistress, Frau von Stein, whose virtual presence adds a further dimension to the trip. It furnished him with a host of observations. He travelled widely and visited sundry mines. On 1 December he visited Elbingerode, noting 'rocks and a mine'. Yet that is by no means all. In the same jotting, he casually announces the opening of a new poem, 'Harz Journey in Winter', which would preoccupy him throughout the trip. Next, he spent about a day and a half in the spectacular Baumann's Cave. Its Devonian limestone, with its striking stalagmites and stalactites, makes this one of the finest sites in Germany. Goethe wrongly believed the rock was 'marble' and sensed that the whole was in some way animate, a sign of the 'ongoing life of nature' (*GLTT*, II, 133).

He assiduously visited further mines daily from 5 to 9 December, travelling from Rammelsberg to Segen and Altenau. On 10 December, he is also occupied with colour theory: 'When, however, the sun inclined to set, with the yellowish tint of the snow, light violet shadows were already visible, yet one had to regard them as deep blue, when an intensified yellow was reflected from the illuminated parts' (*GLTT*, II, 139). Then, another mine: 'Strange feeling . . . to come up here [in Goslar] where the underground blessing [silver, copper, lead and tin] makes the mountain towns prosper joyfully' (*GLTT*, II, 136f.).

Here he arrives at the secret purpose of his visit: a historic ascent of the Brocken. Conditions were atrocious. There had been a heavy snowfall. Nobody before had made a winter ascent; it was supposedly unclimbable.[9] Then, as he observed the mountain, the mist suddenly cleared and he set out. It was an arduous ascent. At the summit he experienced a 'bright, magnificent moment, the whole world in clouds and mist, and . . . everything light. What is man that Thou art mindful of him' (*WA*, III/1, 56–7). In recalling his Creator, Goethe invokes the *topos* from that similarly momentous event, the first modern climb – Petrarch's (1304–1374) ascent of Mont Ventoux.[10] By his evocation of this fabled climb on the

Manuscript of the Poem 'An den Mond' contained in a letter to Charlotte von Stein, 1778.

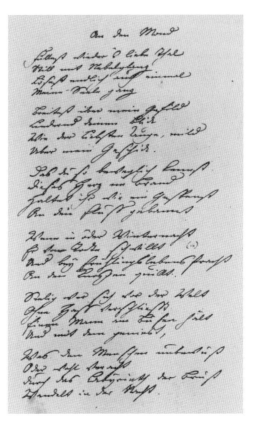

highest mountain in its region, Provence in southern France, 441 years before, on 26 April 1336,[11] Goethe places himself on a par with the founder of modern poetry. Yet he introduces a new form of verse: a poem written in the midst of nature at her wildest, as the voice of experience. Having completed his climb, he, like Petrarch, wrote a letter to confirm the deed, but also produced a drawing: 'Brocken in the Moonlight'.[12] A whole shower of representations – letter, poem, drawing – capture the unique moment. At this point he calls his own character 'symbolic' (*GLTT*, II, 140) – as if he himself were a work of art, a truly universal man. Indeed, insofar as Goethe here generates a new form of adventure – the tour upon a high and dangerous peak, anticipating the men who climbed Mont Blanc, the Matterhorn and Mount Everest – he is indeed symbolic of a modern type. To gauge his boldness, it needs to be remembered that Mont Blanc was not climbed until ten years later, in 1786.

In order to complete his experience, he longs for the full moon:

> Now my dearest I step outside before the door and there
> lies the Brocken in the grand magnificent moonshine
> before me over the pine trees and I was up there today
> and sacrificed to my God my dearest thanks on the Devil's
> Altar [a rock formation on the summit]. (*GLTT*, II, 140)

With a heroic independence, Goethe worships a private god on the altar, and thereby inverts normal values to encompass the extremes of the metaphysical realm, just as he does those of the natural world. The image recalls Goethe's 'peculiar' private religion, as narrated in *Poetry and Truth* (*CW*, IV, 261f.), according to which God had entrusted Lucifer with Creation, and bestowed the entire creative power of the world on him. To assert his own unique perspective, he continues to lace his narrative with lines from his new poem, 'Winter Journey in the Harz' ('Harzreise im Winter'). It is one of his most intractable texts, written in free verse, and has been affectingly set to music by Brahms in his *Alto Rhapsody*. Far from being 'emotion recollected in tranquillity'[13] the poem constitutes the raw stuff of experience. For not only did Goethe pioneer a new form of adventure, he invented a spontaneous poetry to express it. Imitating Pindar's grandiloquent but obscure style, with its diverse complex rhythms, Goethe's poem bursts forth into free verse – a form later adopted by literary modernism:

> To match the hawk,
> Who on heavy clouds of morning

At rest with languid pinion
Seeks out his prize,
Soar now my song. (*SP*, 39)

In adopting a lofty position, the speaker takes the viewpoint of a
god, who soars insouciantly over his creation. The issue is destiny.
The speaker accepts the doctrine of predestination in a particularly
strong form, which recalls the new concept of a scientific law
emerging in the Renaissance:[14]

For a god has
Set for each his course
Predetermined
Which the fortunate
Swiftly runs to its
Joyful term (*SP*, 39)

With a trope typical of the Enlightenment, the speaker's notion of
a human law reflects the strictness of the immutable natural laws
promulgated by Sir Isaac Newton (1643–1727). The magnificent
celestial viewpoint reminiscent of the bird of prey plummets to
earth in order to capture the character of human beings. These are
of contrary types, the joyous and the melancholic:

But if misfortune
Has garrotted his heart
He chafes in vain at
The fatal thread's limit
That tethers like iron . . . (*SP*, 39)

Not for the first time, and certainly not for the last, Goethe
envisions experience in terms of polar opposites – on the one side
the fortunate and on the other the tragic. Thus humanity mirrors

the natural world. The contrary forces that drive creation threaten to tear mankind apart. Here lies the eternal mystery upon which the poem concludes:

> You stand with breast impenetrable
> Mysterious and evident
> Over the astonished world
> And look from clouds
> On all its kingdoms and its glory
> Still nourished by you from the veins of brothers
> Standing beside you. (*SP*, 43)

In a startling personification, the god assumes the character of an inscrutable man, who is simultaneously visible and invisible. The earthly kingdoms here invoked comprise both the Three Kingdoms of Nature and the human kingdoms of the political realm – the world in its entirety. The earth's nurture, according to the paradoxical imagery of the last two lines, stems from the god's kindred spirits who exist on Earth as in Heaven. If this suggests the watery streams nourishing all creation, the word 'veins' also evokes the seams of the mines. By such hints the poem recalls the inflexible world of the Harz which Goethe traversed on his journey. Apart from walking and climbing, Goethe engaged in other forms of exercise, too, such as riding, swimming and skating – a contemporary fashion he introduced to Weimar.

On his third geological visit to the Harz, conducted in summer 1784, Goethe extended his activities, collected samples from the area of the Brocken and drew up a catalogue of the minerals in preparation for their inclusion in his collection:

> From the bare rock on the great Brocken,
> heavily eroded by weathering.
> Under the turf on the Brocken. On the surface

the field-spar is dissolved into china clay.
On the way from the Brocken to the
Arendsklinter Cliffs. (*LA*, I/1, 83)

The transcendent arc traversed in Werther's springtime letter
(quoted in the last chapter) from the infinite to the infinitesimal
continues to define Goethe's own horizon, as in his reflections
he moves from the deity to the earth, including its finest details,
such as the texture and colour of a stone. By suffusing his previous
enthusiasms with a rational analytic, taking in the precise structure
of the globe, Goethe also modifies his spirituality, inasmuch as
he further emancipates himself from Christianity to develop a
new religiosity based on the Jewish Dutch philosopher Benedict
de Spinoza, whom we touched on earlier. Spinoza, who has been
credited with founding the radical Enlightenment,[15] underwent

a revival in Goethe's day, albeit he was notorious for his alleged atheism. Goethe's image of a godhead simultaneously visible and invisible in the 'Harz Journey in Winter', as well as his poem's concept of immutable laws which negate free will, reflects Spinoza's creed. Spinoza's *Ethics* (1677) served him as a model. Perhaps its central tenet for Goethe is Proposition xv: 'Whatsoever is, is in God, and without God nothing can be, or be conceived.'[16] This incisive doctrine, elsewhere expressed as *Deus sive Natura* (God or Nature),[17] underpins every aspect of Goethe's endeavours. It thus enables him to centre all his various interests. For the inner identity uniting creation, both its material and spiritual aspects, establishes a cohesion between every part. Therefore Goethe professed to an 'elective affinity' with Spinoza and revered him as a 'Saint', as he wrote to Charlotte von Stein on 28 December 1784,[18] attributing to him the role as a philosopher in his works that Shakespeare occupied as a writer. In an essay of around 1785 preserved only in the hand of Charlotte von Stein, with whom he studied the *Ethics*, Goethe developed the philosopher's ideas:

> The infinite cannot be said to have parts.
> Although all finite beings exist within the infinite, they are not parts of the infinite; instead, they partake of the infinite. We have difficulty believing that something finite might exist through its own nature. Yet everything actually exists through its own nature, although conditions of existence are so linked together that one condition must develop from the other. Thus it seems that one thing is produced by another, but this is not so – instead, one living thing gives cause to be, and compels it to exist in a certain state. Therefore being is within everything that exists, and thus also the principle of conformity which guides its existence. The process of measuring is a coarse one, and extremely imperfect when applied to a living object.[19]

This conception had important consequences for Goethe's religion. The idea of the omnipresent spirit, as proposed by Spinoza, led him to accept every kind of religion (*HAB*, III, 220). Goethe's view of Spinoza supports many other notions: organic form, living existence, spiritual nature, natural continuity and – in a riposte to Newtonian science – the thesis that living objects cannot be measured. This point provides Goethe with a ground for his qualitative approach to nature, which repudiates the tradition of empirical and mathematical science beginning with Galileo. Yet Goethe did not stick to Spinoza's ideas. His holistic vision, which underwrites his environmental method, goes far beyond Spinoza and the founder of this approach, Baron de Montesquieu (1689–1755), with his belief in the influence of climate on social forms:[20] for Goethe envisages the interaction of climate, geology, plant life and indeed the whole natural habitat on social structures. This also has echoes of Rousseau, and of the great Swiss scientist

Charlotte von Stein, aged 38, silverpoint, presumably a self-portrait.

Albrecht von Haller, who wrote the nature poem 'The Alps' ('Die Alpen'; 1732), which established the link between mountain scenery and political freedom.[21] Goethe employs this approach in his *Letters from Switzerland* (*Briefe aus der Schweiz*; 1779), in a clear echo of Rousseau and Haller.

However, the method that Goethe developed in response to Spinoza met its first success neither in literature nor in geology but in quite a different field, namely zoology. In his first major scientific essay, 'An Intermaxillary Bone is Present in Man as well as in Animals' (*Versuch aus der vergleichenden Knochenlehre dass der Zwischenknochen der obern Kinnlade dem Menschen mit den übrigen Tieren gemein sei*; 1784) (*CW*, XII, 111–16), privately circulated but not published until 1820, Goethe announced his discovery – the presence of a bone in the human skull that (he thought) had previously been believed to exist only in animals.[22] He announced his find to Herder:

> I have found – neither Gold nor Silver, but something
> that delights me unspeakably – into
> the *os intermaxillaria* in human beings!
> I was comparing human and animal skulls with [Justus Christian] Loder, hit up the right track, and behold Eureka! Only, I beg of you, not a word to anyone, for this must be a great secret for the present. You ought to be very much delighted, too, for it is like the keystone to anthropology, and it's there, no mistake! And how! (*HAB*, I, 435f.)

The excitement is palpable. Goethe believed he had found a continuity between man and the animals. Hitherto it was believed that mankind's lack of this bone proved its uniqueness. Man stood out as distinct from other mammals. Now Goethe demonstrated the link that connected man to the higher animals. Even if, unknown to Goethe, the bone had already been noted in 1779 by the French naturalist Pierre Broussonet (1761–1807), this contribution to comparative anatomy marked a breakthrough. Moreover, Goethe placed this discovery into a wider frame: he recognized the force which drives creation, growth, change – and ultimately evolution; and he grasped the evolutionary significance of the environment. This clearly emerges in his poem 'Metamorphosis of Animals' ('Metamorphose der Tiere'; 1806):

> So the shape of an animal patterns its manner of living,
> Likewise their manner of living, again, exerts on the animals'
> Shapes a massive effect; all organized structures are solid,
> Thus, which are prone to change under pressure
> from outward conditions.
> . . .
> So be glad of it, Nature's loftiest creature, now feeling
> Able to follow her loftiest thought on her wing of Creation.
> Stand where you are, be still, and look behind you, backward,
> All things consider, compare, and take
>   from the lips of the Muse then,
> So that you'll see, not dream it, a truth that
> is sweet and certain. (*cw*, I, 161)

The poem perceives a law uniting the animal kingdom, including mankind. As Charles Darwin acknowledged in *On the Origin of Species* (1859),[23] such theses contributed to the theory of natural selection and hence to a general redefinition of man's place on earth.

Goethe planned to synthesize his literary and scientific plans in what he called his *Novel on the Universe* (*Roman über das Weltall*), a title which echoes Lucretius' (*c.* 99 BCE–*c.* 55 CE) cosmological poem, *On the Nature of the Universe* (*De rerum natura*). This work, it has been shown, was of major importance for Goethe.[24] Goethe harboured this 'terrible plan' (*HAB*, II, 372) until about 1799. No drafts survive. The ambition remained a dream, though it infused several later schemes in his poetry, drama and fiction: 'The Metamorphosis of Plants' (*Die Metamorphose der Pflanzen*; 1798–9) and 'Metamorphosis of Animals' (*Metamorphose der Tiere*; 1806), *The Elective Affinities* (*Die Wahlverwandtschaften*; 1811) and *Faust II*. In contrast to Lucretius' opening with the cosmos itself, it appears Goethe might have begun with the origins of the earth, as detailed in the following jotting of 1785:

> When our earth formed itself into a body, its
> mass was in a more or less fluid state.
> This mass was not simple, but the parts of which it
> consisted were closely dissolved in a like manner.
> The solution occurred through an inner fire, or rather, the
> mass was preserved by an inner fire in the same state of
> solution, which cannot be compared to a smelting fire.
> The core of the earth crystallized and is
> probably the greatest mass. (*LA*, I/1, 96)

Goethe teaches himself the art of exact observation and follows Werner in accepting that granite is the oldest rock. The same idea forms the subject for his essay 'On Granite' ('Über den Granit'; 1784), possibly written in connection with his plan for the cosmological poem. The essay is a hymn to stone:

> Every journey into uncharted mountains reaffirms the
> long-standing observation that granite is the loftiest and
> deepest-lying substance, that this mineral, which modern
> research has made easier to identify, forms the fundament
> upon which all other mountains rest. It lies unshakably in the
> deepest bowels of the earth; its high ridges soar in the peaks
> which the all-surrounding waters have never risen to touch.
> . . .

Here you stand upon ground which reaches right down
into the deepest recesses of the earth; no younger
strata, no pile of alluvial debris comes between you
and the firm foundation of the primal world.

. . .

At this moment, when the inner powers of the Earth seem
to affect me directly with all their forces of attraction and
movement, and the influences of Heaven hover closer to me, I am
uplifted in spirit to a more exalted view of Nature. The human
spirit brings life to everything, and here, too, there springs to life
within me an image irresistible in its sublimity. (*cw*, XII, 131f.)

Goethe's vision covers the full range of experience from
naturalism to piety. The primal force of attraction behind creation,
according to Kant's *Universal Natural History and Theory of the
Heavens* (1755),[25] is not just a theory for Goethe, but an experience;
and in reacting to the most ancient rock at the earth's core, upon
which he stands on the most elevated peak, he appreciates the
furthest heavens, as well as the life pulsating in all things. This
could perhaps be called 'lived Spinozism'. The harmony that
Goethe intimates also imbues his most celebrated poem, which he
wrote on 6 September 1780 upon the highest hill in the locality near
Ilmenau – the Kickelhahn, a mere 860 metres (2,820 ft) high – after
a day at the mine. Here is Longfellow's version:

'Wanderer's Night Song'

O'er all the hill-tops
Is quiet now,
In all the tree-tops
Hearest thou
Hardly a breath;
The birds are asleep in the trees:

Wait, soon like these
Thou, too, shall rest. (*CW*, I, 58f.)

Goethe inscribed this magical poem with a pencil into the
wooden frame of the window of the hunting lodge where he stayed,
thereby immortalizing his unpremeditated poem; yet by linking
the three kingdoms of nature – mineral (hill-tops), vegetable (tree-
tops) and animal (little birds) – the seemingly artless lyric evokes a
continuous cosmos. Every feature belongs to the greater whole. The
insightful sincerity, by which knowledge informs the spontaneity,
creates an image in which all nature is imbued with tranquillity.
Once again, Goethe shared his poem with Charlotte von Stein in a
letter. Artfully, he describes its genesis, but does not actually send
her the poem itself. He recalls what preceded the verses: his visit
to a porphyry cave marked by two standing stones and with an
oblong entrance; his kissing the letter 'S' (for Frau von Stein) that
he had carved into the stone on an earlier occasion; his prayer to
Vishnu, who upholds the world; his refuge on the highest peak,
above the woods; and the sunset (*GLTT*, II, 299f.). From these data
it can be seen how Goethe distilled a naturalistic image from his
experience. Although his lover and the Hindu deity were clearly on
his mind at the time, he does not include them in the poem: they
are only suggested by the intimate awe that his words exude. If the
sublime is normally grand and even violent, Goethe's poem evokes
a uniquely gentle sublimity.

Critics do not normally associate this poem with Hinduism,
and so a word may be in order to explain its oriental mythology.
Goethe had come across Hinduism about three years earlier (*CW*, IV,
397), and although he did not find its deities suitable subjects for his
verse, they certainly enriched his views. Goethe's letter to Charlotte
von Stein records that he invoked the god Vishnu just before he
wrote this poem: Vishnu clearly stands behind its imagery as a god
who, according to the *Rig Veda*, has 'measured out the terrestrial

regions', 'established the upper abode', 'upholds heaven and earth', and is 'ever-present within all things as the principle of all.'[26] Vishnu's several attributes underwrite the view of the world in 'Wanderer's Night Song'. Thus a breath of orientalism suffuses the physical geography, the space and the quiet spirituality of Goethe's finest poem, lending a hint at the ultimate unity of the world. With typical secretiveness, Goethe conceals the oriental motif, but leaves it as an 'open secret', to be discovered by the cognoscenti.

It is hard to exaggerate the importance of Charlotte von Stein for Goethe in the first phase of his life in Weimar. Having previously failed to commit himself to his young lovers, Charlotte – a married woman – enabled Goethe to stabilize his relations to the opposite sex. In becoming a *cavaliere servente* (the gallant lover of a married lady, which was a fixed social position in Renaissance Italy), he found a relationship that suited his need to combine intimacy with distance. Charlotte shared his interests, such as reading philosophy, and enabled him to mature in chaste fashion. When they met, Charlotte was a lady-in-waiting. Mother to seven sons, she was an ardent admirer of Goethe and enjoyed a fine reputation. A contemporary describes her as follows:

> Pure, proper feeling combined with a natural, passionless, light disposition have worked together with her own diligence, furthered by the contact to excellent people, that harmonized with her completely fine thirst for knowledge, to form her into a personality whose nature and existence are most unlikely to come about in Germany very often again. She lacks any hint of pretentiousness or affectation; she is open, free in a natural manner, neither too sober nor too light, lacking excessive enthusiasm, and yet, with spiritual warmth, takes an interest in everything sensible and in all that is human, well-informed and possessing a fine delicacy, and even an aptitude for art. (*HAB*, I, 641)

As an older, more experienced partner, locked in a loveless marriage, she served Goethe as a confidante for about twelve years, and introduced him to the manners of polite society, such that he learned to exercise greater self-control, and transmute himself from being the exuberant 'genius' of the *Sturm und Drang* into a gentleman. Their approximately 1,700 letters leave no doubt that this was a grand passion, if almost certainly platonic.[27] His forms of address for her, including 'my angel', 'dearest gold', 'my oracle' and 'sweet heart',[28] betray his ardour; and his little gifts, including 'asparagus', 'a bunch of flowers', 'grapes', 'two pheasants from yesterday's hunt', a 'little casket', several 'saplings' or 'strawberries',[29] indicate his attentiveness. Their relationship helped Goethe to lead a more balanced existence; and in so doing, he acquired a new vision, based in Roman antiquity and the Italian Renaissance. This was the *humanitas* espoused by Cicero and Petrarch. The precept occurs in two of Goethe's hymns of the early 1780s, still written in the free verse of the *Sturm und Drang*, but newly balanced, insightful and wise. 'The Divine' ('Das Göttliche'; 1783) opens thus:

> Noble, let man be,
> Helpful and good!
> For that alone
> Distinguishes him
> From all beings
> That we know. (*CP*, 44–6)

With these few words, an ethical imperative enters Goethe's universe, a noble law that impels a man to pursue right action. The morality is resolutely man-centred: it cuts out the beasts, and it presupposes sociability as the basis of life. Above all else, the poem asserts what Iris Murdoch (1919–1999) calls 'the sovereignty of good': the maxim that goodness constitutes the supreme value, and that only the good can bring about the good life.[30] Goethe is paraphrasing a famous passage in Plato's *Republic* (*c*. 380 BCE), where Plato defines the 'higher' place of good: 'Now that which imparts truth to the known and the power of knowing to the knower is . . . the Idea of the good.'[31] Goodness constitutes the archetype upon which all other concepts hinge. Herein lies its superlative power. Moreover, as Goethe's text observes, mankind is endowed with choice, the ability to exercise judgement. From this gift – as in the Old Testament – arises man's divinity. A critical feature of the human condition is sociability, as the earlier of these two hymns, 'Limits of Human Nature' ('Grenzen der Menschheit'; 1779–81), concludes:

A little ring
Confines our life,
And many generations
Link up, enduring
On their existence's
Endless chain. (*CW*, VII, 84f.)

The Great Chain of Being, that *topos* so familiar from Goethe's earlier writing, here serves as the matrix for the human family, linked together in historical time. The idea rehearses Cicero's noted definition of humanity, the watchword for Renaissance humanism, which affirms the absolute value of community: 'in the whole moral sphere . . . there is nothing more glorious or of wider range than the solidarity of mankind.'[32] The essential *humanitas*, the concept of which originated with Cicero, and which was revived by Petrarch (who likewise treats goodness as the highest value),[33] assumes a fresh and vital form with Goethe.

Shaking off the particularism of the *Sturm und Drang*, Goethe now joined the vanguard of the humanist revival in Germany. This was the movement inaugurated by Lessing in his *Education of the*

Human Race (*Die Erziehung des Menschengeschlechts*; 1780) and was subsequently developed by Herder, beginning with his *Ideas for the Philosophy of History of Humanity* (*Ideen zur Philosophie der Geschichte der Menschheit*; 1784–91).[34] 'Let Humanity be our goal,' Goethe declared in 1818 (*WA*, 1/16, 271), placing the concept at the centre of his aspirations. This universe of the mind he did so much to create is one of the glories of German civilization.

Goethe's letters to Charlotte von Stein effortlessly elide into poetic expression, giving the impression that he lived in a state of continuous inspiration, as when he expounds on 'mankind's miraculous fates'.[35] The same thought provides the subject for his most affecting love poem of these years, 'Why Confer on us the Piercing Vision?' ('Warum gabst du uns die tiefen Blicke'; 1777),[36] in which he reverts to the idea of 'sympathy', but imbues it with a new, self-reflective sobriety. Yet beneath the surface of their harmonious relationship, problems lurked which would ultimately destroy it. As early as May 1776, when their relationship had barely begun, Goethe commented: 'I want to bathe once again in the melancholy of my former fate.'[37] As with his earlier lovers, the liaison with Frau von Stein ended in abandonment, when he abruptly left the scene while sojourning at Karlsbad, and departed for Italy on 3 September 1786 without a word of farewell.

The tensions Goethe experienced at court likely impacted on his next great play, in style if not in chronology, namely *Egmont* (1774–87). The tortuous genesis of this work indicates not just recalcitrant material but Goethe's own inner contradictions: in the years leading up to the French Revolution, while serving an absolutist state, he was occupied with a drama on liberty. The clash of the *ancien régime* with the new era that he experienced locally manifests itself in the fate of the romantic hero, Egmont, and that of his young lover, Klärchen. G. H. Lewes praises these characters as 'bright, genial, glorious creations, comparable to any to be found in the gallery of Art' but, like many other critics, he finds the construction deficient.[38] Yet this does scant justice to the play's brilliant design. The theme involves one of the greatest imperial powers the world has known, the Spain of Philip II (r. 1556–98), for which the phrase was coined 'an empire on which the sun never sets', and one of its dominions, the Spanish Netherlands, which revolted against foreign taxation and the persecution of the Protestants. As in *Götz*, Goethe has fastened on a nodal point in history through which to place freedom against oppression, life against sterility, youth against decrepitude and – this time – a nascent, budding sovereign state with a burgeoning future against an empire tied to the past.[39]

The characters fulfil their destiny with a terrifying fatalism. This takes the art of German tragedy to a new height. *Egmont*'s tragedy ensues from a seemingly inevitable collision between figures who represent contrary world-views. The main character, Egmont, is shown in the round. He is a 'whole man'. A statesman. A lover. His young mistress, Klärchen, is the first of many exquisite Goethean females, whose song 'Gladdened/ And saddened/ And troubled in vain' (*cw*, VII, 1160) epitomizes romantic love. Alba, the Spanish duke, is cold, ideological, bigotted. There is also a full social range in the play. Apart from the political figures, there are the burghers, the tradesmen and the common people. These Dutch citizens represent the freedom and humanity that are pitted against the brutality and domination of the Spaniards. The tragic clash between these two sides, an aggressive ideology and a libertarian *Weltanschauung*, runs through every aspect of the play. Indeed, this conflict between a cold, repressive, rationalistic, colonial regime, with all the instruments of a military machine, and a small, free-thinking, glorious, unarmed and subjugated people, anticipates the horrors that have since become typical of the modern total state. The grand debate between Egmont and the Duke of Alba, conducted in a set-piece, reflects the classic arguments between Machiavellianism, typified by the demagogy in which verbal meaning is reversed to assert control, and naive realism, anticipating the inevitability of a future liberation. Naked power in all its brutality proves to be the cowardly opposite of the heroic impotence it persecutes and ultimately condemns to death.

Whereas *Götz* comes to a political dead-end, *Egmont* heralds a Golden Age by investigating the roots of the religious and the socio-economic forces that later gave rise to such artists as Frans Hals (1580–1666), Rembrandt (1606–1669) and Vermeer (1632–1675) and Ruisdael (1628–1682). Just as Shakespeare provides a model for *Götz*, Rembrandt and Spinoza serve as examples for *Egmont*. The play is Dutch in theme, form and philosophy. Spinoza's views on democracy underpin the play's quest for sovereignty. In examining the basis for the sovereignty of the Dutch nation, Goethe has hit on a central political concept for the definition of a modern state.[40] His text follows Spinoza when Egmont demands that the former constitution of the United Provinces should be restored and its sovereignty reinstated.[41] The vague national aspirations of the *Sturm und Drang* here take on the form of a credible political philosophy. As to Rembrandt, Goethe adored the Dutch painter, having studied him intensively since his Leipzig days. He immersed himself in his art and played a major part in the modern Rembrandt revival: 'I live entirely in Rembrandt,' he wrote.[42] He followed the Dutch master in his own drawings. Rembrandt's engraving, sometimes called *A Thinker in his Study* and sometimes called *Faust*, is said to have had a major impact on Goethe's *Faust*.[43] Goethe taught himself to adopt Rembrandt's vision and to view the world through his eyes (*cw*, IV, 241). The innovative construction of *Egmont*, with its fine visual settings, owes much to Rembrandt. Indeed, Rembrandt is key for the play's iconography. For Rembrandt taught Goethe to tame his creative energies in well-constructed scenes, which pass before the audience as pictures at an exhibition. Like Rembrandt, too, Goethe wishes to depict 'the history of mankind' (*HA*, XII, 26). The tableaux culminate in a virtuoso finale: Klärchen's apotheosis, redolent of a 'transfiguration' in the manner of Rembrandt, anticipates Dutch freedom. The stark contrasts in the play's lighting also derive from the Dutch master: the basic contrast is that between darkness (Alba) and light (Klärchen). The moment when Egmont reveals himself to Klärchen in his finery is also pure Rembrandt. And the citizens in the play recall the free burghers who so proudly prepare to defend their city in Rembrandt's *The Night Watch* (1642). Enlightened. Sober. Proud. Humane. The parallel is heightened by the fact that this picture, the masterpiece of the Dutch Golden Age, celebrates the end of the Eighty Years War: the moment towards which the entire action of Goethe's play tends, and which was prompted by Egmont's execution.

The Night Watch enshrines a girl at the centre – just as *Egmont* revolves around Klärchen – to celebrate liberty. In both these works it is not so much the armed men but the girl that triumphs. The 'colour of the soul' in the play is a 'sign of Protestantism'. As such, it suggests a new era.[44] Although the actual conclusion is often regarded as an incoherent volte-face, if interpreted as the climax to a philosophico-visual design, it constitutes a logical end. Klärchen's gloriole signals the future political liberty that, as the audience knows, lies ahead. Indeed, this finale also affords a dramatization of Spinoza's political vision: the 'civil rights' of the individual manifest as they 'conserve themselves in their own condition'; for this is an act which is determined not by the 'sovereign power' of another state but by the individual's own liberty.[45] Egmont's expression of personal freedom foreshadows the forthcoming sovereign liberty of the Dutch state.

The play culminates with the terrible necessity of sacrifice. Without sacrifice, the ideal cannot be attained. Klärchen gives up her life for the sake of Egmont. This is the private gift of love. Then, with confident nobility, Egmont faces his beheading. This is the public deed, the leader's gift to his nation. The conclusion signals one of the progressive bifurcations in Goethe. Whereas he remained in the employ of an absolute ruler, his play advocates

Johann Heinrich Lips after Rembrandt, 'Faust in his study', frontispiece for Goethe's *Faust: A Fragment* (1790).

the liberation of a people which wishes to found a republic. Such tacit advocacy of democracy represents a conundrum. How could Goethe take this self-contradictory line? He refuses to be intimidated by the terror of the single point of view, which in the end is nothing less than dogma, and instead embraces the multiplicity of viewpoints to do justice to the fullness of life.

This is a creative ambiguity, a life-enhancing plurality, which mirrors the fecundity of creation itself. Goethe rejoiced in such contradictions. This was a matter of principle. Only opposites could encompass life as a whole. In a noted aphorism he remarks: 'Every word that is uttered provokes its opposite.' (CW, XI, 191)

Finally, *Egmont* reverts to ritual and thereby restores the motive force of ancient tragedy. With a difference. The catharsis, normally distributed among the audience, transforms the characters themselves – both Klärchen and Egmont – who experience a purification. Their redemption elevates the end to a transcendental level, consonant with a spirit of idealism.[46] The audience apprehends Egmont's imminent execution. That is the shock and the horror. The cruelty cannot be gainsaid. Yet in diagnosing Egmont as a tragic charismatic figure,[47] the play foreshadows the magnetic impact his personality will achieve beyond the grave. This recalls Max Weber's idea of the charismatic leader who owes his power to a quasi-religious source.[48] Goethe calls this the 'demonic'.[49] Thus *Egmont* is a kind of martyr drama in which the hero imitates Christ, both in his innocence, his naivety and in his willingness to die so others may live.[50] Goethe fuses Rembrandt's humanism with Spinoza's vision. Like Rembrandt's *The Night Watch,* his masterpiece is a study in political chiaroscuro, which presents the same stark contrasts as those set forth by Spinoza: 'the fundamental principle of the state . . . is not to dominate or control people by fear or subject them to the authority of another. On the contrary, its aim is to free everyone from fear so that they may live in security.'[51] These complexities were understood by Beethoven, the master of musical contrasts, in his *Incidental Music for Egmont,* Opus 84 (1810). He captures the play's every mood – from the mechanistic oppression of the military to the sublime. The triumphant finale, echoed by Tchaikovsky in his *1812 Overture,* has become the standard of liberty.

4

The Italian Turn

Having established himself by exploring his German cultural roots, as advocated by Herder, and settling in a pocket-sized Protestant Duchy in the north of the Holy Roman Empire, Goethe next gave a new direction to his affairs by turning south and travelling to Italy, the heartland of Catholicism. This marked an incisive new phase in his life. In actual fact, most of Italy was a kingdom of the Holy Roman Empire – which retained a nominal claim to it in the eighteenth century when it was ruled by the emperor's plenipotentiaries and, in part, by Austria, until the latter was expelled by Napoleon – which meant that in travelling south, Goethe remained within his own hereditary cultural circle.[1] Yet the journey meant far more. It brought him into direct contact with the Renaissance; from there, it introduced him to ancient Rome; and finally, it linked him with the world of the ancient Greeks. Indeed, though he never ventured to Greece, some places that he visited – notably Sicily – had once belonged to Magna Graecia, or Greater Greece. The journey itself could be understood as an attempt to create a wider horizon, and to heighten his intellect, just as states in that time buttressed their hegemony by enhancing their cultural heritage, to which they attached as much importance as military might.[2]

In taking this trip, Goethe followed in the footsteps of countless travellers, such as the philosopher Thomas Hobbes (1588–1679) and the poet John Milton (1608–1674), who visited the ancient sites and

Goethe, *Eruption of Vesuvius*, 1787, watercolour.

met such luminaries as the scientist Galileo Galilei (1564–1642);[3]
but his father and Winckelmann were the most immediate models.
However, Goethe's trip differed from the general run of the Grand
Tour – which normally took in Flanders, France, Italy, Germany
and Holland – by focusing on Italy alone. There was no set route,
though the major towns and scenery were de rigueur, and in this
regard Goethe's trip was not unusual, but the length of his stay
was less typical. Even such practices as travelling in disguise were
common.[4] He produced a book in the tradition of travel writing,
like Tobias Smollett's *Travels through France and Italy* (1766), but
his *Italian Journey* (*Italienische Reise*; 1813–17), which he based on
his diary and his letters to his friends, created a new style (CW, VI,
1–489) and changed the course of travel writing. This can be seen
most clearly in Charles Dickens's celebrated *Pictures from Italy*
(1846), which followed Goethe by privileging the Roman Carnival,
or in Henry James's *Italian Hours* (1909).

The range of Goethe's Italian interests was remarkable. He studied 'individuals, the people, the state, government, nature, art, customs, and history'.[5] This inclusivity, which should be fleshed out by adding the antiquities,[6] recalls the theories of the philosopher of history Giambattista Vico, whose seminal *The New Science* (*La scienza nuova*; 1725) Goethe read in Naples (*HA*, XI, 191–2).[7] According to Vico all aspects of a culture must be studied in their totality. But Goethe's fusion of experience and aesthetics, of anthropology and science, is perhaps unique, and more closely resembles the accounts met among eighteenth-century explorers such as Captain Cook (1728–1779), albeit the subjective element is new. As W. H. Auden rightly points out, *The Italian Journey* is 'a psychological document of the first importance'.[8] With all its subtleties, it likely inspired later aesthetic visions of Italy such as that of John Ruskin (1819–1900).[9]

The scion of independent Frankfurt delighted in contradicting the standard views, as in his account of Venice, which Lewis Mumford (1895–1990) has celebrated as the 'Utopian city'.[10] Byron (1788–1824) likewise elevates Venice:

> I stood in Venice, on the Bridge of Sighs,
> A palace and a prison on each hand:
> I saw from out the wave her structures rise
> As from the strokes of the Enchanter's wand.[11]

Unlike Byron, Goethe foregrounds anthropology. Spurning such fantasies as Byron's, he finds Venice's defining feature in its 'people': 'a large mass, a necessary, an instinctive existence' (*HA*, XI, 67). Where others see the origin of the modern city, Goethe reaches to that more fundamental, inchoate entity grounding modernity – the human 'crowd', a topical concept born of the ideas that led to the French Revolution, albeit some trace it to the Renaissance.[12] In a peculiar phrase, Goethe echoes René Descartes' (1596–1650) categories of 'clear and distinct ideas',[13] with which he originated modern philosophy, when asserting that he formed a 'completely clear and true image' of Venice (*HA*, XI, 99). He thereby intimates that his view is foundational. This very modern humanism, which recognizes not the individual but the multitude as the true measure, indicates how deeply Goethe participated in that wider shift marked by the Revolution. But behind this view lies the insight he achieved into the citizens of the ancients, the *populus Romanus*, as made tangible in the Forum and in edifices such as the Coliseum – a building which caused him to shudder (*HA*, XI, 555). In this manner, through delving into Italy Goethe came to better understand the civil society of his own era, and, in a new take on the collective, to recognize that each individual human being is 'only a supplement of all the rest' (*FA*, XV/1, 371). Goethe would have had occasion to discuss such matters with the celebrity thinker Gaetano Filangieri (1752–1788), whom, like many other travellers, he visited in Naples (*HA*, XI, 191f.).[14] The impact of Filangieri's constitutional theory extended to the French Revolution as well as to Napoleon. Some of its tenets proved pivotal for Goethe, notably the duty 'of contributing as far as individually possible, to the good of the society to which one belongs.'[15] Filangieri's political theory remained an ideal to conjure with well into Goethe's late period, when he recalls it in *Wilhelm Meister's Travels* (*HA*, VII, 66). Yet his view is tempered by realism, as also formulated in Italy, in the phrase: 'the more I see of the world, the less I can hope that it will ever become a single, intelligent, wise and happy mass.' (*HA*, XI, 322) Thus Goethe sets himself against the most powerful theories of his day, which entail social harmony – as willed by Rousseau in *A Discourse on Inequality* (1755) and *The Social Contract* (1762) – as well as Jeremy Bentham (1748–1832), who held that the legislator must promote 'happiness'.[16] It is as well to bear this scepticism in mind when assessing Goethe's political vision.

Goethe began his Grand Tour in peculiar circumstances. On 3 September 1786, while on furlough in Carlsbad, he 'stole away'

Goethe, *The Pyramid of Cestus*, 1788, watercolour.

(*CW*, VI, 13) unannounced on his 'hegira' (flight),[17] leaving behind
Frau von Stein, and his duties in Weimar, from which Karl
August later granted him retrospective exemption until his
return almost two years later. He returned imbued with new
experiences, enriched by new ideas and bringing with him a
significant collection of artworks, not least his own drawings. The
chief places he visited were Lake Garda, Verona, Vicenza, Padua,
Venice, Ferrara, Bologna, Arezzo, Perugia, Assisi, Rome – where
he stayed four months – and Naples. Here he inspected Pompeii,
Herculaneum and Paestum. He then travelled south and embarked
for Sicily, where he visited major sites including Palermo, Catania
and Taormina. On his return he sojourned for almost another year
in Rome, occupying himself with the antiquities, before heading
home via Siena and Florence, Parma and Milan, to reach Weimar
on 18 June 1788. Henceforth, as a quotation from Ovid suggests at
the end of *The Italian Journey* (*CW*, VI, 448), he regarded himself as an
exile from Rome.

Goethe's yearning for Italy originated in his childhood (*FA*,
XV/2, 1,041ff.). It was inspired by his father's Italian journey – as his
friend Friedrich Schiller observed (*FA*, XV/2, 1,042) – and focused
chiefly on three idols: the art historian Winckelmann; the painter
Raphael (1483–1520); and the architect Andrea Palladio (1508–1580).
Rome was intended as the focal point, the place Winckelmann
celebrated as the 'true university' of the world (*FA*, XV/2, 1,048).

Goethe arrived with the unlikely plan of becoming a painter. His set in the celestial city chiefly comprised artists. He roomed with Johann Heinrich Tischbein (1751–1829), living in the middle of town at 18 Via del Corso; and it is the latter's painting, *Goethe in the Campagna* (1787), which gives us the finest full-length study of the poet. A notable friend was Angelica Kauffmann (1741–1807), a painter whose portrait of Goethe, though less successful, shows him from a more vulnerable side. The only writer of note whom Goethe befriended was Karl Philipp Moritz, who had recently published a *Bildungsroman, Anton Reiser* (1785). When Moritz broke his arm, Goethe tended him and organized a nursing rota; indeed, Goethe rarely felt so close to anyone, writing that 'Moritz . . . is like a younger brother to me.'[18]

The most striking liaison Goethe formed was with a young Roman widow, the waitress Faustina di Giovanni, with whom he had a passionate affair. This is documented in the 24 *Roman Elegies* he composed back in Weimar (1788–90). At the same time, these poems also celebrate his new mistress Christiane Vulpius (1765–1816). One of the poems recalls how he made his assignations with Faustina at her inn by writing secret messages in wine spilled on the table. Originally titled *Erotica Romana*, these poems, which are written in the style of the Roman love poets, introduce a new openness to the body. This was the sensuality suppressed by Christianity but supposedly typical of the ancients. The poems thus continue Petrarch's humanist project, for just like Petrarch, Goethe invokes antiquity to ground a new sensibility, an ethic of emancipation. Indeed, it is Petrarch's dream of a resurgent Rome that animates Goethe's entire cycle, echoing the Italian poet's wonder: 'Who can doubt that Rome would rise up again if she but began to know herself?'[19] Goethe too seeks the eternal city: 'I want to see the enduring Rome, not the one that passes away every ten years.' (*CW*, VI, 125f.) The city enabled Goethe to create a new identity:

> *Saget Steine mir an, o! sprecht, ihr hohen Paläste.*
>> *Straßen redet ein Wort! Genius regst du dich nicht?*
> *Ja es ist alles beseelt in deinen heiligen Mauern*
>> *Ewige Roma, nur mir schweiget noch alles so still.* (*FA*, I, 393)

Speaking in the elegiac couplets of the classical poets, Goethe extols the city that his predecessors admired above all others, as a location animated by life itself and empowered by love. John Whaley's translation perfectly captures Goethe's elegiac couplets:

> Tell me, stones, and call out, O speak, you lofty palazzi!
>> Streets, O talk to me now! Genius, will you not stir?
> Yes, all is animate here, within your sanctified ramparts,
>> Rome everlasting; from me only its voice is withheld. (*SP*, 57)

Never before had a German poet captured the essence of a city, or, for that matter, written such luminous verse:

> *Eine Welt zwar bist du, o Rom, doch ohne die Liebe*
>> *Wäre die Welt nicht die Welt, wäre denn*
>> *Rom auch nicht Rom.* (*FA*, I, 393)

The elegiac couplets figure the harmony of ancient art:

> You indeed are a world, O Rome; but failing love's presence
>> World would not truly be world, nor then would Rome
>> still be Rome. (*SP*, 57)

The osmosis by which Goethe transforms his own character, like Keats's 'chameleon poet',[20] enabled him to re-orientate German poetry and to imbue its culture with a vibrant classicism. Although this has been called 'the tyranny of Greece over Germany',[21] the term belittles the way in which a culture can regenerate itself by

Goethe, *Italian Seacoast*, 1789, watercolour.

absorbing alien influences. What Goethe now learns is a new holism, by virtue of which he can re-centre his activity, to fuse life and love, sense and intelligence, learning and art, pleasure and instruction, into a single uplifting experience:

> *Froh empfind ich mich nun auf klassischem Boden begeistert,*
>   *Lauter und reizender spricht Vorwelt und Mitwelt zu mir.*
> *Ich befolge den Rat, durchblättre die Werke der Alten*
>   *Mit geschäftiger Hand täglich mit neuem Genuß.*
> *Aber die Nächte hindurch hält Amor mich anders beschäftigt,*
>   *Werd ich auch halb nur gelehrt, bin ich doch*
>   *doppelt vergnügt.* (FA, 1, 405)

The loving tone is shot through by a charming humour, as when the speaker imagines himself tapping the rhythm of the hexameter on his beloved's back; in fact, Goethe was not entirely secure in his metrics and asked August Wilhelm Schlegel (1767–1845) to correct his versification. The rise and fall of the verse is well captured by John Whaley's translation:

> Now on Classical ground, I'm happy to find it inspires me;
>   Past and present speak louder, exciting me more.
> Here I heed good advice, I leaf through the books of the ancients
>   With an assiduous hand, daily delighting anew.
> But when it comes to the nights I'm thoroughly taken by Amor;
>   And if I'm only half-learned, doubly I'm happy instead. (*SP*, 57f.)

In his deft conclusion, Goethe implicitly substitutes the political triumvirate, Pompey, Crassus and Caesar, with the trio of love poets – Catullus, Propertius and Tibullus. By this means he tacitly upholds Vico's tenet, so key for the Enlightenment, and not least for the duchy of Weimar, that power resides not in military might, but in the arts.[22] The *Roman Elegies* demonstrate the survival of art through the ages, and its capacity to humanize and to enrich. But Goethe supplements the humanism of the book by a humanism of the body. Frequently, love poetry concerns love as an abstract quantity, as for instance in Shakespeare's 116th sonnet, 'Let me not to the marriage of true minds':

> Love's not Time's fool, though rosy lips and cheeks
> Within his bending sickle's compass come:
> Love alters not with brief hours and weeks
> But bears it out even to the edge of doom.
> If this be error and upon me proved
> I never writ, nor no man ever loved.[23]

Goethe's lyric eliminates Shakespeare's rhetoric. Shakespeare's absolute love cannot be bounded, but Goethe's Roman elegy is directed towards a real, living lover; his point that he not only

Wilhelm Tischbein, *Goethe Looking Out of His Window in Rome*, 1787, mixed media.

luxuriates in love, but engages in 'intelligent conversation' with his mistress is just slightly off-key – loving, but also a touch patronizing. Another defect is perhaps that Goethe occasionally shows traces of the utilitarianism that was his bourgeois birth right. This is exemplified in his brilliant if reductive view, 'was fruchtbar ist allein ist wahr' ('only that which is fruitful is true' (*sp*, 152)). The critique was made by Heinrich Heine, who has left a sardonic account of his visit to Weimar.[24] In the end, however, these are minor flaws in a splendid love poem which is also a celebration of Rome, the eternal city: enriching the genre of love poetry, the elegies fuse body with the mind, the senses with the intellect, love with learning and pleasure with self-knowledge. If poetry often dwells on heartache, the *Roman Elegies* are rare in creating a poetry of fulfilment. The antiquities' role is key, not least in revealing the eternal power of art. Goethe dilates on this effect towards the end of the *Italian Journey*:

> In general . . . the most marked effect of all artworks is that they put us back into the situation of the time and the individuals that produced them. Surrounded by ancient statues, we feel ourselves in the midst of a vigorous natural life, we become aware of the diverseness of human forms and are led directly back to the human being in his purest state, with the result that the observer himself becomes alive and purely human . . . Being able to enjoy such surroundings every day in Rome, one begins at the same time to covet them; we want to set up such figures next to ourselves . . . On opening our eyes in the morning, we feel stirred by such splendid things; all our thinking and musing is accompanied by such figures, and consequently it becomes impossible to sink back into barbarism. (*cw*, vi, 441)

Goethe treats art as mankind's supreme product: in edifying and ennobling, it fuses ethics and philosophy, scholarship and law, in a manner more effective than either politics, trade or commerce; for in large part, it is art that drives and perfects our civilization. Such is the religion of high art that Goethe established in Germany: art's role lies in its transformative power. It is through art that culture survives; and through art that it can be reborn. What he does not state, though, is that such change requires effort. His first sight of a Doric temple in Paestum is a case in point: 'My reaction was purely one of astonishment. I found myself in a totally alien world.' But then 'I soon pulled myself together, remembered my art history, bore in mind that the spirit of those times was in keeping with such architecture . . . and in less than an hour I felt reconciled.' (*CW*, VI, 179) Paestum contains three temples, but Goethe singles out only one, the best kept, a massive Temple to Hera. This creates a dramatic effect in his narrative. He thus focuses on a particularly early example of Greek architecture, from the sixth century BCE. Compared to later temples, its columns are massive, with a strong 'entasis' or swelling near the centre. The surviving example includes a nearly complete entablature. Its frontal view is indeed daunting. One seems to be faced by a god. In presenting the process of appreciation, Goethe's description offers a glimpse of art history as the interaction between object and observer, whereby the structure impresses itself on the viewer through the eye, persuading him to adopt a positive attitude. Note how he ties knowledge to experience, and captures the sublime ('uncomfortable', 'intimidated') via a precise grasp of the columns ('blunt, skittle-shaped, dense columnar masses') as well as the roof. He actually forces himself to appreciate what at first strikes him as alien, and thereby subjects himself to the superior power of ancient art.

The *Italian Journey* repeatedly compares sculpture, architecture and the human being. In Rome, Goethe confesses:

I am like an architect who wants to raise a tower but has laid a poor foundation for it . . . May God grant that when I return,

the moral consequence of having lived in a wider world will
also be manifest to me. Yes, along with my artistic sense my
moral one is undergoing a great renovation. (*cw*, vi, 123)

The trip impressed upon Goethe the need to change the premise
of his life. He now rejected the national base of his art, hitherto
rooted in the acceptance of local tradition, and embraced the
cosmopolitanism of the ancients. This is Socrates' doctrine, as
quoted by Plutarch: 'I am not an Athenian or a Greek, but a citizen
of the world.'[25] In Roman culture, it is said, the best expression
of cosmopolitanism is in Marcus Aurelius, whose statue Goethe
saw in Rome, and who had concluded that all mankind are
'common citizens' and the whole world 'a kind of state'.[26] In the
Enlightenment, Kant's *Anthropology* (1785) developed this ideal:
he defined what he called a 'regulative idea' by which to overcome
social division and form a 'cosmopolitan society'.[27] Goethe builds
on Marcus Aurelius and Kant. He makes his point in in two witty
epigrams, writing that Germany possessed no political reality,
which we quoted earlier; instead, the Germans should expend their
efforts on becoming human beings (*FA*, I, 507–95). In pursuing this
goal, he transfers the Roman ideal of a state based on the unity
of all mankind, *humanitas*, to the Holy Roman Empire.[28] Greek
architecture, with its propensity to travel across time and space,
to reform and to adapt, represents the universal language of this
cosmopolitan society. In Goethe's optimistic view, the Greeks
provided the basis upon which to erect a new German identity.

The prism through which Goethe viewed antiquity was the
work of Andrea Palladio.[29] This was the most successful of all
Neoclassical architects, who transferred the ancient structures
into modern dwellings and thereby started a fashion that spread
from the Veneto across the world, influencing such figures as Inigo
Jones (1573–1652) and Sir Christopher Wren (1632–1723) as well as
Thomas Jefferson (1743–1826). Even the American Capitol is built

in the Palladian style. Goethe venerated Palladio. One senses he identified with him. When he writes that Palladio was 'thoroughly imbued with antiquity' (cw, vi, 63), he sounds like a tutelary genius; likewise when he calls him 'a great man' who 'reacted to the pettiness of his own times . . . not surrendering but determined to remodel everything in accord with his noble ideas' (cw, vi, 63), one senses that Goethe gained strength from his example. He bought Palladio's manual, *The Four Books of Architecture* (1570), and avidly studied its theory.[30] He made the architect's maxim his own:

> Beauty will result from the form and the correspondence
> of the whole, with respect to the several parts, of the parts
> with regard to each other, and of these again to the whole;
> that the structure may appear an entire and complete
> body, wherein each member agrees with the other, and
> all necessary to compose what you intend to form.[31]

The same ideas run through Goethe's classical aesthetic almost verbatim. Goethe too regarded 'proportion' (HA, xii, 743) and 'noble correspondence' (HA, xii, 726) as defining features of beauty. In an essay by Moritz which he quotes in *The Italian Journey*, beauty is similarly defined as being 'complete in itself' (cw, vi, 433). Palladian masterpieces such as the Olympian Theatre and the Basilica in Vicenza greatly attracted him. But above all he admired the Villa Rotunda – an iconic building with an audacious dome echoing the Roman Pantheon that continues to fascinate:[32] it was here, for example, that Joseph Losey filmed his version of *Don Giovanni* (1979). Goethe's homage to Palladio is contained in his description of this villa, which is one of the set-pieces in *The Italian Journey* (cw, vi, 50). Yet to understand Goethe's appreciation of Palladio's style,[33] and his insight into Palladio's reliance on nature, it is necessary to examine Goethe's absorption of these principles in his own work, both literary and scientific.[34] Moreover, Palladio furthered

Goethe's growing encyclopaedism, inasmuch as by including both the sciences and the arts in his purview, Goethe represents the Renaissance ideal of the *uomo universale*.[35]

The first fruit of Goethe's dialogue with Palladio was his play *Iphigenia in Tauris* (*Iphigenie auf Tauris*; 1779) that he brought with him to Italy in a prose format, written in a mere six weeks, and which he now set about recasting in verse. Palladio's harmonies in the Villa Rotunda recur in the drama.[36] The characters are grouped symmetrically. The five acts are balanced geometrically around a central axis, just like the villa, in a structure that is radial rather than axial.[37] Moreover, just as Palladio revives antiquity in a new, humanist style, Goethe's play lends a new, moral ethos to ancient tragedy. In his diary, Goethe mentions working on the play in conjunction with Palladio's book (*FA*, xv/1, 685), and this would appear to confirm their closeness. But Goethe's contemporaries completely missed the point. His closest friend, Schiller, observed:

> It is so completely modern and un-Greek that it is impossible
> to understand, how it could ever have been compared to
> a Greek play. It is purely moral, but the sensual power,
> life, movement, and everything that specifies a work as
> truly dramatic is completely lacking. (*FA*, iii/1, 764)

Schiller loses sight of the changes demanded by Neoclassicism, which require the dramatist to accommodate his subject to his own age. He also exaggerates the play's moral core to the exclusion of its vitality. Likewise, more recent critics have assailed Goethe for his alleged 'avoidance of tragedy', ignoring the very real tragic dimension in the play – and the fact that Goethe's model, Euripides' *Iphigenia in Tauris*, also lacks a terrible end, in the rather narrow sense that there is no catastrophe.[38] These supposed weaknesses evaporate when the play is considered as a sequel to Palladian humanism.

Iphigenia continues the innovative trajectory begun in Goethe's first great play. About seven key shifts occur: 1) the dethronement of the deity; 2) the re-centring of the self; 3) the defence of feminism; 4) the purgation of evil; 5) cultural relativism; 6) conflict resolution; 7) the civilizing process. Together, these themes redefine mankind, developing the views championed by G. E. Lessing in *Nathan the Wise* (1779) and Mozart in *The Magic Flute* (1791). These three dramatic masterpieces constitute the trilogy of German tolerance. They are effectively a joint project that set forth the ideals of reason and truth, justice and virtue, tolerance and brotherhood. This cultural achievement should be better recognized. In comparison to its French equivalent, the German *Aufklärung* is too little known. As T. J. Reed argues so eloquently, it deserves to be recognized as one of the splendours of Western civilization.[39]

The most radical element in *Iphigenia* is its displacement of the gods. In the place of transcendence the play introduces the power of the individual conscience. This is a thinly veiled assault on Christianity. The central figure acts autonomously. She is a free spirit. She, not the gods, is the true shaper of destiny. It is she who decides the characters' fate. Thus she supplants the metaphysical order and replaces it by an earthly power – humanity itself. Once again one detects Spinoza's doctrine of freedom. The change in world-view is accomplished in a Copernican Revolution, comparable to that which Kant achieved at about this time in *The Critique of Pure Reason* (1781) and developed in *The Critique of Practical Reason* (1788) – a parallel Goethe himself later noted (*CE*, 11 April 1827, 24).[40]

In *Iphigenia* Goethe presents what he variously calls the 'soul', the 'breast' or the 'heart' as the organ through which the subject understands the world. He thus disposes of what the rationalists call the 'mind' or the 'thinking substance', and locates intelligence in the organ of feeling, by which the individual grasps reality.[41] By different routes, therefore, both Goethe and Kant overcome the

Maria Wimmer as Iphigenie and Hermann Schomberg as Thoas in a production of *Iphigenie in Tauris* at the Schiller Theater, Berlin, 1957.

dualism which had typified philosophy since Descartes; in Kant's case by idealism, and in Goethe's by a direct, haptic apprehension of the object. This can be observed near the start of *Iphigenia*, when the Greek priestess disputes with the barbarian king, who wishes her to marry him:

IPHIGENIA My lord, do not speak ill of our poor sex.
    A woman's weapons are not glorious
    Like those of men, yet they are not ignoble.
    Believe me, here I am a better judge
    Than you of what is in your interests.
    You do not know yourself nor me, and yet
    You think we could find happiness together.
    Full of this confidence, in all good will,
    You urge me to consent to what you wish;
    And here I thank the gods that they have given me
    The strength that will not let me undertake
    This marriage bond which they have not approved.
THOAS This is no god, but your own heart that speaks.
IPHIGENIA Their only speech to us is through our hearts.
THOAS And have I not the right to hear it too?
IPHIGENIA The storm of passion drowns that gentle voice.
THOAS Only the priestess hears it, I dare say.
IPHIGENIA A king should hearken to it most of all.
THOAS Your sacred office and your family's
    Celestial dining-rights no doubt bring you
    Nearer to Jove than a mere earthborn savage.
IPHIGENIA This is how you reward me for the confidence
    You forced from me.
THOAS I am no more than human. (*CW*, VII, 13)

The dispute about the 'heart' forms the pivot of the play. It is an argument about rights and power. Both the king and Iphigenia, however, ultimately accept their own humanity:

THOAS Do you expect the crude and barbarous Scythian
    To hear the voice of truth and human kindness
    When Atreus, the Greek, was deaf to it?
IPHIGENIA All men can hear it, born in any land. (*CW*, VIII, 48)

Iphigenia asserts the view that runs through the play that all men (and women) are essentially the same. Every human possesses the same understanding. The same feelings. But Goethe expands the 'heart' into the primary organ. It is a complex sensorium: the seat of the emotions; the means of understanding; consciousness; the conscience; and the means by which to know the world. He first presented this theory in a poem to Frau von Stein (*cw*, I, 61). It lies at the centre of his classicism. In some ways these ideas anticipate the work of the American philosopher Susanne Langer by offering a holistic, concrete and tactile approach to knowledge; from Susanne Langer, Goethe's ideas passed to America's foremost mid-century critic, Susan Sontag; and thence directly to today's leading philosopher of feeling, Martha Nussbaum. The modern theory of emotion as a way of knowing rests squarely on Goethe's achievement.

Goethe also subscribes to the cultural relativism of the Enlightenment. This can be noted inter alia in the king's sarcastic dismissal of Tantalus, Iphigenia's ancestor, whose 'celestial dining rights' consist of Tantalus boiling his son Pelops alive and serving him up to the gods: the Greeks are even more barbaric than the barbarians. This relativism derives from one of Goethe's spiritual 'friends' (*HA*, IX, 480), Michel de Montaigne (1533–1592), who proposed it in his celebrated essay 'On the Cannibals';[42] the idea then became widespread in the Enlightenment via Montesquieu's *Persian Letters*.[43] Goethe was perhaps the first to transpose it into the drama, and thereby to transform an ancient tragedy into a piece of progressive philosophy: there is no essential difference between a civilized man and a barbarian; civilization itself can be as bad as savagery – an insight that the twentieth century more than confirmed. Goethe thus recognizes the dark underside of the Enlightenment, as highlighted by T. W. Adorno (1903–1969) and Michel Foucault (1926–1984).[44] But he shows how the darkness may be combatted, in this case by the purgation of Orestes, and the king's exercising of self-control. By exorcizing the curse of her ancestors, Iphigenia initiates a healing action, which inaugurates a civilizing process on the island.

As in *Egmont*, Goethe includes key ideas from political philosophy in his play, in order to come to terms with topical problems. Just as Thomas Hobbes's *Behemoth* (1668) had long before set out the programme for the Enlightenment by proposing a route from savagery to civilization, Goethe's play depicts the process of Enlightenment, reverting to the ideas of the friend of Montaigne, Étienne de La Boétie's (1530–1563) *The Politics of Obedience* (*Le Discourse de la servitude volontaire*), and (as T. J. Reed was the first to show; *GHB*, II, 214) anticipating the educative procedure Kant later outlines in his essay, 'What is Enlightenment?' (1784).[45] Just as La Boétie attacks 'voluntary servitude', Kant rails against 'voluntary tutelage'. Personal freedom also lies at the heart of Goethe's drama. All the main characters – Iphigenia, Thoas, Pylades – undergo a transformation and experience a self-improvement that amounts to liberation. This is the freedom from 'tutelage' Kant defines as the essence of Enlightenment. In this sense, *Iphigenia* dramatizes modern philosophy, and foreshadows Norbert Elias's *The Civilising Process* (1939);[46] for as with Elias, the key to civilization in *Iphigenia* lies in self-restraint.

The deeply political character of Goethe's play sets *Iphigenia* in the vanguard of proto-feminism.[47] While he does not plead for women's rights, Goethe's treatment of Iphigenia's 'virtue' as identical with that of men fully accords with the view advocated by Mary Wollstonecraft in *A Vindication of the Rights of Woman* (1792).[48] Likewise, the point that women enrich civilization also features here.[49] In proving herself not just equal, but superior to the men in the play, Iphigenia stakes out a claim for political equality.

Her chief political act is to persuade the king to change the ancient law according to which strangers to the island must be executed. This barbaric rite ceases by her intercession. Her action needs to be understood as introducing international law to the island – what the eighteenth century called the 'Law of Nations'. The principle she espouses can be directly traced to Enlightenment international law. It comes from Emer de Vattel's *The Law of Nations* (1758): nations can only discharge their duty if they love one another; this is 'the pure source' of all 'humanity'.[50] According to de Vattel, international law enables nations to unite: it spreads humanity throughout the world. In adopting this axiom, which is also reflected in the American Constitution, Goethe places law – the subject he studied at university – into his drama. It thereby becomes the means to achieve conflict resolution. Thus Iphigenia cements the rule of friendship between Greeks and barbarians: she overcomes the distinction in the handshake with which the play concludes – in contrast to the hostile end to Euripides' play. Law is the vehicle by which to consolidate society and to forge international relations. Intriguingly, and as has hitherto escaped notice, in this regard Goethe was following in the footsteps of his great-great grandfather, Johann Wolfgang Textor (1638–1701), who taught international law at the University of Altdorf. No less a figure than Leibniz was among his pupils. Like his great ancestor, Goethe revered the 'law of nations', and placed it at the climax of *Iphigenia*. The age understood: the play was performed in Vienna to great acclaim on 9 June 1815, when the Treaty of Vienna was signed.[51] This treaty put an end to the Napoleonic wars and created a new and peaceful world order. The play thereby helped to forge what has come to be known as 'the collective conscience of humanity.'[52] Thus *Iphigenia* affirms a belief in cosmopolitan humanity, in which human beings share their values, goodness and truth, justice and humanity.

The three great areas that impacted on Goethe in Italy were mankind, art and nature. Of the three, it was nature that guided his concerns and animated his endeavours. The seminal idea that occupied him in Italy, upon which he brooded in the Botanical Gardens at Padua – one of the oldest such gardens in

the world – as well as in Naples and at Palermo, was the notion
of the 'archetypal plant' or *Urpflanze*. Earlier eighteenth-century
botany was dominated by Carl Linnaeus (1707–1778). The system
that Linnaeus devised involved a classification of the plant world.
It depended on the analysis of every part of a plant, placing the
data into a formal structure and giving each part a Latin name.
This hierarchical taxonomy lent a definitive order to the vegetable
kingdom. The method has since been recognized as typical of the
eighteenth-century's episteme – the nexus of concepts by which
the epoch understood the world.[53] Linnaeus' *Species plantarum*
(1753), which forms the internationally accepted basis of modern
botany, describes 7,300 species, and it establishes an 'organography'
with which to represent an exact model of nature in a hierarchy
of distinct concepts.[54] Goethe was deeply influenced by this work,
noting that 'apart from Shakespeare and Spinoza', nobody had
affected him more than Linnaeus (*LA*, 1/9, 16); but this was an
antithetical impact, for whereas Linnaeus 'separated' phenomena,
Goethe felt impelled to 'unify' them (*LA*, 1/9, 16). In almost every
way, his theory was the opposite of Linnaeus'. Goethe's approach
effected a major paradigm shift, of the type noted by Wolf Lepenies,
by replacing Linnaeus's rigid system by organic flexibility.[55] This led
from the static model typical of classical botany to the nineteenth-
century dynamism that produced evolutionary theory. The central
concept Goethe introduced to effect this change was that of the
Urpflanze, which he developed in Italy: 'Please tell Herder', he writes
to Frau von Stein on 23 March 1787, 'that I will soon be ready with
the archetypal plant' (*WA*, 1/31, 75). Then, writing from Palermo on
17 April, he fancies that he might actually discover it: 'For surely a
plant like that exists!' (*WA*, 1/31, 147) Finally, in a letter to Herder from
Rome on 8 June 1787 he observes:

> The *Urpflanze* will be the most extraordinary creation in
> the world, one that nature herself might envy me. With this

model and the key to it one can go on and on indefinitely inventing plants which must be consistent, I mean plants which, even though they do not exist, might exist, not just picturesque and poetic shadows or semblances, but possessing the quality of inner truth and necessity. The same law will be applicable to all living things. (*WA*, IV/8, 232–3)

Thus Goethe announces his discovery of the law of plant growth, the law governing the development of every species. It is simple, structural, generative and universal. Indeed, it may well be the first organic law in modern science. By aspiring to explain *all* life, moreover, Goethe's theory anticipates the science of genetics. Goethe described his theory in a short study, *An Essay to Explain the Metamorphosis of Plants* (*Versuch die Metamorphose der Pflanzen zu erklären*; 1799) (*CW*, XII, 76–97). Later he summarized his thesis in an evocative poem written in elegiac couplets, 'The Metamorphosis of Plants' ('Die Metamorphose der Pflanzen'; 1798). This is his earliest and most successful attempt to fuse science and literature in the manner of Lucretius' *De rerum natura*.[56] Addressing his beloved, in a gesture reminiscent of eighteenth-century women's writing,[57] Goethe begins with the confusion that appears to reign in the plant kingdom and seeks to resolve it:

> *Dich verwirret Geliebte die tausendfältige Mischung*
> *Dieses Blumengewühls über dem Garten umher,*
> *Viele Namen hörest du an und immer verdränget,*
> *Mit barbarischem Klang, einer den andern im Ohr.*
> *Alle Gestalten sind ähnlich und keine gleichet der andern*
> *Und so deutet das Chor auf ein geheimes Gesetz.* (*FA*, I, 639)

The poem recalls the verbal chaos of Latin plant names which confuse the would-be adept. Instead it sets up a 'secret law' governing the whole plant kingdom. This unitary law simplifies

Goethe's sketches showing development of stems from nodes and leaves, *c.* 1790.

the plant world. What counts is not the flowers' visible diversity, but their common origin and development. Goethe calls this 'metamorphosis'. John Whaley captures the tone of the original in his translation:

> This confuses you, dearest, these modes
> of thousands of minglings
> In the riotous flowers spread through the garden all round;
> Many names you hear with respect, and each one's barbaric
> Sound will always displace each that you heard just before.
> All forms are like in their structure, and
> none equates with the other;
> And this common accord points to a mysterious law,
> To a sacred enigma. (*SP*, 77)

Goethe believes he has discovered the structural plan common to all plants, by virtue of which every plant is unique in shape, yet identical with every other in form.[58] This discovery became the subject of a famous dispute between Goethe and Schiller at their first meeting on 30 July 1794. After Goethe described his archetypal plant, Schiller retorted: 'That's not an observation. That's an idea.'

To this Goethe sardonically replied: 'Then I'm happy to have ideas without knowing it.' (*cw*, XII, 20)

The importance of Goethe's contribution to botany has been stressed by the British botanist Agnes Arber, who translated his essay and analysed his findings at length.[59] She also confirms the impact of Goethe's ideas on Darwin, suggesting that they constitute a proto-theory of evolution. Moreover, the wider discipline Goethe founded with his 'morphology' (*cw*, XII, 53–72) – a neologism of Goethe's – is a field Darwin calls 'the most interesting department of natural history' and 'its very soul'.[60] Nothing more clearly shows the role of Goethe's endeavours in the development of modern science. Goethe's morphology, as I have indicated, decisively influenced the emergence of genetics, as it both contributed to the tradition that led to Gregor Mendel's (1822–1884) discovery, and inspired Mendel himself, who was well acquainted with Goethe's biology. Goethe is still cited in scientific papers on molecular genetics.[61] Indeed, no less a person than an editor of the science journal *Nature* has drawn attention to the link between Goethe's morphology and the science of DNA: his theory of the spiral-form of life appears to anticipate the structure of the double helix.[62] After Mendel and Darwin, his morphology also made its way into the theory of transformations proposed by D'Arcy Thompson in his monograph *On Growth and Form* (1917), which lists Goethe's ideas as its precursor.[63] From here Goethe's innovations have become subsumed under the discoveries of that other universal genius, Alan Turing.[64] The so-called 'Turing Patterns' constitute a vital continuation of Goethe's morphology. Turing's classic paper on 'The Chemical Basis of Morphogenesis' (1952) laid the foundations of modern theoretical biology: in a Goethean manner reminiscent of the 'archetypal' plant Turing showed the emergence of patterns – stripes, spots, whorls – from a homogeneous state. Thus Goethe's discoveries continue to shape the cutting edge of contemporary science.

5

The Classical Centre

Goethe constantly surprises his reader with new ideas.[1] Yet there is a continuity that defines his work, characterized by such motifs as nature and subjectivity. One of his most striking innovations is to break with the concept of a coherent personality and to introduce the notion of a multiple self, as we later find in the work of Walt Whitman (1819–1892) and Marcel Proust. In a conversation with Frédéric Soret (1795–1865), a Swiss private scholar and tutor to the future Grand Duke of Weimar, conducted in the poet's last year, Goethe observed: 'Mon oeuvre est celle d'un être collectif qui port un nom: Goethe.' (My oeuvre is that of a collective being that is called Goethe.)[2] Walt Whitman presents a similar view: 'Do I contradict myself?/ Very well then I contradict myself;/ (I am large, I contain multitudes.)'[3] Whitman seems to have been well acquainted with Goethe, as appears from some absorbing notes, in which, with reservations, he praises his German predecessor as 'the most profound viewer of Life known'. In a separate comment he observes how Goethe 'united qualities seemingly the most incompatible.'[4] Whitman specifically singles out Goethe's poems for being 'as great as the antique'.[5] Whitman thereby signals the major phase inaugurated after Goethe's return from Italy when, under the impact of antiquity, he switched his allegiance to the classical era. To some extent Shakespeare was now replaced by Homer, who stands behind Goethe's short verse epics *Reinecke the Fox* (*Reinecke Fuchs*; 1792) and *Hermann and Dorothea* (*Hermann und*

Dorothea; 1797); Latin poets such as Catullus, Ovid, Propertius and Tibullus inspired the *Roman Elegies*, and Lucretius, a significant model in the Enlightenment,[6] lay behind 'The Metamorphosis of Plants' (1790) and 'Metamorphosis of Animals' ('Metamorphose der Tiere'; *c.* 1798–9). Thus Goethe combined the qualities of 'the ancients' with those of 'the moderns', bridging the gap between opposites, as discussed by Nicolas Boileau-Despréaux (1636–1711), who argued for the ancients, and Bernard Le Bovier de Fontenelle (1657–1757), who defended the moderns. The debate had racked the intellectual world since the Renaissance.[7] Goethe's apparent reneging on his earlier principles as a modern in actual fact constituted an expansion of his allegiance, by virtue of which he subsumed his previous ideas under a new and timeless form. Initially he hesitated to regard himself as a classicist: 'We are convinced that no German author thinks of himself as a writer of classics.'[8] Yet with time, notably in his essay 'Winckelmann and his Age' ('Winckelemann und sein Jahrhundert'; 1805), he summarized antiquity in a manner redolent of his own achievement:

> Man can achieve much through the appropriate use of his individual abilities, and can achieve extraordinary things if several of his talents are combined. But he can only accomplish the unique, the wholly unexpected, if all his qualities unite within him and work together as one. (*CW*, III, 100f.)

Here is the 'wholeness' Goethe sought by virtue of which the individual unites his diverse faculties into a single power, focused and concentrated, such that the elements of his nature merge, enrich and empower one another so that they operate together as a single force.[9] This defining feature of his classicism – so opposed to modern fragmentation – helped to enable Goethe's mature diversity.

Johann Heinrich Meyer, *Christiane Vulpius with her Son August*, 1792, watercolour.

Goethe returned to Weimar from Rome on 18 June 1788, at a time when the French Revolution was already brewing, with an insurrection in Grenoble which was to dispose of the *ancien régime* and to change Europe – and Goethe's life – forever. Yet the transformation that most preoccupied him at this time was his meeting with the young Christiane Vulpius on 12 July. It seems they became lovers that same night. The actress Karoline Jagemann (1777–1844), the mistress of Duke Karl August, to whom she bore three children, has left us a lively portrait of Christiane. She had known her since childhood, and continued to observe her at close quarters:

> In my childhood [Christiane] lived next door to us and was a
> pretty, friendly, hard-working girl; out of her fresh face, which
> was as round as an apple, a pair of blazing jet-black eyes shone

forth, her slightly upturned mouth showed that she liked to laugh, she had a row of lovely white teeth, and her dark brown and full tresses fell onto her forehead and her nape. She kept her pensioned father and an aged aunt by her skill at making artificial flowers, and Goethe met her in this impoverished state; translated to superfluity and encouraged to lively new pleasures, she not only caught up with what she had missed, but ate and drank so much, that her childish and naive traits adopted the expression of a Bacchante while her form tended to excess.[10]

There seems no doubt that Christiane took to the bottle. Yet given Karoline's dislike of Goethe, who offended her in his role as the Weimar Theatre Director, and her constant intriguing against him, which eventually resulted in his resignation (1817), a certain prejudice towards Christiane cannot be ruled out. Karoline took particular offence at Goethe's patriarchal manner: all-knowing, controlling and authoritarian.[11] A drawing by the Swiss artist Johann Heinrich Lips (1758–1817) of Christiane seated with a book in her lap shows a rather modest and demure young lady. Christiane and Goethe lived together out of wedlock, yet he regarded it as a true marriage and celebrated their 'wedding anniversary' each year. Goethe and Christiane had five children, only one of whom survived, August (1789–1830); an unnamed child (1791); Caroline (1793); Carl (1795) and Kathinka (1802).

The relationship between Goethe and Christiane scandalized Weimar (not least Charlotte von Stein, who broke with Goethe), and contributed to the poet's reputation for immorality. Ever since the publication of *Werther* he had been regarded as immoral. Subsequent works did little to dispel that reputation, including *Faust: A Fragment* (*Faust, Ein Fragment*; 1790) and *Wilhelm Meister's Apprenticeship*, with its alleged promiscuity, not to mention *The Elective Affinities* and its depiction of adultery. Both Coleridge and De Quincey confessed to disquiet over Goethe's morals. Whitman

Karl Joseph Raabe, *August von Goethe*, 1811, miniature.

also condemned his 'wickedness'. Goethe's alleged immorality certainly harmed his reputation, but by and large, the charge diminished as the nineteenth century wore on.[12]

A charming poem drawn from life and published in 1796, which has the ring of truth, combines the manner of a Latin love poem with modern domesticity:

Der Besuch

Meine Liebste wollt ich heut beschleichen,
Aber ihre Türe war verschlossen.
Hab ich doch den Schlüssel in der Tasche!
Öffn' ich leise die geliebte Türe!

Auf dem Saale fand ich nicht das Mädchen,

Fand das Mädchen nicht in ihrer Stube,
Endlich da ich leis die Kammer öffne,
Find' ich sie, gar zierlich eingeschlafen,
Angekleidet auf dem Bette liegen.

Bei der Arbeit war sie eingeschlafen,
Das Gestrickte mit den Nadeln ruhte;
Zwischen den gefaltnen zarten Händen.
Und ich setze mich an ihre Seite,
Ging bei mir zu Rat', ob ich sie weckte?

Da betracht' ich den schönen Frieden,
Der auf ihren Augenlidern ruhte;
Auf den Lippen war die stille Treue,
Auf den Wangen Lieblichkeit zu Hause,
Und die Unschuld eines guten Herzens
Regte sich im Busen hin und wieder.
Jedes ihrer Glieder lag gefällig,
Aufgelöst von süßem Götterbalsam.
. . .
Lange saß ich so, und freute herzlich
Ihres Wertes mich und meiner Liebe,
Schlafend hatte sie mir so gefallen,
Daß ich mich nicht traute sie zu wecken.

Leise leg' ich ihr zwei Pomeranzen
Und zwei Rosen auf das Tischgen nieder,
Sachte, sachte schleich' ich meiner Wege.

Öffnet sie die Augen, meine Gute,
Gleich erblickt sie diese bunte Gabe,
Staunt, wie immer bei verschloßnen Türen
Dieses freundliche Geschenk sich finde. (FA, I, 697–8)

The unknown translator has nicely captured the intimacy of
Goethe's poem, which is less well-known than it deserves to be:

'The Visit'

To-DAY I thought to steal upon my darling,
But the door was closed of her apartments.
Of a key, however, I am master;
Noiselessly I glide within the doorway.
In the salon found I not the maiden,
Found the maiden not within the parlour,
But on tiptoe entering her chamber,
There I find her, sunk in graceful slumber,
In her robes, upon the sofa lying.

At her work had slumber overtaken her;
And the netting, with the needles, rested
'Twixt the fair hands that hung crosswise folded.
Silently I sate [*sic*] me down beside her,
And awhile I mused if I should wake her.

Awed me then the peace so sweet and holy,
Which upon her drooping eyelids rested:
On her lips abode a trustful quiet,
Beauty on her cheeks, the home of beauty;
And the tranquil movement of her bosom
Showed how innocent the heart that moved it.
All her limbs, so gracefully reposing,
Lay relaxed by sleep's delicious balsam:
There I sat enraptured, and the vision
Curbed the impulse I had felt to wake her,
With a spell that close and closer bound me.

. . .

137

Long while thus I sat, with heart elated,
Thinking of her worth and my devotion;
Sleeping, she with rapture so had filled me,
That I did not venture to awake her.
Placing softly down upon her table
Two pomegranates and two half-blown rosebuds,
Gently, gently, glide I from the chamber.
When she opes her eyes, my own heart's darling,
And they rest upon my gift, with wonder
Will she muse, how such fine token ever
There should be, and yet her door unopened.
When to-night again I see my angel,
Oh, how she will joy, and twofold pay me,
For this tribute of my heart's devotion![13]

Goethe, 'Christiane Vulpius on a Sofa', 1788/9, pencil drawing.

A matching drawing of this scene created in 1788 or 1789 places this portrait in the first year or so of their 'wild marriage'. The likely source for the theme of a sleeping lover is in Propertius' Elegies, 1.3; but Goethe has toned down the eroticism, creating a gentler, more intimate portrait than his Latin predecessor.[14] The symbolism of the pomegranates (an erotic image of abundance) and the roses creates a sense of splendour, intimating the joys that await the couple when she awakens, as well as the fertility of their love. No less a witness than Goethe's mother wrote of Christiane on the occasion of the latter's visit to Frankfurt: 'We were very happy and cheerful together. You can thank God! You rarely find such a dear – unspoilt, magnificent child of God. How my mind is at rest, since I know her completely, regarding *everything* concerning your good self.'[15]

Goethe's correspondence with Christiane provides a sincere source concerning their relationship and dispels the negative image spread by gossips and nay-sayers. Of their letters, 354 by Goethe and 247 by Christiane survive. They cover every aspect of their life together and exhibit tenderness and yearning, familiarity and gratitude. The charge that Christiane inhibited Goethe's talent is refuted by his exceptional creativity in their years together as well as by the stream of poems she inspired (*GHB*, IV/1, 393). His poem for her written on their 25th anniversary commemorates their meeting in tender fashion. Unusually, he sent it in a letter, on 26 August 1813:

Gefunden

Ich ging im Walde
So für mich hin,
Und nichts zu suchen
Das war mein Sinn.

Im Schatten sah' ich
Ein Blümchen stehn,

Wie Sterne leuchtend,
Wie Äuglein schön.

Ich wollt' es brechen;
Da sagt' es fein:
Soll ich zum Welken
Gebrochen sein?

Ich grub's mit allen
Den Wurzeln aus,
Zum Garten trug' ich's
Am hübschen Haus.

Und pflanzt es wieder
Am stillen Ort;
Nun zweigt es immer
Und blüht so fort. (*FA*, II, 20)

Even when he was over sixty, Goethe could still write with the innocence of youth. As ever, John Whaley's version hits just the right note:

'Found'

Once in the forest
I strolled content,
To look for nothing
My sole intent.

I saw a flower
Shaded and shy,
Shining like starlight,
Bright as an eye.

I went to pluck it:
Gently it said:
Must I be broken,
Wilt and be dead?

Then whole I dug it
Out of the loam
And to my garden
Carried it home.

There to replant it
Where no wind blows.
More bright than ever
It blooms and grows. (*cw*, 1, 191f.)

No one can fail to note the echoing of the form of Goethe's 'May Song' and the theme of Goethe's 'Rose on the Heath' written a full 42 years earlier: the abandon with which the youth uprooted the rose contrasts markedly with the tenderness the speaker here displays in carefully removing the unnamed flower from the ground, together with the surrounding earth, in order to ensure its survival. The gentle eroticism (Goethe often associates shining eyes with sexuality) invokes the bliss of a well-matched couple, while the lover's beauty ('More bright than ever') suggests an affection heightened by spirituality. Notwithstanding his dominance, the poem exudes a sense of mutuality, which is typical for Goethe and Christiane, and more generally for his love poetry. Few poets (one thinks of Donne) so represent the bliss of joint possession. Yet by all accounts Christiane was a feisty and spirited woman. She showed courage when, after the Battle of Jena on 14 October 1806, the invading French forces plundered Weimar and threatened their home. She defended Goethe and their property from the assault until he himself was able to intercede with the commanding officer.

Goethe's summer house, Weimar, from *Park um Weimar* (1958).

Five days later, he married her – partly no doubt in gratitude, partly to secure her inheritance in the case of his death, but, as has been argued, chiefly for love.[16] Her death ten years later, on 6 June 1816, devastated him. He locked himself in his room, refusing to accept that she had died. As he wrote: 'I do not wish to deny it to you – why should one play at being great? – for my condition is close to utter despair.'[17] The frequent asseverations of Goethe's 'happiness' cannot gainsay the depths he plumbed when hurled into grief.[18] Although Goethe rarely displays his suffering in his poems, he certainly explores it in his dramas.

In his most mature plays, *Iphigenia in Tauris* and *Torquato Tasso*, Goethe comes to terms with the ravages of suffering in a classical form. Both plays keep to the three classical unities of time, place and action, as first defined by Aristotle in his *Poetics* and given their final form by the French dramatist Pierre Corneille in his 'Discourse on the Three Unities' (1660).[19] Yet as C. M. Wieland (1733–1833) observed, both *Iphigenia* and *Tasso* contain elements of three distinct styles: the naturalness of Shakespearean drama, the simplicity of the Greeks and the good taste of French Neoclassicism.[20] Goethe's revival of classicism amounted to a dual clarification: he looked back both to Greek and Roman antiquity, and to the Italian Renaissance, and transplanted their style to Weimar. The resulting world-view has become known as Weimar Classicism. This achievement required a major act of the imagination on Goethe's part. The idea of the Renaissance had not yet been invented in historiography. The first historian to describe it was Jules Michelet, who devoted a volume to the topic, *Renaissance et Réforme* (1855), in his massive history of France. It was subsequently adopted by Jacob Burckhardt.[21] Goethe's Neoclassicism in his plays and essays and translations helped to pave the way for this very modern understanding of the Renaissance.

Goethe did not gain this insight at a single stroke. The developments emerged gradually. *Iphigenia in Tauris* cost him years, and *Torquato Tasso* also had a long gestation: he noted the theme on 30 March 1780, took the manuscript to Italy, and announced the play's completion almost a decade later on 8 August 1789. His polish often stems from exacting and tortuous labour. The discovery of the Renaissance derives from wrestling with the past, both to write his play, to achieve self-understanding, and to attain a new vision of history. This enabled him to locate Tasso in a (late) Renaissance context, the Court of Ferrara, and so to offer the first modern depiction of the period.[22] As with Michelet, Goethe's Renaissance marks 'the discovery of the world, the discovery of man.'[23] *Tasso*'s hero is a Renaissance man not in the sense that he possesses an encyclopaedic talent, but because he appears – like a sculpture by Michelangelo – in all his raw emotions as a passionate, suffering human being. The Renaissance mood appears in the play's opening scene, when Leonora of Este observes the revolution that led from medieval 'barbarism' to modern civilization. She singles out Petrarch for special mention, who is credited with inventing the idea of the Middle Ages, and with bringing about the rebirth of culture.[24] Speaking to the princess, she explains exactly how cultural change occurs. In doing so she uses the imagery of the celestial spheres – a scientific conceit in itself typical of Renaissance thinking:

A noble man attracts more noble men
And has the power to hold them, as you do.
Like calls to like; your brother and yourself,
Magnetic centres, draw into your orbit
Minds great as you and as your forbears were.

Robert Hart and Raphael Morghen, *Torquato Tasso*, 1834, stipple and line engraving on paper.

Here happily the splendid light was kindled
Of Science and of bold untrammelled thought,
When barbarism's murky twilight still
Concealed the wider world. (*cw*, VII, 57)

Leonora envisages the Renaissance as an event typified by the
new philosophy ('bold untrammelled thought') and by 'Science',
which spreads its 'light' upon the Middle Ages ('barbarism's murky
twilight') and thereby ushers in a new age. These are indeed the
hallmarks of the Renaissance. In a move that has become a topos of
modern historiography, she cites Petrarch, the first humanist and
the founder of the new poetry:

My father in his praises linked Ferrara
With Rome and Florence. Often then I longed
With my own eyes to see it. Now I'm there.
Here Petrarch was hospitably received. (*cw*, VII, 57)

Thus the opening sets the scene in the Renaissance. It also
introduces the all-pervasive Platonism of the age (*cw*, VII, 61).[25]
By its references to Renaissance philosophy and science, poetry
and politics, Goethe's *Tasso* establishes the paradigm shift which
heralded modernity.

In accord with this break, in the person of Tasso Goethe also
creates a new form of dramatic hero, comparable to Oedipus
and Hamlet: the poet as hero. Giorgio Vasari (1511–1574) first
paid homage to the ideal of the artist hero in connexion with
Michelangelo's *David* (1501–4),[26] but Goethe perhaps first treated
the artist as a hero in a work of literature. This changed the way
artists came to be seen. Thomas Carlyle, a great admirer of Goethe,
adopted his position in *On Heroes, Hero-worship, and the Heroic in
History* (1841):

The Poet is a heroic figure belonging to all ages; whom all ages possess, when once he is produced, whom the newest age as the oldest may produce; – and will produce, always when Nature pleases. Let Nature send a Hero-soul; in no age is it other than possible that he may be shaped into a Poet.[27]

Carlyle observes: '*Sincerity*, a deep, great, genuine sincerity, is the first characteristic of all men in any way heroic.' And he notes that the hero is 'an *original* man'.[28] By juxtaposing Tasso, the representative of the *vita contemplativa* with Antonio, who embodies the *vita activa*, Goethe treats the poet's sufferings as comparable to the labours of a man of action. This revaluation of the artist's inner life raises the theme of *Werther* to a higher level.[29] By taking the life of a major poet from the late Renaissance as its hero – Torquato Tasso (1544–1595), who was incarcerated in Ferrara as a madman – Goethe once again foregrounds an outsider, a misfit who cannot accommodate to society, and treats man's existential dilemma. Tasso's introspection, his destiny as a poet, threatens his very existence. The novelty of the play is its interiority. As Goethe noted: 'Everything in it only occurs inwardly; hence I am always afraid that it won't emerge clearly enough externally.'[30] The play is focused on Tasso's psychology. The action, minimal as it is, serves to illuminate his inner world.

It is often maintained that *Tasso* represents the tragedy of the artist.[31] But it is no more the tragedy of an artist than *Oedipus Rex* is the tragedy of a king, or *Hamlet* the tragedy of a prince. Tasso is the mouthpiece of human suffering. In antiquity – the world of outward action – a monarch could best epitomize the human lot; in modernity, the era of privacy and inwardness, it is the poet who can best illuminate what it means to be a human being. More particularly, Tasso, the poet imprisoned by the state, symbolizes the individual in the sense defined by the sociologist Norbert Elias,[32] as a Renaissance man torn apart upon the rack that stretches between the Middle Ages and modernity. Modern civilization, according to Elias, hinges on self-restraint, and this is the very quality that Tasso must learn. As he states towards the end when suffering overcomes him:

> TASSO And am I, then, as wretched as I seem?
>   As feeble as I show myself to you?
>   Is everything lost? And has my agony,
>   As though the ground were quaking, quite reduced
>   The building to a gruesome heap of rubble?
>   Have I no talent left, a thousandfold
>   To entertain, distract, sustain my mind?
>   Has all that energy failed that in my heart
>   At one time stirred? Have I annulled myself,
>   A nothing now, mere nothing?
>   No, all is there, and only I am nothing;
>   To myself I am lost, and she to me! (*CW*, VIII, 138)

Tasso experiences virtual death over his relation to the princess and the court. This sense of nothingness, which threatens to destroy him, leads him to tragedy. In response, Antonio, the man of action, calls upon Tasso to practice Socrates' wisdom and to know himself:

> ANTONIO But if you seem to lose yourself entirely,
>   Compare yourself! Remember who you are! (*CW*, VIII, 138)

Antonio leads Tasso towards a positive response. Yet he nonetheless endures the tragic clash between his individuality and the world. The words 'compare yourself' alter the conventional Greek wisdom 'know thyself'. Goethe, as has been said above, mistrusted the ancient idea. He argued instead that 'The human being only knows himself insofar as he knows the world.' (*CW*, XII, 39) Antonio wishes to lead Tasso back to the world. But every aspect of his life seems under threat: his links to his epic poem; to his patron, Alfonso II, Duke of Ferrara; to the princess, whom he loves; and to the statesman, Antonio, his rival for the duke's attention. He thus endures the clash that G.W.F. Hegel (1770–1831) sees as the essence of tragedy. This is a manifestation of the Divine, 'as it enters the world of the individual action.'[33] Indeed, the agony Tasso endures bears comparison with the 'piercing wounds' that the blinded Oedipus suffers when he exclaims 'the gods long since abhor me',[34] or with Lear's despair in the monosyllabic 'Howl, howl, howl, howl! O ye are men of stones:/ Had I your tongues and eyes, I'd use them so/ That Heaven's vault should crack.'[35] Whether in Oedipus' 'gods' or Lear's 'Heaven', a token of the Divine makes itself felt in tragic drama. This is also Tasso's case:

> TASSO Yes, at the right time you remind me of it! –
>
> . . .
>
> No, it's all gone! – One thing alone remains:
> Nature endowed us with the gift of tears,
> The agonised outcry when at last a man
> Can bear no more – and me above all others –
> In pain she left me euphony and speech
> To voice the deepest amplitude of my grief!
> When in their anguish other men fall silent
> A god gave me the power to tell my pain.
> (*CW*, VIII, 138)

In contrast to Oedipus or Lear, Tasso experiences the divine as an inner presence. This is truly modern. By virtue of his god-given gifts Tasso can express the suffering that overwhelms humanity. His inner world fractures, and by psychologically annihilating himself, he undergoes a virtual suicide. The experience of destruction is Tasso's total lot.

When Goethe completed his *Tasso*, the French Revolution had just begun with the siege of the Bastille on 14 July 1789. That day and its consequences were to occupy him for the rest of his life. As he remarked in a letter to F. H. Jacobi of 3 March 1790, 'You can easily imagine that the French Revolution was a revolution for me, too.' It was for him 'that most terrible of all events', which 'consumed' his talent 'to no purpose' (*cw*, XII, 40). This was not exactly true. He produced several fine works centred on the events: the plays *The Great Cophta* (*Der Gross-Cophta*; 1791), *The Bourgeois General* (*Der Bürgergeneral*; 1793) and *The Natural Daughter* (*Die natürliche Tochter*; 1801–3); the cycle of novellas *Conversations of German Emigres* (*Unterhaltungen deutscher Ausgewanderten*; 1795); and the short epics *Reinhardt the Fox* (1796) and *Hermann and Dorothea* (1797). Against the tumult and the destruction of the age, he proposes a credo of stability: 'For in an unstable time, if a man himself is unstable/ He will increase the unrest and spread it further and further;/ But he who holds firmly to his purpose gives shape to his whole world.' (*cw*, VIII, 306) For Goethe, who placed little faith in political action, only personal responsibility can afford a defence against chaos: right action alone can provide security and positively affect the world.

Goethe was nonetheless dragged into the vortex of the revolution. Against Goethe's advice, Karl August participated in the War of the First Coalition against France, and Goethe had no choice but to accompany him.[36] He set down his experiences in *Campaign in France, 1792* (*Campagne in Frankreich*; 1819–22). The book has a dual character: on the one hand, it glorifies Goethe as a hero at the centre of events, while on the other it attacks the warfare. It is an early example of anti-war literature. Both themes climax in the depiction of the Battle of Valmy on 20 September 1792. Although he was a non-combatant, and while Karl August retreated to the safety of a nearby hill, Goethe played the part of a Romantic hero by exposing himself directly to the French cannonade, and risked being blown to smithereens. He notes the strange sound made by the cannon balls, 'as though composed of the hum of a top, the bubbling of water, and the whistling of a bird'; and his own physical sensation, 'as though I were in a very hot place' – so-called 'cannon fever' (*cw*, v, 651f.). This dicing with death saw the poet place his fate into the hands of the gods, like an ordeal by fire, from which he emerged stronger and purer. Goethe's view of the battle has been disputed by scholars, who regard it as an insight *post festum*, but there is no reason to doubt his veracity: 'From this time forth a new epoch will begin, and you will be able to say that you were there.' (*cw*, v, 66) This was indeed a stunning victory for the untried French forces. Mere conscripts beat the well-tried Prussian army, and stopped the allies in their tracks en route to Paris. The impact of this achievement was incalculable: the revolutionary troupes celebrated by singing *La Marseillaise*, and the news travelled straight to Paris, where the National Convention sat, abolished the monarchy and declared the Republic. To make his prediction Goethe needed to be no more astute than the rest of his contemporaries. Even at the time the victory was widely recognized as epoch-making. Thus, in dramatically presenting the Battle of Valmy, Goethe situates himself as a witness to a turning-point in world history, and as the prophet of its future unfolding.

Goethe's project depended heavily on his collaboration with the poet, dramatist and philosopher Friedrich Schiller, together with whom he developed Weimar Classicism. Schiller settled in Weimar in 1787 and in Jena in 1789, where he held the Chair of History at the University, which it was Goethe's role to oversee. He was an immensely popular teacher. Goethe described his original meeting with Schiller in his essay 'Memorable Encounter' ('Glückliches Ereignis'; 1817) (*cw*, xii, 18–21), in which he presents the pair of them as opposites, representing the two contrary theories of modern philosophy: rationalism (on Schiller's part) and empiricism (on Goethe's). When Goethe described his 'archetypal plant' as an

Ludovika von Simanowitz, *Friedrich Schiller*, 1793, oil painting.

empirical observation to Schiller, the latter responded that it was not a fact, but an 'idea'. From that point on, they tried to mediate these positions and Goethe learned to incorporate idealism into his thinking. They both profited greatly from their collaboration. They met regularly, corresponded frequently, and discussed their ideas and their researches and debated each other's work-in-progress. Every one of Goethe's major works from this period benefited from Schiller's input, including *Wilhelm Meister's Apprenticeship* and *Faust I* (1808), besides which they stimulated each other to take new directions, as in the so-called Ballad Year of 1797, when they each wrote half a dozen ballads. They also collaborated on the satirical *Xenia* (1796), totalling 696 epigrams in all. These little texts often dealt lightly with the most urgent matters. In the following couplets, Goethe adopts the views of Adam Smith (1723–1790) on that most topical issue, the means by which to secure a universal peace, and then continues in the spirit of Voltaire (1694–1788),[37] with a response on the inevitability of war:

> *Zum ewigen Frieden*
> *Bald, kennt jeder den eigenen Vorteil und gönnet dem andern*
> *Seinen Vorteil, so ist ewiger Friede gemacht.*

> *Zum ewigen Krieg*
> *Keiner bescheidet sich gern mit dem Teile der ihm gebühret,*
> *Und so habt ihr den Stoff ewig und ewig zum Krieg.* (*FA*, 1, 500)

As ever, Goethe seeks out first principles. Here, he finds a characteristic polarity in the alternation of peace and war:

> *On Eternal Peace*
> Soon, everyone will know his own interest, and grant the other
> His interest, too, which is how we will make an eternal peace.

> *On Eternal War*
> Nobody gladly accepts the portion that he rightly deserves,
> And so you have grounds eternal, ay eternal, for an unjust war.

The cynicism Goethe and Schiller often display in these poems suits the genre – satire – as exemplified by the Roman poet Martial. But it does not necessarily represent their last word. If they had fun writing these poems, however, they did not necessarily enhance their reputation.

Schiller even wrote a distich to explain the form. It was translated by Coleridge, an avid follower of the German scene:

The Ovidian Elegiac Metre Described and Exemplified
In the hexameter rises the fountain's silvery column;
    In the pentameter ay, falling in melody back.[38]

The collaboration on *Xenia* was so successful that authorship
cannot readily be distinguished: this testifies to a remarkable
symbiosis between these two giants of German literature.

Schiller wrote some of his finest plays at this time, and the works
the two writers then produced represent the canon of Weimar
Classicism. The fullest theoretical expression of their ideals appears
in Schiller's *On the Aesthetic Education of Man in a Series of Letters* (*Über
die ästhetische Erziehung des Menschen in einer Reihe von Briefen*; 1794).[39]
This provides a philosophical response to the French Revolution,
but unlike other counter-revolutionary blasts, chief among them
Edmund Burke's *Reflections on the Revolution in France* (1790), Schiller
produces a positive construct whereby to preserve humanity from
conflict. Central to his thesis is the view that the modern citizen is
as yet unprepared for a republic and needs to acquire the moral and
intellectual skills necessary to fit himself for government. He makes
the point by comparing modernity with ancient Greece:

The polypoid character of the Greek States, in which every
individual enjoyed an independent existence but could, when
the need arose, grow into the whole organism, now made
way for an ingenious clock-work, in which, out of the piecing
together of innumerable but lifeless parts, a mechanical kind
of collective life ensued. State and Church, laws and customs,
were now torn asunder . . . Everlastingly chained to a little
fragment of the Whole, man himself develops into nothing
but a fragment . . . Weary at last of sustaining bonds which
the State does so little to facilitate, positive society begins
. . . to disintegrate into a state of primitive morality.[40]

This analysis of modern ills anticipates Karl Marx and Herbert Marcuse (1898–1978),[41] albeit Marx drew the opposite conclusion: he wanted to change society in order to transform the individual. Schiller's response involves restoring individual 'wholeness', an idea linked back to Joseph Addison's (1672–1719) phrase, 'the whole man is to move together'.[42] He places his faith in the so-called 'aesthetic state' as the instrument to restore the lost harmony of humanity: 'In the Aesthetic State [there] is a free citizen, having equal rights with the noblest . . . Here therefore, in the realm of Aesthetic Semblance, we find [the] ideal of equality fulfilled'.[43] Goethe, while sharing with Schiller the imperative to establish 'wholeness', did not accept this raptness, and took a more practical approach in *Wilhelm Meister*.

Goethe's *Wilhelm Meister* belongs to that handful of novels that possess world-historical significance.[44] This was recognized by his contemporary Friedrich Schlegel (1772–1829), the leading proponent of early Romanticism, who claimed that the three great 'tendencies' of the age were J. G. Fichte's *Science of Knowledge* (*Wissenschaftslehre*; 1794), Goethe's *Wilhelm Meister* and the French Revolution.[45] For all the strange juxtaposition, as Schlegel himself noted, there is a strict alignment between the three, which can be put thus: Fichte accomplished a revolution of the spirit whereby the ego became the dominant category in philosophy; Goethe completed a revolution in art, through which the individual achieved supremacy in the world; and the French Revolution marked a political reversal, inasmuch as the people assumed the dignity of their own rule. By transforming the novel into a form of wisdom literature and treating it as a genre comparable to philosophy,[46] Goethe uses it to come to terms with political philosophy: thus the narrative culminates in its adoption of social contract theory,[47] as it dominated political thought from Hobbes to Kant.

The kernel of the novel and its *Weltanschauung* can be found in a statement Wilhelm makes in a letter: 'To put it to you in a *single* word: to fully educate myself, just as I am, was always my obscure

Print by L. Schütze of Goethe's house on the Frauenplan, Weimar, after a drawing by Otto Wagner, 1827.

wish and my intention, ever since my earliest youth.' (*CW*, IX, 174) The German verb *bilden* here means 'form', 'fashion', 'shape' and not just 'educate': it involves drawing out the whole person until it becomes a harmonious and complete member of society. Often interpreted as a form of inwardness, *Bildung* actually leads to socialization.[48] This vital concept of individual growth, developed from Goethe's studies in natural science by analogy with plants and animals, breaks with the mechanistic view of man promulgated in the Enlightenment by philosophers such as La Mettrie in *L'Homme Machine* (Man a Machine; 1747), and supplants it by the image of the individual as an organic being. The educational novel itself was pioneered by Rousseau in *Émile* (1762). In a typically contrarian gesture, Goethe takes issue with Rousseau's thesis, as contained in *Émile*'s opening sentence: 'God makes all things good; man meddles with them and they become evil.'[49] *Wilhelm Meister* reverses this vision by demonstrating the moral ascent of an individual via trial and error. To treat the ideal of *Bildung* as 'ironic', as sometimes occurs today, denies the evidence so apparent in Goethe's rebuttal of Rousseau: *Émile* preaches self-control, *Meister* inculcates freedom; *Émile* argues that a mistake can undo a character, *Meister* shows how it fosters maturity; and *Émile* claims the distinction between child and adult, whereas *Meister* shows a miraculous continuity.[50] George Eliot's (1819–1880) praise of Goethe seems apposite:

> Everywhere he brings us into the presence of living, generous humanity – mixed and erring, and self-deluding, but saved from utter corruption by the salt of some noble impulse, some disinterested effort, some beam of good nature.[51]

There is a galaxy of characters in the novel, each of whom pulses with energy. Each of them is memorable. Each unique. Each lives by an inner rule. While being consistent, they are never predictable, and this lends them their colourful truth. From Wilhelm's first love, the actress Marianne, who cross-dresses as a soldier, to the flirtatious Philine and the tragic Mignon, with her moving songs, or the homely Therese and the noble Natalie, the sarcastic Jarno, the deranged Harper and the wise Abbé, Goethe has peopled his novel with unforgettable characters. These richly drawn figures, with all their failings, are as generous as they are instructive, and thereby contribute to Wilhelm's formation. It is, the reader understands, not only maxims but life that provides education. We observe 'the whole human being' that Goethe and Schiller set at the core of their humanism; for here, that 'awareness of the possibilities of life' enters fiction, which F. R. Leavis (1895–1978) considered the hallmark of great writing:[52] sexuality plays as much a role as abstinence. The individual must not only acquire knowledge and skills, but cultivate the body and its movements to achieve a harmony. The emphasis on 'life' occurs in a memorable apothegm which is given a prominent place towards the end: 'Remember to live.' (*cw*, IX, 331) This inverts the old maxim, *memento mori*. Goethe

'Wilhelm with Mignon and the Harpist', 19th-century postcard.

is the poet of affirmation. His faith in life as the highest good recurs throughout his work, issuing in the lapidary formula: 'However it may be, life itself is good' (*CW*, I, 264–7). As a celebration of life in all its variety, *Meister* affords its reader a rare pleasure, and inculcates both empathy and insight. The impact it has had on German

Circle of Joseph Nicolas Peroux, *Marianne von Willemer*, 1809, watercolour.

culture can be measured, inter alia, by its probable influence on Jewish emancipation.[53]

The novel provided the archetype for Romantic poetry, as expressed by Friedrich Schlegel in the celebrated 116th *Athenaeum Fragment* (1797). *Wilhelm Meister* exemplifies this ideal by comprising every genre: the epic narrative; the drama, as contained in the episode on theatre; the lyric, present in the evocative songs; criticism, in conversations on Shakespeare; and wisdom literature, in the maxims and aphorisms. As I have suggested, it also aspires to philosophy, for example in the Certificate of Apprenticeship (*cw*, ix, 303): when Wilhelm is told, 'Nature has given you your freedom' (*cw*, ix, 304) he finally leaves the state of nature and, as Hobbes understands it, becomes bound by the social contract with society.[54] Thus – once again Goethe positions himself against Rousseau's *Émile* and contradicts *The Social Contract* – society here represents the realm of freedom.[55] This alters social contract theory, as advocated in the French Revolution, for in Goethe's view, man in society already possesses freedom; it needs, however, to be achieved not by a change in society, but by personal emancipation.[56]

It should be amply clear that this is a novel that repays our attention by enlarging our capacity to think, and that it does so by raising literature to the level of philosophy. Though not the first such German *Bildungsroman*, it inspired many others and founded a long tradition in which bourgeois culture fashioned itself:[57] for example Stendhal's *La Chartreuse de Parme* (The Charterhouse of Parma; 1839), Balzac's *Illusions perdues* (Lost Illusions; 1843), Dickens's *David Copperfield* (1849–50), James's *Roderick Hudson* (1875), Flaubert's *L'Éducation sentimental* (A Sentimental Education; 1869) and Joyce's *A Portrait of the Artist as a Young Man* (1916). As Franco Moretti has shown, these texts helped to shape the life of the modern bourgeoisie.[58]

6

The Intellectual Capital of the World

Goethe changed the face of the world by the force of his genius
and lent Weimar that cultural prestige which, as Morgenthau
has shown, equals power in the political realm.[1] He thereby
heightened the legitimacy of a minuscule state, such that it became
an international centre.[2] Goethe and Schiller together exercised
a powerful attraction over their divided country in the latter part
of the century. The University of Jena, where Schiller taught and
which Goethe oversaw in an official capacity, became the focal
point for Romanticism, so that it may in retrospect be called the
Intellectual Capital of the World.[3] The greatest philosophers of
the age, inspired by Kant's discoveries, sought to outdo him with
their systems. This led to the finest flowering of any single group of
thinkers since ancient Greece. No less than four major philosophers
taught in Jena: K. L. Reinhardt (1757–1823), J. G. Fichte, G.W.F.
Hegel and F.W.J Schelling (1775–1854). In addition, the critic and
philologist Friedrich Schlegel (1772–1829) worked there, founding
the Romantic manifesto *Athenaeum* (1798–1800) with his elder
brother August Wilhelm. Others who joined them included the
philologist Wilhelm von Humboldt (1767–1835) and his brother
the scientist Alexander (1769–1859).[4] Two budding poets also
studied here, attracted by Schiller's teaching: Novalis and Friedrich
Hölderlin – whose *entrée* with Goethe completely misfired. The
Romantics debated philosophy and poetry, politics and linguistics,
law and science, labour and society, and many other areas. All this

Caroline Rehberg, *Friedrich Schlegel*, before 1800, drawing.

provided a match for Goethe's own encyclopaedic interests. The ideas envisioned in Jena or in direct proximity helped to shape modernity.[5] Hardly an area remained untouched, and its results can be seen across the continent – in Germany and Britain, France and Spain, Italy and Bohemia, Poland and Russia. Although the Romantics never formed a coherent group, but comprised overlapping circles, they nonetheless both affirm the centrality of Jena in the intellectual world and demonstrate Goethe's ability to assemble around him a galaxy of talent. Moreover, his sociability and curiosity guaranteed him an ever-expanding circle of friends. The Romantic manifesto itself, as formulated by Friedrich Schlegel in the 116th *Athenaeum Fragment* (1798), echoes Goethe's multiplicity:

> Romantic poetry is a progressive universal poetry. Its purpose is not merely to reunite all of the different genres and to put poetry in touch with philosophy and rhetoric. Romantic poetry wants to and should combine and fuse poetry and prose, genius and criticism, artistic poetry and nature poetry. It should make poetry lively and sociable, and make life and society poetic. It should poeticize wit and fill all of art's forms with sound material of every kind to form the human soul, to animate it with flights of humour. Romantic poetry embraces everything that is purely poetic, from the greatest art systems, which contain within them still more systems, all the way down to the sigh, the kiss that a poeticizing child breathes out in an artless song.[6]

This aesthetic reverberated throughout Europe in subsequent Romantic literature. The work that chiefly prompted this universalism was *Wilhelm Meister*, in which all such diversities merged.[7] Moreover, Goethe's studies of nature also inspired Romantic science,[8] affecting Novalis, Schelling, Humboldt, J. W. Ritter (1776–1801) – the discoverer of ultraviolet light – as well as Henrik Steffens (1773–1845) and Lorenz Oken (1779–1851), who founded the first German scientific society. But it was Novalis who developed these ideas most radically in his plans for a 'Romantic Encyclopaedia' or a 'scientific Bible'.[9] Even Wordsworth's aesthetic looks back to Schlegel's ideas. In Wordsworth's celebrated 'Preface' to the *Lyrical Ballads* (1798) he maintains the fitness of chemistry, mineralogy and botany for inclusion in verse. To such diverse fields the poet lends his 'transfiguration'.[10] Goethe himself was not best pleased by the Romantics' tendency to take his ideas to new extremes and soon found himself in opposition to the movement. In his most critical comment, in a conversation with Eckermann of 2 April 1829, he observed: 'I call the classic healthy, the romantic sick.'[11]

It was not actually the Romantics who established the Goethe cult that dominated German culture in the nineteenth century, and which has continued in a lesser form until today. It was begun by the Berlin *salonnière* Rahel Varnhagen (1771–1833). Rahel belonged to a small group of emancipated Jewesses who held dazzling salons.[12] 'Our circle' (as she called it) formed in 1790. It was a shining mix. Visitors included the Romantics Friedrich Schlegel, Ludwig Tieck (1773–1853), Clemens Brentano (1778–1842), Heinrich von Kleist (1777–1811) and Heinrich Heine; the diplomat Friedrich von Gentz (1764–1832), who played a leading role in the Vienna Conference; and it also provided a platform for Beethoven's friend, the Prussian composer Prince Louis Ferdinand (1772–1806). According to the Danish literary scholar Georg Brandes (1842–1927), this salon was the first place in Germany to manifest world citizenship – an ideal directly linked to Kant and Goethe. The latter's name runs like a red thread through Rahel's voluminous correspondence. He warmed to Rahel, whom he met twice, describing her in the highest terms as a 'beautiful soul' – the acme of womanhood. Goethe also proved hospitable to her close friend, the doctor David Veit (1771–1814), who has provided a fine pen-portrait of the writer:

He is far taller than usual, and fat and broad shouldered in proportion to his size . . . His forehead is exceptionally fine, finer, than I have ever seen; his eyebrows are as in the painting [by Johann Heinrich Lips], but his completely *brown eyes* are turned down further than there. There is much spirit in his eyes, but not the devouring fire which people speak of so much. He already has folds under his eyes and quite considerable sacks; altogether one can recognise his age of forty-four to forty-five . . . His nose is a real hawk's nose, only that the bend in the middle loses itself quite gently . . . His mouth is very beautiful, small, and capable of exceptional movement; only he is disfigured by his unusually yellow, crooked teeth.[13]

Rahel and her circle did not just read Goethe; they imagined themselves as his creations and lived through his imaginings.[14] Her salon had the resonance and longevity to promote Goethe's reputation – which was by no means as secure around 1800 as it appears today – on a truly national basis. If she and her illustrious friends did not actually invent Goethe, they established his renown. Yet it was another woman – of whom Rahel had a somewhat low opinion – namely Mme de Staël, in her book *De l'Allemagne* (Of Germany) of 1813, who most contributed to his international reputation.[15] For Mme de Staël, Goethe was the representative German, and one of the great conversationalists of the age:

When Goethe is induced to talk, he is admirable; his eloquence is enriched with thought; his pleasantry is, at the same time, full of grace and philosophy; his imagination is impressed by external objects, as was that of the ancient artists; nevertheless his reason has but too much the maturity of our times. Nothing disturbs the strength of his mind, and even the defects of his character, ill-humour, embarrassment, constraint pass like clouds round the foot of that mountain on the summit of which his genius is placed.[16]

This encomium is among the finest portraits of Goethe by one of his contemporaries.

Goethe's main scientific interest, his studies of colour, issued in his *Contributions to Optics* (*Beiträge zur Optik*; 1791–2), which subsequently led to his magnum opus, his chief scientific work, *Theory of Colours* (*Zur Farbenlehre*; 1810).[17] Nothing he did filled him with so much pride. Nothing he did has been subject to such vilification. Nicholas Boyle scathingly speaks of his experiments with the prism as 'a tissue of ingenious and obstinate error'.[18] This is a common view, but wrong all the same. As will shortly be seen, Goethe's theory is accurate and cannot really be faulted as an explanation of colour. Goethe himself must share a large part of the blame for the hostility it encountered. He presented his findings as a critique of Newton's *Opticks* (1704), which he owned in the form of the definitive fourth edition (1730). He attacked Newton often and intemperately. Yet as he later saw (*LA*, 1/8, 205), he was not dealing with optics at all, the mathematical theory of light, but with colour.[19] As a result of this misprision Goethe's theory has been almost universally ridiculed. No less a scientist than Helmholtz saw fit to rebut it.[20] To reinstate it, one of our best scholars has re-interpreted it – somewhat implausibly in my view – as a 'colour theology'.[21] This is a rather wayward reading, which depends on supposing that when Goethe believed he was doing science he was really studying God. There is no reason to accept that Goethe could have been quite so misguided. Indeed the theological interpretation does not bear scrutiny. It simply takes a metaphor for the fact. For the sake of clarity in this tricky matter, therefore, I shall rehearse the central point of the theory, and will then attempt a vindication.

At this point it may be helpful to say a word about method. It was more than a century ago that Wilhelm Dilthey (1833–1911) expounded the difference between the human sciences based on 'understanding' and the natural sciences concerned with 'explaining';[22] but the discussion of Goethe's colour theory too frequently relies on an outmoded and thoroughly discredited methodology. Literary scholars habitually critique Goethe's views in positivistic terms instead of expounding his ideas. Yet nowhere in the history of science, not least since the pioneering studies by Joseph Agassi and Imre Lakatos, would such a method be acceptable today.[23] It is anachronistic to mock Copernicus's circular orbits, Kepler's geometrical cosmology, Descartes' spirals or indeed Newton's alchemy.[24] It is similarly inappropriate to condemn Goethe's view of Newton. His attitude was common: Leibniz stressed the weaknesses of Newton's concept of gravity;[25] Bishop Berkeley (1685–1753) criticized his theory of motion; David Hume had strong reservations about his science in general. In critiquing Newton, Goethe was not atypical. As is well established, moreover, Hume sought to replace Newton's world system by a 'science of man'.[26] In the same way, Goethe placed the human being into the centre of his theory. This was the model that later taught Einstein to turn the prevailing view of the physical universe around and to start with the observer: that meant the end of the absolute world system and the origin of the special theory of relativity. Thus Einstein's endorsement of Goethe's epistemology established a new cosmology.

Goethe, Schiller and the Brothers Humboldt in Schiller's Garden, after a 19th-century drawing by Andreas Lauber.

In his essay 'The Experiment as Mediator between Object and Subject' ('Der Versuch als Vermittler zwischen Objekt und Subjekt', 1792 (*cw*, XII, 11–17)), Goethe sets out his method. It is clearly argued in opposition to Newton. The latter's method is based on a mathematical analysis of colour: he argues in terms of definitions, axioms, proposition and proofs. His optics is a quantitative science. Goethe takes the opposite line. He wishes to discover causes which lie behind the appearance of colour in nature. Newton analyses. Goethe synthesizes. Since it is how colours arise in the natural world that interests Goethe, he is not concerned with geometrical proofs, but with what happens on the surface of an object when a colour is created. He therefore tries to establish a sequence of experiments that does not follow logical or mathematical criteria, as Newton's do, but which replicates nature itself:

> As worthwhile as each individual experiment may be, it receives its real value only when united or combined with other experiments. However, to unite or combine just two somewhat similar experiments calls for more rigour and care than even the sharpest observer usually expects from himself. Two phenomena may be related, but not nearly so closely as we think. Although one experiment seems to follow from another, an extensive series of experiments might be required to put the two into an order actually conforming to nature. (*cw*, XII, 13–14)

Goethe's method does not, as I have said, attempt to construct a mathematical theory, but to understand nature's own operations. This explains his scepticism towards constructing hypotheses on the basis of isolated facts, what he calls 'an individual experiment' to prove 'an idea already formed' (*cw*, XII, 14). In physics, however, proofs depend on a so-called 'crucial experiment' – a single experiment that could make or break a theory. From Goethe's point of view this approach is artificial: it does not represent nature, but an abstract idea. Although Goethe's view was ridiculed as naive for over a century, as the historian of chaos theory James Gleick (b. 1954) observes, today Goethe's method has come to be accepted, precisely because it follows the complexities of natural events.[27] For, as Ludwig Wittgenstein was the first to point out, Goethe's theory does not at all depend on a so-called *experimentum crucis*, but reveals the phenomena of colour as they appear in series of interconnected events.[28] Instead of Newton's separate geometrical proofs, therefore, Goethe proposes a series of interlocking experiments; and then invites the scientist to repeat these experiments, in order to understand his conclusions. For him, the crucial experiment has no validity because it is an isolated event, and could never exist in nature. Such experiments trash the plenitude of nature; and indeed, there are many truths in nature that cannot be subjected to such a test at all (*FA*, 1/10, 760). Whereas Newton is a mathematician, Goethe is a radical empiricist. It is this empiricism which underlies the *Contributions*, whose lack of a theoretical framework somewhat reduces their comprehensibility. Yet this deficit is more than mitigated by the style. Its charm introduces a beauty to scientific writing on a par with Gilbert White's *Natural History of Selbourne* (1789).

Whereas Newton sets out to 'explain the properties of light', as he writes at the beginning of the *Opticks*, Goethe – I repeat – wants to understand 'colour'.[29] These goals are antithetical and lead to opposite conclusions. Far from making a 'great error',[30] Goethe was breaking new ground in establishing a phenomenology of colour. In other words, as Dennis Sepper shows, he effected 'a reconstitution of chromatics, the science of colour'.[31] While Newton separated the colours contained in white light, Goethe examined the effects of light in producing colour. He adopts the position taken by Keats at a legendary dinner hosted by the painter Benjamin Haydon (1786–1846) and also attended by Wordsworth and Charles Lamb (1775–1834). On this occasion Keats claimed that Newton 'destroyed

all the poetry of the rainbow, by reducing it to prismatic colours'.[32]
Goethe, in a similar vein, explains his thesis as follows:

> The condition of space around us, when we cannot see any
> objects before us with healthy eyes, we call darkness. We
> think it abstractly without an object as a negation, it is,
> like rest, welcome to the tired, unpleasant to the lively.
>
> We cannot, however, ever conceive of light in abstracto,
> for we become aware of it as the effect of a particular
> body, which exists in space, and by means of this same
> effect makes other bodies visible. (*cw*, XII, 15)

Goethe always begins with observable nature, with the immediate
experience of the senses, and places the position of the observer
into the centre of his analysis, which here means the organ of
perception itself, the 'healthy eye'. This holism never separates the
observer from what he observes. Such extreme empiricism is more
radical than that commonly adopted in the sciences since the time
of Galileo. As Goethe says in *Theory of Colours*:

> Colours are the actions and reactions of light. In this
> sense we can expect them to tell us something about light.
> Although it is true that colours and light are intimately
> related to one another, we must consider both as belonging
> to all nature. Through them nature seeks to manifest itself,
> in this case to the sense of sight, to the eye. (*cw*, XII, 158)

In contrast to Newton, who sees colours as being contained in light,
Goethe regards them as its products. His theory is that colour occurs
when 'light' and 'dark' meet in the medium of an 'opaque body':[33]

> The highest degree of light, such as that of the sun . . . is for
> the most part colourless. This light, however, seen through a

medium but very slightly thickened, appears to us yellow. If the density of such a medium be increased, or if its volume become greater, we shall see the light gradually assume a yellow-red hue, which at last deepens to a ruby colour. If on the other hand darkness is seen through a semi-transparent medium, which is itself illumined by a light striking on it, a blue colour appears: this becomes lighter and paler as the density of the medium is increased, but on the contrary appears darker and deeper the more transparent the medium becomes: in the least degree of dimness short of absolute transparence, always supposing a perfectly colourless medium, this deep blue approaches the most beautiful violet.

This interaction between light and shade constitutes what Goethe calls an 'original phenomenon', an *Urphänomen*. Such phenomena are irreducible facts. They produce the full range of other phenomena in their respective areas. Goethe derives them from 'empirical' facts, which in turn are subsumed under 'scientific categories', and these lead on to 'even higher levels':

In the process we become familiar with certain requisite conditions for what is manifesting itself. From this point everything gradually falls into place under higher principles and laws revealed not to our reason through words and hypotheses, but to our intuitive perception through phenomena. We call these phenomena *archetypal phenomena* because nothing higher manifests itself in the world . . . What we have been describing is an archetypal phenomenon of this kind. On the one hand we see light or a bright object, on the other darkness, or a dark object. Between them we place turbidity and between them and through this mediation colours arise from the opposites; these colours, too, are opposites . . . (*cw*, xii, 194f.)

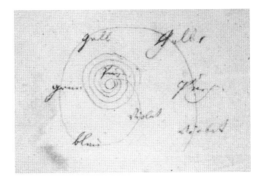

A design in Goethe's hand of a colour spiral, showing the emergence of all colours from purple by a process of intensification.

This description contains the quintessence of Goethe's thought on colour. The archetypal phenomenon forms the ultimate point that science can reach. The physicist Werner Heisenberg (1901–1976), to whom we owe the discovery of the uncertainty principle, argues that Goethe's view is non-Cartesian;[34] but more fundamentally, it is anti-Galilean: what Goethe opposes is the entire drift of the modern physical sciences, the mathematization of the world picture.

Goethe's epistemology in his colour theory derives from the Neoplatonic philosopher Plotinus (204–270), who systematized the idea of the Great Chain of Being. This belief in a continuous chain connecting every sphere from the divine to the lowest forms underwrote the philosophy of the Renaissance.[35] It also underlies the continuity Goethe sees in nature. His reversion to Plotinus signifies his faith in a spiritual order suffusing creation. The doctrine features in a little poem near the beginning of his colour theory which tells how the eye as the organ of perception shares an affinity with the perceived – in other words, how the physiological colours in the eye enable the subject to see colour in the natural world:

Wär' nicht das Auge sonnenhaft,
Die Sonne könnt es nie erblicken;
Lag nicht in uns des Gottes eigne Kraft,
Wie könnt uns Göttliches entzücken? (FA, I, 645)

At his lyrical best, Goethe writes with an artless purity that defies translation; it is impossible to convey the richness or the beauty of the original:

If the eye were not like the sun,
The sun it could never see;
If the god's power did not dwell in us,
How could we perceive Divinity?

Goethe knows how to shock in the most ingratiating manner; for this poem places him at odds with the two dominant schools of epistemology, empiricism and rationalism. Basing himself on the belief in man's divinity Goethe establishes an analogy between the sun and the eye.[36] There is a discrete cosmology here. The eye serves as a tiny planetary orb with respect to the entire universe. Their bond enables human vision; and from vision the apprehension of colour arises. By invoking a cosmos structured on inner similarities, Goethe opposes both rationalism and empiricism. Thus, in a light and gentle vein, the poet as scientist tilts at Newtonian mechanics. Yet elsewhere his assault was more often intemperate, and this has caused much puzzlement. But it is not really hard to explain. In berating Newton's 'partial madness' (*LA*, 1/6, 262), Goethe combats the abstraction of the world picture wrought by physics: he thus defended the spiritual unity of creation. It was a doctrinal combat. What was at stake was the intellectual leadership of modernity. Goethe wished to install his humanism into a scientific context, in order to combat what he saw as the de-humanizing dangers of modern physical science. This faith in the spirit, although questioned in the more secular context of the anglophone world, survived in Germany with its adherence to *Kultur*.[37]

Goethe recognizes five archetypal phenomena: (1) magnetism; (2) electricity; (3) the action of light and shade to make colour; (4) the archetypal plant; and (5) the archetypal animal (*GHB*, IV/2, 1080–82). In each of these he finds 'attraction and repulsion', what he came to call 'polarity',[38] an idea he gave its definitive formulation in 1828:

> the two great driving wheels in all nature: the concepts of *polarity* and *intensification*, the former a property of matter insofar as we think of it as material, the latter insofar as we think of it as spiritual. Polarity is a state of constant attraction and repulsion, while intensification is a state of ever-striving ascent. (*CW*, XII, 6)

These are the forces at work in both impelling the plant to grow and in causing colour to appear in the natural world: thus, from the polar action of light and shade, an act of intensification causes the colour purple to form. By looking at the emergence of colour in this way, Goethe created a colour circle as an explanatory tool. He began by applying the theory of attractions to colour and made a drawing of the spectrum shaped like a magnet in 1798 (*LA*, I/3, plate xxiii). He discussed this with Schiller, who took an active part in his researches. It was Schiller in fact who proposed a term for generating colour that prompted Goethe's own terminology: a so-called 'common' mixture produces green, and a process of 'intension' – what Goethe later called 'intensification' – creates a 'noble mixture', or purple (*GHB*, III, 721). Such interactions give rise to every colour. Although the analogy with magnetism may seem curious, with respect to the history of science it makes sense, for Goethe (*HA*, XIV, 156) implicitly reverts to that foundational text of modern physics, William Gilbert's *On the Magnet* (1600). This impressed thinkers like Galileo and Hobbes with its empirical method, and influenced many later scientists.[39] Goethe may well have been inspired by Gilbert's discovery of thermal magnetization and demagnetization, whereby magnets undergo a colour change (like any heated or cooling iron).[40] That would point to a unity in

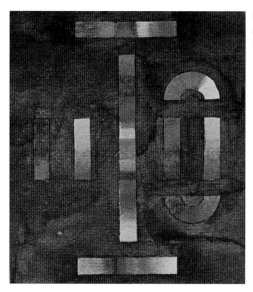

Goethe, *Spectrum in the Shape of a Magnet*, 1798.

nature linking physical forces to chromatics. By intimating this, Goethe approaches an issue also debated in Newton's *Opticks*: 'The changing of Bodies into Light, and Light into Bodies, is very conformable to the Course of Nature, which seems delighted with transformations.'[41] The forces Newton infers in these operations are those of attraction and repulsion[42] – the very ones noted by Goethe – but Newton did not extend this insight to develop the notion of polarity.

Let us revert to the question of method. Notwithstanding the criticism – not to say opprobrium and ridicule – heaped on Goethe for his critique of Newton, he would have found strong support in at least one quarter. As noted above, David Hume held the same view.[43] Hume's impact on the German *Sturm and Drang* is well-attested,[44] and Goethe knew Hume's work (*FA*, I, 606). Like Hume in *A Treatise of Human Nature* (1739), he pursues a 'science of man', and shares Hume's belief, expressed in the *Treatise*, that one must not overstep knowledge of the external properties of bodies.

Thus Hume argues against Newton that it is 'beyond the reach of human understanding' to 'penetrate into the nature of bodies, or explain the secret causes of their operations'.[45] This is the very position adopted by Goethe. Likewise Hume maintains that we must 'confine our speculations to the appearances of objects to our senses, without entering into disquisitions concerning their real nature and operations.'[46] Hume is here sceptically critiquing Newton's concept of force,[47] but the same argument holds for his analysis of colour. Far from being an outdated adversary of Newtonianism – an 'embarrassment', as has so often been claimed – Goethe, like Hume, is sceptical as regards to its abstractions. In point of fact, he seeks to overcome the dualism of experience and science that has exercised some of the best philosophers of science, including E. A. Burtt (1892–1989), A. N. Whitehead and Ernst Cassirer.[48] Both Whitehead and Cassirer are explicit advocates of the Goethean viewpoint.

Although Goethe's colour theory has been vindicated for almost sixty years, this has yet to percolate into scholarship. Around 1964 Mitchell Feigenbaum, in conducting the research that led him to Chaos Theory, examined Goethe's colour theory and decided that it was correct.[49] This led him to transfer Goethe's methodology into his own field. That was a signal success for Goethe's mode of procedure. But the substance of Goethe's findings has also been shown to be valid. For even earlier than Feigenbaum, Edwin Land's keynote paper in *Scientific American* in 1959 had proposed a two-colour theory.[50] Land asks: 'Is there something "wrong" with classical theory?'[51] Unaware of Goethe's work, he studied 'colour vision under natural conditions in complete images' and concluded, in terms of physics, that 'colour in the natural image depends on the random interplay of longer and shorter wavelengths.'[52] This is Goethe's view translated into the terminology of modern optics. Although the theory is now accepted, it took almost half a century for the agreement with Goethe to be noted in the scientific literature, and the fact has still to be more widely registered.[53] Yet Land's clear and well-argued paper lays to rest a long and fractious debate. Goethe's bicolour theory works. His status as a scientist is vindicated. Since Land's position is universally accepted by the scientific community, it is therefore time to recognize that Goethe's much disparaged theory of colour is actually right. Newton and Goethe's analyses are not competing theories, but complementary.

Goethe's colour theory has enjoyed a rich afterlife. It has had a profound influence on art, philosophy and – of course – colour theory. In 1841 *Theory of Colours* became the first book to be borrowed from the London Library.[54] Among those it influenced were the painters Philipp Otto Runge (1777–1810) and Johannes Itten (1888–1967); and the modernist advocates of abstraction Paul Klee (1879–1940) and Wassily Kandinsky (1866–1944); but perhaps the most important reception was by J.M.W. Turner (1775–1881), whose painting *Light and Colour (Goethe's Theory) – The Morning after the Deluge – Moses writing the Book of Genesis* (*c.* 1843) explicitly refers to Goethe. It may have been through Turner that Goethe's thesis that 'colours are the actions and reactions of light' (*cw*, xii, 158) entered the world-view of the Impressionists: for this conception provides the ground to their approach. Hence, if Goethe did not alter physics, he certainly helped shape modern art. Two philosophers also studied him. Arthur Schopenhauer was a follower of Goethe in his own study, *On Vision and Colour*, published in 1816.[55] And about a century later, Wittgenstein came to terms with his ideas; he appears to accept Goethe's critique of science and even adopts his concept of the *Urphänomen*.[56] More significantly still, it has been argued that Goethe's method had a decisive impact on his later philosophy and influenced the approach in his *Philosophical Investigations*.[57]

Goethe's scientific writings merged with his poetry in a remarkable series of poems published as 'God and World' ('Gott und Welt'; 1815). Since his return from Italy he had set his sights on uniting science and literature:

Johann Heinrich Lips, *Goethe*, 1791, chalk drawing.

nobody would admit that science and poetry could be united. People forgot that science had developed out of poetry, and they did not consider that after a revolution of the ages, the two could meet again in a friendly manner, for their mutual advantage, and on a higher level. (*LA*, I/9, 67)

Goethe here recalls the writings of the pre-Socratic philosophers such as Empedocles (*c.* 459–530 BCE), which present scientific ideas couched in verse. By envisaging a paradigm shift whereby the two fields reunite, he creates a new genre – distinct from the didactic verse of his predecessors Alexander Pope (1688–1744) and Albrecht von Haller (1707–1777) – which is lyrical, scientific and philosophical. It is the lyrical dimension that sets Goethe's verse apart. For he makes ideas sing. These poems do not replicate Goethe's pre-existing views. They express their own unique cosmology. In this sense they 'do' science in lyric form. In 'World Soul' (*Weltseele*; 1798–1802 (*GHB*, I, 280–82)), for example, Goethe offers an exuberant prophecy depicting the human spirit as a constituent part of creation. It opens as follows:

Friedrich Tieck,
F.W.J. Schelling,
c. 1805, drawing.

Weltseele

Verteilet euch nach allen Regionen
Von diesem heil'gen Schmaus!
Begeistert reißt euch durch die nächsten Zonen
In's All und füllt es aus!

Schon schwebet ihr in ungemessn'nen Fernen
Den sel'gen Götterraum,
Und leuchtet neu, gesellig, unter Sternen
Im lichtbesätem Raum.

Dann treibt ihr Euch, gewaltige Kometen,
Ins Weit' und Weitr' hinan.
Das Labyrinth der Sonnen und Planeten
Durchschneidet eure Bahn. (*FA*, II, 491f.)

In poems such as this, with their sumptuous diction and
innovative language, Goethe fulfils his dictum that science and

poetry, having once been conjoined in the writings of the pre-
Socratics, will one day reunite (*LA*, I/9, 67). The genre that Goethe
invents to achieve this end is that of the cosmological lyric. Here,
in this version, the translator John Whaley is fully on form with a
masterly rendition of Goethe's text:

'World Soul'

Depart the feast of sacred dedication
And search all worlds about!
Rush through the universe in pure elation,
Enthuse and fill it out!

In blissful soaring through unfathomed distance
The dreams of gods you dream,
With stars and seeding light in new existence
You join in space and gleam.

Then, mighty comets, thrusting through the notion
Of far and further space
You intersect the labyrinthine motion
The suns and planets pace. (*SP*, 81)

The event commemorated here appears to be the so-called
Romantics' Meeting held in Jena on 11–15 November 1799, when the
guests debated the new movement's principles. This foundational
act gathered together the main protagonists of early Romanticism,
including Novalis and Schelling, with Goethe in attendance.
The young men decided the programme that would take Europe
by storm. Goethe's poem takes its title from Schelling's book of
that name and elaborates the latter's thesis that according to the
law of 'polarity' a single principle unites inorganic and organic
life.[58] The astronomy in the poem is indebted to the discoveries of

William Herschel's drawing of nebulae, 1811.

William Herschel (1738–1822), notably his so-called 'nebulae' which include galaxies beyond the Milky Way. In varying the old dream of intergalactic travel, Goethe imagines the young Romantics as astronauts launching their careers into interstellar space. Like Schelling, he passes through a whole series of distinct phenomena to indicate a natural chain. Into this model he inserts the aperçu – reversing the notion of a God-driven world – that the human spirit itself forms an active part of the universe. The fusion of science and myth, religion and love lends this poem a unique appeal. Indeed, the cosmos itself – echoing views stretching from Plato's *Timaeus* (*c*. 360 CE) to Johannes Kepler (1571–1630) – is seen to be alive.[59]

7

The Faustian Age

Goethe left his imprint on Germany both culturally and politically.
The Austrian dramatist Franz Grillparzer (1791–1872) described the
very affecting impression Goethe made on him at a visit, appearing
'half like a father and half like a king.'[1] The modern visitor to
Weimar can still trace his footsteps from his palatial home on
the Frauenplan, with its grand staircase, classical sculptures and
attractive garden where he oversaw the planting, to his modest
summer cottage, a short walk away across the River Ilm. Partly at
Goethe's instigation, in 1788 the garden on the Ilm was redesigned
in the fashionable English style. Goethe did not just influence
Weimar's cultural life, he helped to shape its topography. In a very
real sense the town bears his imprint. Other buildings, such as
the rather ugly castle that was destroyed by fire in 1774 and rebuilt
under Goethe's direction, also testify – in more ways than one – to
his impact. As a politician, though conservative, he introduced
reforms, notably halving the army's size (to cut expenses), and he
also made improvements to the roads, bridges and waterways;
but after returning from Italy, he turned more to cultural affairs,
directing the theatre and overseeing the art academy, the medical
and scientific institutions, as well as other bodies (such as the
libraries). He took a dour view of the matter: 'In political affairs
people behave as if they were on a sick-bed and toss themselves
from one side to another in the mistaken belief that they will
be more comfortable.'[2] With his career, his position advanced.[3]

Against the will of the nobility, Karl August had appointed Goethe to the Privy Council – which made all the duchy's political decisions – in 1776, and to buttress this position, by intercession with the emperor, he had him ennobled in 1782. Eventually, upon the elevation of Weimar into a grand duchy after the Vienna Congress, in 1815 Goethe advanced to become a Minister of State. By thus fusing the 'contemplative life' with the 'active life', his trajectory rehearsed the ideal of a Renaissance man. By his achievements as the national poet, whose cult was inaugurated by Rahel Varnhagen and her influential salon,[4] he brought to his duchy what Morgenthau calls 'the power of prestige'.[5] Thanks to Goethe's contribution Weimar attained world-historical importance.

As Goethe grew in years and in stature he increasingly understood himself as a historical personage. Augustine had first presented himself in an autobiography, and Rousseau then established the genre with his *Confessions* (1782–9); but Goethe produced a sequence of six confessional works and developed the art into a supreme mode of self-representation in his own autobiography *Poetry and Truth*. By this means he created a veritable encyclopaedia of the 'I'. He aimed not just to tell his life story, but to locate himself in relation to major figures in literature, such as

Josef Stieler, *Goethe*, 1828, oil painting.

Klopstock, and historical figures like the Holy Roman Emperor. By this means he created the myth of himself as the representative man of his age – and has been rewarded in German historiography, which speaks of 'The Age of Goethe'. Through the medium of conversation Goethe also expanded his identity, notably in those with Chancellor von Müller and Eckermann. With some exaggeration, Nietzsche regarded his conversations with Johann Peter Eckermann, as 'the best German book that there is'.[6] In this relaxed form Goethe developed a well-nigh infinite series of insights. He even historicized his scientific work. *Theory of Colours* contains a historical section, and his papers on botany contain an essay on their place in his biography. Goethe hereby continues the transformation of history writing from a rational to a mythical mode that, according to Hayden White,[7] began with Herder; but Goethe applies this mythical vision to himself as a representative individual.[8] The chief work in which history occupies a central place is *Faust*.

Faust busied Goethe for his whole life. A vast trove testifies to its genesis.[9] The main phases are *Urfaust* (*c.* 1772–5), *Faust: A Fragment* (1790), *Faust: A Tragedy* (1808) and *Faust II* (1832). At 12,111 lines, it is probably the longest play in the German language. It is a pioneer of 'open form', breaking with the unities of Aristotelian drama. Instead it presents a montage of scenes, one as short as six lines, others around four hundred, and creates a vivid phantasmagoria. Goethe's other plays follow an encyclopaedic pattern with forms as diverse as morality, Shrovetide, classical, pastoral and Elizabethan; but *Faust* drives this further by introducing elements from each while also exploiting the 'world theatre' of Calderón (1600–1681).[10] The poetic diction, subtle and sharp, tender and profound by turn, is the richest in German. Nowhere else does Goethe risk such heterogeneity.[11] This results in a Romantic form – bizarre yet unified. Mikhail Bakhtin (1895–1975) regarded carnival as an essential feature of Goethe's creativity,[12] using it as a spur to his literary theory, and if we want to appreciate *Faust* fully, we must rejoice in its burlesque variety. The sixteenth-century comic dramatist Hans Sachs gave the form; the biblical Book of Job stands behind the story; Dante furnishes a model. The themes range from the pre-Socratics to magic, alchemy, ethics, ontology, epistemology, psychology, government, economics and land reclamation – not to mention its affecting two love stories with Gretchen and Helena respectively. There is a vast cast, and there are dizzying time shifts and rapid scene changes from Heaven to Faust's study, the Brocken, the Throne Room, ancient Greece and distant mountain gorges. The 'Prelude on the Stage' (*CW*, II, 3–7, ll. 22–242) adumbrates its tensions. A refusal to be bound by rules testifies to the Faustian urge. Different eras co-exist: ancient Greece, the Middle Ages, the Renaissance, Reformation and modernity. The style is by turns realistic, mythical and symbolic. All this tests theatre to the limit. Applying the insights he had acquired as a theatre director, Goethe knew how to turn this gallimaufry into a coherent spectacle. The version directed by Andy Serkis with Simon Callow as Faust at the Lyric Theatre in Hammersmith, London, in 1988, showed how it can work in translation; and Peter Stein's fifteen-hour uncut staging, performed over four nights in Germany and Austria in 2000, finally proved that it convinces in its entirety. The mix of lofty ideas and bad jokes, sublime and low-life settings, tenderness and bathos, magic and myth and (against Aristotle, again) history and tragedy effect a truly cosmic drama – 'From Heaven, through the World, to Hell.' (*CW*, II, 7, l. 242)

Goethe's starting points are the puppet theatre versions of Faust performed in eighteenth-century Germany, not to mention Christopher Marlowe's play of 1604 and the original *Faust Book* of 1587.[13] The core of the myth is, first, Faust's unquenchable zest for knowledge; and, second, his pact with the Devil to satisfy that desire. Goethe changes both of these features. Instead of knowledge, his Faust wants experience. Instead of a pact, he makes a wager with the Devil. Instead of a flat character, he is a highly complex figure. The terms Faust sets make a mockery of the Devil's plans. In place of a fixed term of 24 years, Faust lays a bet: 'It is to strive with all my might/ that I am promising to do.' (*cw*, II, 45, l. 1,742) What he actually offers is his own life's span:

> If on a bed of sloth I ever lie contented,
> May I be done for then and there!
> . . .
> If I should ever say to any moment:
> Tarry, remain! – Thou art so fair,
> Then you may lay your fetters on me. (*cw*, II, 44, ll. 1,692ff.)

In the place of the supernatural knowledge desired by Marlowe's Faust, Goethe's Faust wants the Devil to help him to become an all-round human being:

> And I'm resolved my inmost being
> Shall share in what's the lot of all mankind,
> That I shall understand their heights and depths,
> Shall fill my heart with all their joys and griefs,
> And so expand myself to theirs,
> And, like them, suffer shipwreck too. (*cw*, II, 44, ll. 1,770–75)

Goethe's Faust desires to be a Renaissance man with a difference. In the first place, he contracts Mephistopheles to allow him the full span of his life; in the second, he asks to be granted both suffering and joy. Whatever happens to him at the end counts for nothing: he tricks the Devil by making a wager that he cannot lose. The Devil gains nothing. He forfeits Faust's soul and loses the wager even before the action begins. In becoming a universal man, and experiencing both ecstasy and anguish, Faust wins all, experiencing pain and joy in equal measure as a result of his bet. Unlike the flat character in the chapbook, moreover, Faust is a complex,

'The Appearance of the Earth Spirit', in *Faust I* (1810–12).

self-contradictory character. And in a further departure from the old story, his innermost self is defined neither by a rational mind nor by overweening ambition, but by the heart, the feeling self. As he declares: 'Happiness! Heart! Love! God!/ I have no name to give it./ Feeling is everything.' (*CW*, II, 89, ll. 3,554ff.)

A large part of *Faust I* is taken up by a typical *Sturm und Drang* plot – the Gretchen Tragedy – which, with its poignant echoes of

Ophelia's fate, almost stands alone. The tale of meeting, wooing, temptation, seduction, loving, matricide, romance, ecstasy, pregnancy, scapegoating, agony, infanticide, prison, insanity and execution possesses all the power of a ballad, the intensity of lived experience and the catharsis of an ancient tragic drama. By virtue of the compassion bestowed on Gretchen, the play elevates the victim into a moral victor. It was a topical theme.[14] The choice of this subject – the girl who kills her mother and her child – instantiates the kind of retrospective justice Michel Foucault achieves in *Moi, Pierre Rivière . . .* (I, Pierre Rivière; 1973).[15] Yet in this instance the dramatist alone plays a lawyer, psychiatrist, expert witness, judge and priest to defend Gretchen before the court of public opinion. The display of injustice puts the world on trial, and judgement is left to a heavenly voice: 'She is saved.' (*cw*, II, 119, l. 4611) Kant opposed capital punishment for child murderesses on the grounds that the birth and death occurred outside the law.[16] The play likewise treats Gretchen's execution as an outrage. Yet she does not capitulate in the face of shame, as has been claimed. Enlightenment Germany was not a shame but a guilt culture.[17] She accepts her guilt and expiates it by willing her own execution. By means of divine intervention (a true *deus ex machina*) the play then vindicates Gretchen, who, in a paradox around which the plot revolves, though she is legally guilty, proves to be morally pure. This reflects the ethical reversal typical for the age, whereby the woman's lapse comes to be seen as virtue.[18] This did not always go down well. After a conversation about Faust with Goethe in 1804, Mme de Staël observed that he had a 'deep-rooted immorality shrouded in mysticism'.[19] The drama of the outcast as we later meet it in Büchner's *Woyzeck* (*c*. 1836) now enters the European stage.

It has been claimed that Goethe's exoneration of Gretchen must be hypocritical. Yet he had written years before: 'I have completely separated my political and social life from my moral and poetical life.'[20] To segment one's personality is not an act of hypocrisy but an existential necessity, which everyone must do to some or other degree to accommodate to society. It is, moreover, a category error to treat a writer's poetic views as if they were undermined by his politics. Goethe himself recognized this tactic of his critics, arguing that since they could not question his talent, they attacked his character.[21] It has often been noted that although he showed sympathy towards Gretchen, in a similar case before the Privy Council on 4 November 1783 he voted for the death penalty for Anna Katharina Höhn. She, like Gretchen, had killed her child.[22] Does this invalidate his attitude in *Faust*? Karl August's alternative, to incarcerate the guilty girl for life but to subject her to annual public humiliations and beatings, was hardly merciful.[23] The most thorough study to date concludes that both alternatives were inhumane.[24] What of Goethe's role? To decide this question, and remove it from subjectivity, the critic needs a secure principle. A basic rule that also applies here is that 'the more difficult interpretation must be preferred' (*lectio difficilior potior*).[25] Whereas Goethe's vote in the Privy Council of 1783 contradicts the view in *Urfaust*, its retention years later in *Faust I* of 1808 takes on a new meaning: it refutes the poet's vote. The poet Goethe – as so often – sits in judgement on the man. Thus the play is an exercise in self-criticism. Martha Nussbaum's view applies here: a poet may be a judge;[26] in the same spirit, Goethe the poet sits in judgement of Goethe the man. As with Goethe's other weaknesses, since he puts them on plain show, nothing is easier than for a critic to condemn him by a display of moral superiority. But this is to mistake sanctimony for criticism.

Faust addresses himself as unaccommodated man:

> Unconstant, homeless,
> A restive brutal creature with no purpose
> That like a cataract has stormed in greedy fury
> From rock to rock toward the abyss below. (*cw*, ii, 86, l. 3,348)

The point has been made that this cannot represent the poet's inner self given his privileged life,[27] and in fact it comes from an early layer of the play; however, since the inner self lies within, by definition it remains inaccessible and so *a fortiori* – given the absence of other evidence – we must accept expressions such as this as proof of the poet's feelings, for which we also have independent evidence.

The restlessness evident here is apparent from Goethe's constant movement. For although he appears to have led a sedentary existence, he was always on the move. Apart from the journeys to Switzerland and Italy and the campaign in France, there were the trips to Jena and Ilmenau, the celebrated journey to the Harz or, in later years, the regular visits to the spa at Carlsbad in Bohemia – thirteen in all, for a total of 885 days (*GHB*, IV/1, 596ff.). The stays much enlarged Goethe's circle. He met politicians and scholars, scientists and artists, high officials and dignitaries. The contact extended to royalty: the Prussian king Frederick William III (1770–1840) and the Austrian empress Maria Ludovica (1754–1806) belonged to his company. No less a figure than Prince Metternich (1773–1859), one of the leading statesmen of his day, was also an acquaintance. Flirtations were common too – what Goethe called 'little eyes' (*Äugelchen*), maybe half-a-dozen in all, not to mention a big romance. Perhaps the most noteworthy encounter, however, occurred at Teplitz, another Bohemian spa, where he met Beethoven in the summer of 1812 – just at the time when Napoleon, Beethoven's former idol, was marching on Vitebsk and hoping to conclude the first phase of his Russian campaign.[28] The composer had previously sent Goethe his *Incidental Music for Egmont*, which the poet promised to perform with the play, and had also bought a copy of *Wilhelm Meister*, presumably to prepare for the encounter. This is best remembered by an incident which probably never happened. The artist Carl Röhling produced an engraving in 1887 that shows Goethe making way for the empress and bowing to her while Beethoven strides on regardless: the image depicts the contrast between two personalities, two aesthetics and two eras whose customs divide the traditional court poet from the modern artist. The results were mixed. While Goethe admitted that the latter's 'talent astounded' him, he deplored his 'completely unruly behaviour', while Beethoven complained: 'Goethe is too comfortable in the Court air – more than it behoves a poet.'[29] Behind this disapprobation one senses that Goethe may have been less comfortable in his role as a courtier than it seems. Beneath the outer veneer there presumably lurked those darker forces he only permitted to surface in his writings. Goethe's capacity to depict restlessness and even abject despair points to the presence of a tempestuous inner world that his Olympian exterior – so offensive to visitors such as Heine, who called him a 'superannuated god' (GHB, IV/1, 480) – kept thoroughly hidden from view.

Wisdom and how to transmit it much preoccupied the older Goethe.[30] He lived in dialogue with other minds: the Bible and Plato, Rousseau and Kant, Homer and Shakespeare. The moralists La Rochefoucauld (1613–1680) and La Bruyère (1645–1696) afforded a model for his own *Maxims and Reflections* (*Maximen und Reflexionen*; 1833), which emphasize the dialogic nature of the mind. Disavowing their barbs and spite, however, he prefers a mellow note with a typically rising tone: 'Everything intelligent has already been thought; one just has to try to think it again.' (*HA*, XII, 415) His aphorisms can best be understood as messages to the soul: verbal artefacts designed to transmute the inner nature of his reader. To remove the sting of an aphorism, however, means to risk pomposity, as sometimes happens with his weaker maxims. Yet he certainly knew how to be tough: 'It is better for you to suffer injustice than for the world to be without law. Therefore everyone should bend to the law.' (*HA*, XII, 379) This somewhat unpalatable rigour hardly becomes a poet. To risk pomposity: the more differentiated viewpoint since taken by H.L.A Hart, who stresses the morality of law, is better suited to the arts.[31] Yet although Goethe matches neither Pascal's (1623–1662) searing honesty nor Lichtenberg's

Carl Röhling, *The Incident at Teplitz*, 1812, oil painting.

(1742–1799) sardonic brilliance, his best apophthegms are wise and meditative, being both heartfelt and intimate communications to a distant reader. Among the finest are those on nature. He desires a 'gentle empiricism' (*HA*, XII, 435), and lays out his own epistemology: 'Everything which is in the subject is in the object.' (*HA*, XII, 436) It follows that he sometimes assumes the pose of a prophet, as when he foretells a new science, and instructs the nineteenth century to change its scientific method (*HA*, XII, 440). The form of the aphorism suits his leaning towards open-endedness. He shuns closure. This is one reason for his anti-clericalism – so typical of the Enlightenment: 'The church debases everything it touches.' (*HA*, XII, 376)

The closest he came to voicing a credo is perhaps in this letter:

> I for my part in consideration of the manifold directions of
> my nature cannot have enough with one mode of thinking;
> as a poet and artist I am a polytheist, however as a natural
> scientist I am a pantheist, and the one as decidedly as the
> other. If I need a God for my personality as a moral being,
> that is taken care of too. Heavenly and earthly matters
> are so extensive a kingdom that only the organs of every
> creature taken together may comprehend the whole.[32]

Both the individual and the world are a manifold: the person divides, and society unites in order to grasp the divinity. Interestingly, the idea of such combinatorial worship has its roots in the Talmud, where only the totality of explanations can explain a sacred text. Such multiplicity enables Goethe to propel his creativity to ever new heights.

Goethe is always a rewarding critic. In his essay on Winckelmann, he gave his humanism its most sublime expression:

> When man's nature functions soundly as a whole, when he
> feels that the world of which he is a part is a huge, beautiful,

admirable and worthy whole, when this harmony gives him pure and uninhibited delight, then the universe, if it were capable of emotion, would rejoice at having reached its goal and admire the crowning glory of its own evolution. For what purpose would those countless suns and planets and moons serve, those stars and milky ways, comets and nebulae, those created and evolving worlds, if a happy human being did not ultimately emerge to enjoy its existence? (*cw*, III, 100f.)

The imagery resembles the universe of Giordano Bruno (1548–1600) with its 'countless suns' and 'infinity of worlds', but whereas Bruno places the 'intellect' into the centre of the scene,[33] Goethe envisages a 'happy human being'. He counters fear, Pascal's anxiety: 'Le silence éternel de ces espaces infinis m'effraie.'[34] ('The eternal silence of these infinite spaces fills me with fear'.) If 'anxiety' is the keynote of modernity, Goethe celebrates 'Glück' – not 'happiness' but 'joy' and 'good fortune'. He is also a great risk-taker, a frequent iconoclast, who for all his traditionalism enjoys upturning the status quo, as here, where he imagines an evolving, joyous and man-centred universe.[35] This transcends Newton's static picture, replicates Kant's system of 'a cosmos . . . in motion', and so, as an organic process, anticipates the modern model of an expanding universe.[36] T. S. Eliot (1888–1965) opined that Goethe 'merely dabbled in poetry and philosophy'.[37] That sounds like sour grapes. It would be truer to say that his assay affords one of the most comprehensive reappraisals of Western culture ever attempted.

Goethe never lost his ability to shock. In his third novel, *The Elective Affinities* (*Die Wahlverwandtschaften*; 1809), he evokes the sexual experimentation and the infidelities of his Romantic friends. Friedrich Schlegel had prepared the way with his risqué novel *Lucinde* (1799) – a tale that scandalized his contemporaries. They identified the protagonists with Schlegel and Dorothea Veit

Anton Graff, *Dorothea Schlegel*, *c.* 1800, oil painting.

(1763–1839). Dorothea was a daughter of the noted philosopher and leader of the Jewish Enlightenment, Moses Mendelssohn (1729–1786). She married the banker David Veit, from whom she divorced, only to live with Schlegel for several years before their marriage. Another Romantic with a colourful history was an intelligent woman whose liaisons can only be summarized with difficulty: Caroline Schelling (1763–1809), née Michaelis, widowed Böhmer, divorced Schlegel, married Schelling. In this circle – as with the English Romantics – sexual liberation was a form of intellectual adventure. Universal poetry found its correlative in free love. Goethe, as a serial romancer, was perhaps closer to these votaries than he cared to think. He surely knew how to enter into their minds. In doing so in his most lucid novel he, too, caused a scandal. Even Metternich was outraged – although his own closest collaborator, the brilliant Friedrich von Gentz, was known for his licentiousness during the Vienna Congress (1814–15) – and henceforth took a dreary view of Goethe's morals.[38] The Berlin salons and Romantic circles were abuzz.[39] But reactions were mixed. Achim von Arnim (1781–1831) wrote to his brother poet Clemens Brentano (1778–1842) – who jointly edited the anthology of folksongs *Des Knaben Wunderhorn* (*The Youth's Magic Horn*; 1805) – that the book was 'boring' (*HA*, VI, 660). And Wilhelm von Humboldt dourly observed that Goethe had insufficient 'strength' to weld the parts into a 'whole': 'But one mustn't tell him anything like that. He's tight in relation to his own works and grows completely silent if you voice the slightest criticism.' (*HA*, VI, 664)

Schelling and his followers enthused (*HA*, VI, 662), for they misguidedly took the chemical imagery adumbrated in the title as evidence for *Naturphilosophie*, as if the novel proved a homology between man and nature. For the title term stems from the Swedish chemist Torbern Olof Bergman (1735–1784), who coined it to define a chiastic process of a double exchange: $AB + CD > AD + BC$, comparable to what is now called double decomposition.[40] The formula belongs to the eighteenth-century theory of chemical attractions. This aimed to classify the affinities of all known substances (elements had not yet entered the picture). It was meant both as a practical tool and to isolate the cause of chemical action. The goal, then, was to discover the forces that conjoin the smallest particles. Goethe transferred this model to the human sphere: it forms the pattern of the plot; suggests an analogy between love and chemistry; and implies that contrary to the will, the root cause of human behaviour lies in the unconscious self or in a natural process – the human equivalent of universal attraction. The analogy strikes at the root of Enlightenment thought. From Montesquieu to David Hume, philosophers had transferred the principles of Newton's mechanics to political theory as well as to philosophy and psychology.[41] In changing the paradigm from dynamics to chemistry, Goethe replaces a quantitative with a qualitative model which is more appropriate to organic life. This procedure belongs with Goethe's constant attempts to introduce an organic world-view,[42] a picture of the world modelled on man.[43]

Hans Meid, *Eduard and Ottilie Watching the Firework Display*, c. 1932, etching.

He reverts to this point in *Faust*. In both works, literature affords a surrogate for science. In the first climactic episode in the novel, around which the action revolves, the husband and wife, Eduard and Charlotte, betray each other while making love in their marital bed: he thinks of his beloved Ottilie; she envisages the captain as her sexual partner. This double adultery replicates elective affinity, but in a psycho-physical exchange. The tragedy that unfolds from this episode proves to be as clear in structure as it is impossible to construe. Yet as Nicholas Boyle has recently argued,[44] the central episode may actually be elsewhere, and more surprising than was once thought: for it seems likely that the captain and Charlotte made love, in an episode discreetly hidden from the reader's gaze, and that he must accordingly be the father of her mysterious child. If this is the case, *The Elective Affinities* has a fair claim to be regarded as the most scandalous work in all German literature.

Goethe's tragic parable responds to Pierre Choderlos de Laclos' *Dangerous Liaisons* (*Les Liaisons dangereuses*; 1782), replacing its libertine antics by a psychological dilemma suffused with irony, ambiguity and paradox.[45] Each of the characters proves equivocal. None remains without guilt. All succumb to self-deception. Yet in this capricious world, values such as honesty and goodness, humility and devotion, service and sacrifice, or loyalty and love remain alive and immanent as the only feasible principles. Although every character fails, they all represent a value, an inherent quality that redeems them notwithstanding the wrong they do. However, they seem predestined for disaster: Charlotte, the undersexed wife; her husband Eduard, the emotional fantasist; the captain, a 'practical man'; and Ottilie, the spiritual beauty. If character is fate, the wrong mixture is tragedy. That is, these figures are drawn from life. Goethe had already done that in *Wilhelm Meister*. Here, however, he shows the figures in a close and inextricable bond, whereby not just every deed, but every thought, affects the outcome. It is perhaps this constant transmutation of ideas into reality, of reality into ideas – echoing his own *Naturphilosophie* – that accounts for Schelling's liking the novel: 'Nature should be the visible spirit,' he wrote, 'and the spirit should be invisible Nature.'[46] Like Schelling, the narrator focuses on the unconscious.[47] Once again Goethe follows Spinoza, too, to whom Goethe confessed to having an 'elective affinity' (*w*, 1/28, 289). In the spirit of the *Ethics*, Goethe's announcement for the novel gives its theme as 'the unity of nature' (*ha*, vi, 639). Yet, notwithstanding its metaphysics, it never loses touch with the quiddity of life.[48] Thanks to its concern with social interaction, moreover, *The Elective Affinities* can be read as the first sociological novel. Its central formula represents a mechanism for social change. Previous novels had shown characters interacting; *The Elective Affinities* explore the principles of such interaction. This, as has been noted, was recognized by Max Weber, who uses its central idea in his sociology: Goethe's concept of 'elective affinity' forms an important category both in Weber's *The Protestant Ethic* (1905) and in his *Economy and Society* (1922).[49] For Weber as for Goethe, 'elective affinity' provides a key for how all societies operate.

The form of *The Elective Affinities* is harmonious, balanced and classical; the subject matter eruptive, uncontrolled and romantic. This tension between form and content is one of the work's mysteries: the transparent representation of an opaque meaning. To this end the novel sets the events into a specific space, Eduard's country estate, which unfolds lucidly before the reader as the action proceeds, ranging from the mansion to a summer house, a mill and a chapel, and all the aspects of nature. These include the ominous three lakes that are merged into one. Thus the landscape provides a mirror of the action. The constant mirroring of the natural and the human is typical of Goethe's symbolism. Moreover, as contemporary readers often note, the novel seems to treat every 'fashionable' issue (*HA*, VI, 655): marriage and society, etiquette and manners, chemistry and mesmerism, art and architecture, landscape gardening and churchyards, reading and painting, love and death. This integrative attitude became a model for another admirer of Spinoza – George Eliot.[50] Her novel *Middlemarch* (1871–2), with its own scientifically defined social scene, translates Goethe's classical style into the realistic mode. From here the novel's impact again entered sociology, this time in the celebrated book *Middletown* (1929) by Robert S. Lynd and Helen Merrell Lynd. Yet the sense of contemporaneity in *The Elective Affinities* is deceptive. In the contrast between the rationally paired Charlotte and the captain with the emotional Eduard and the intuitive Ottilie, the novel intimates the epochal turn from the Enlightenment to Romanticism. In this reversal the entanglements entrap the characters as much as they perplex the reader. Most crassly, is Eduard a childlike fool or a rogue? Is Charlotte a wise or a cold wife? Is the captain a good friend or a schemer? And is Ottilie a sinner or a saint? Just as the characters lose their moral bearings, the reader finds judgement increasingly hard, as there is no objective viewpoint – the narrator is one of the figures – that could offer an authoritative perspective. This moral ambiguity without the denial of morality leads to that very modern territory which Henry James, a great admirer of Goethe,[51] later made his own in *The Portrait of a Lady* (1881), *What Maisie Knew* (1897) – which recalls Ottilie's lot – and *The Wings of the Dove* (1902). Even the tragedy of *The Elective Affinities* is shrouded in ambiguity. If Ottilie's end arouses 'fear and pity' in Aristotle's sense, the possibility that it may be self-willed raises questions, as does the closing arabesque. Critics have discerned a certain coldness in the work; but the ultimate impression is that of a tragic novel.[52]

Ottilie, even if she willed her end, did not act entirely freely. She is trapped in several ways, both by the relational tangle, by the clash of personal and social forces and by Eduard's ordinance not to leave the estate. Her pitiful death leaves an inescapable sense of what A. C. Bradley (1851–1935) calls 'tragic waste'. Here too Goethe recalls Shakespeare: 'With Shakespeare, at any rate,' as Bradley writes, 'the pity and fear which are stirred by the tragic story seem to unite with,

François Truffaut, *Jules et Jim* (1962). The film is based on Goethe's *Elective Affinities*.

and even to merge in, a profound sense of sadness and mystery, which is due to this impression of waste.'[53] One of the novel's first readers was reminded of *King Lear* (*HA*, VI, 657). The saintly aura surrounding Ottilie and even Eduard's death by imitation foster this mystery, heightened doubtless by the fact that such terrible chthonic powers are released in a privileged, highly educated circle in the midst of civilization. The muted echo of the Napoleonic era – Napoleon had just defeated the Coalition at about the time Goethe began the novel – is clear. Since the 'chemical revolution' of the late eighteenth century was often likened to the French Revolution,[54] there is also a political take to the chemical analogy: the provincial drama in which natural forces are destructively released reflects a wider European turmoil.

Although Goethe appears to have led a sheltered life, he endured the violence of the age and escaped from its upheavals into the realm of art. He responded to violence by a search for stability in beauty: 'In the most terrible and unbearable eras, from which I personally could not escape, I fled into those regions where my heart and my treasure dwell.'[55] He achieved this sublime reversal in his last great poetic cycle, *The West-Eastern Divan* (1819) (*GHB*, I, 306–435):

> *Nord und West und Süd zersplittern,*
> *Throne bersten, Reiche zittern,*
> *Flüchte du, im reinen Osten*
> *Patriarchenluft zu kosten,*
> *Unter Lieben, Trinken, Singen*
> *Soll dich Chisers Quell verjüngen.* (*HA*, II, 7)

At the age of almost seventy, Goethe renewed his style by introducing a new fluidity to German verse. His writing is perhaps more supple than that of any other poet I know – a homage to the Oriental writing he had come to admire as an ideal. He supplemented the poems in the *Divan* with a series of 'Notes and

Essays', and these are included in the edition by Martin Bidney, whose translations are always creditable:

> North and South and West – they shake!
> Thrones are cracking, Empires quake,
> To the purer East, then, fly
> Patriarchal air to try:
> Loving, drinking, songs among,
> Khizar's rill will make you young. (*WED*, 1)

Goethe forged a vibrant link: an exchange between East and West. Having immersed himself in German translations of the Persian poet Hafiz, he produced over two hundred poems in his manner – deliciously sensual and yet loftily spiritual. He collaborated in this venture with the delightful Marianne von Willemer (1784–1860), who wrote several of the poems, and to whom from 1815 he was bound by a passionate but platonic love. Her husband, the banker J. J. von Willemer (1760–1838), actively fostered their relations and in 1816, after the death of Goethe's wife Christiane, even invited Goethe to live with them in a *ménage à trois*. This odd liaison never came about. Indeed, Goethe inexplicably broke with Marianne that same year, after his carriage axle fractured as he set out to visit her, and – superstitious as ever – he abandoned the trip. His willingness to curtail awkward liaisons remained as intact as his *esprit*.

The poems of the *Divan* celebrate the Orient as a palace of fulfilment. Having steeped himself in its lore, he transforms himself into a poet inspired by Sufism and adopts a new mask, a new persona, joking and loving, adoring and teasing, wooing and playing, chiding and admiring, speaking with both the zest of youth and the wisdom of age. This is perhaps his most perplexing self. Tiny details that he observes make for a surprise, like a lover ensnared in hair (*WED*, 31); or a botanical peculiarity such as the leaf of a gingko, which provides him with a symbol (*WED*, 92f.); and of course the wine flows freely, too (*WED*, 123ff.). The best poems are profoundly mysterious. In 'Phenomenon' ('Phänomen'), a nocturnal rainbow presages love (*WED*, 9). In 'Blissful Longing' ('Seelige Sehnsucht') the speaker imitates a moth drawn to the flame. This invites the allegory, 'die and become!' (*WED*, 16f.) The ageing poet speaks with the innocence of youth as he artfully reveals an 'open secret' (*WED*, 25); the intermingling of elements brings about an affirmation of life as a whole: 'What is ugly don't deride;/ This, like beauty, too, let live' (*WED*, 7f.). Then, to conclude, Goethe includes the superlative 'Notes and Essays' at the end of the collection. These range over many diverse fields, as Goethe explores an alien culture. With this book, the idea of a national literature becomes defunct. Instead, 'world literature' begins.[56] The 'Notes' comprise an absorbing poetics, and provide an early foray into this genre:

> *Wer das Dichten will verstehen,*
> *Muß ins Land der Dichtung gehen;*
> *Wer den Dichter will verstehen,*
> *Muß in Dichters Lande gehen.* (*HA*, II, 126)

Goethe's comments on poetics are relatively sparse, which lends a particular importance to each remark. This little poem illuminates the symbiotic relationship of poetry and culture, geography and environment: verse is bound to its territory, and to fully absorb its meaning, the reader must explore the poet's homeland. In a sense, this is a variation on the theme of poetry and nationhood, but the links here are deeper, more complex, more anthropological:

> Poetry if you would know,
> To its country you must go;
> If you would the poet know
> To the poet's country go. (*WED*, 175)

Goethe's poetics here introduce the new method that French sociologists from Durkheim to Halbwachs, using Goethe's terminology, were later to call 'social morphology': the study of environmental impact on social forms.[57] Like a modern anthropologist Goethe wishes to understand a distant culture. Once again he proves a pioneer; this time in his championship of Islam.[58] Indeed, the devotion with which he approaches the Orient adumbrates a wider cultural rapprochement.[59]

With his last novel, *Wilhelm Meister's Travels* (1821; 1829), Goethe jettisons conventional form yet again. This wild invention anticipates modernism inasmuch as it is based less on narrative than on montage. This foreshadows both Joyce's *Ulysses* (1922) and Hermann Broch's *The Sleepwalkers* (1930–32). Goethe called it 'one of my most incalculable works, to which I almost lack the key myself' (*CE*, I, 110). What serves as a plot comprises sundry novellas and aphorisms, and even documentary passages on the Industrial Revolution, loosely strung together by an unreliable narrative frame. Moreover, through its dialogues and apophthegms, Goethe transforms the novel into a form of wisdom literature. Topics range freely from geology to astronomy, from medicine to law and from history to romance, education, philosophy, science and religion. Two themes stand out: the imperative to live in the present (*cw*, x, 435), and to be constantly active (*cw*, x, 424). The novel wages a continual battle with mediocrity. When Wilhelm asserts that the truth lies between two extremes, he is told sharply that it is not truth, but the 'problem' that lies in the middle (*cw*, x, 280). There are countless original adages, such as this one on the relationship between activity and reflection: 'Thought and action, action and thought – that is the sum of all wisdom.' (*cw*, x, 280) The chiastic pattern impels the reader to put this idea into practice.

Just as Goethe comes to terms with modern science in his colour theory, in his later works he struggles with that other great issue of today's world, political economy, and I shall therefore pay particular attention to this question. From the growth of an individual in *Wilhelm Meister's Apprenticeship*, Goethe now enlarges the focus of his book to encompass society as a whole. In doing so he grapples with the same problems of early capitalism which Marx was to wrestle with a generation later. Unlike Marx, however, his utopia does not involve communism, but returning to the ideals of an early modern artisan (*CW*, x, 381–5). His thinking anticipates the theories of John Ruskin and William Morris (1834–1896) as they were practiced in the British Arts and Crafts Movement. Both Morris and Ruskin knew Goethe's book, but also recognized its limitations. Morris complained: 'Goethe must have been asleep', when he wrote *Wilhelm Meister*, 'but 'tis great all the same.'[60]

The overarching structure in the book is often referred to as a social 'circle', an idea that subsequently resurfaces as the central form in Georg Simmel's *Sociology* (1908).[61] Simmel's precept accords with the novel's treatment of both haphazard and more formal relationships as the vehicles by which the individual is formed in society. Like Goethe, Simmel examines how relationships expand from the family into ever more ramified networks. These enrich the personality yet simultaneously lead to specialization – just as in the novel. In Simmel's view, also relevant, modernization involves the membership of an ever-increasing number of circles. His conclusion also reflects Goethe's insight: 'The number of different circles the individual occupies is one of the measures of culture.'[62] This theme as a structural motif underpins the novel's coherence as it panoramically depicts a series of seemingly unconnected circles in a variety of novellas – ideally suited in form to this thesis – and shows various types of labour, from craftsmanship, mining and agriculture to spinning and weaving.[63] Goethe was fascinated by the technical and economic aspects of the new 'technology' and quotes in detail from a description prepared for him by a friend (*FA*, I/10, 878–8). The book discusses features such as the different types of yarn, the mechanical procedure and the yield (*CW*, x, 332–6).

Johannes Schliess, *Weavers at Work in Eastern Switzerland*, *c.* 1830, watercolour.

Around 1790 about one-third of all Swiss workers were employed in the textile industry. The symbolic importance of Goethe's choice of subject is clear: it represents the origins of the Industrial Revolution with the introduction of the Spinning Jenny in Britain – a development which reached the German lands only belatedly. But the imagery also recalls the Luddite riots of 1811–13. In fixing on the cotton industry, Goethe has focused on the 'vehicle' of the Industrial Revolution.[64] This is the precise point, the transition from a cottage industry to a factory, against which the Luddites launched their attack.[65] This popular protest against the Industrial Revolution in the United Kingdom belongs to the novel's political context.

The novel tackles what Karl Polanyi (1886–1964) calls 'the great transformation': the economic, social and cultural changes brought about by the Industrial Revolution. Goethe explores what Polanyi treats as the 'embeddedness' of economics in society,[66] and proposes his own method for preserving the advantages of a long-standing value system within the context of a modern, technological society. Contrary to the rioters' indignation, the novel depicts the possible beneficent effect of technology in the form of 'peace' (*cw*, I, 340f.). This is an industrial idyll. It is to be accomplished by forming a new kind of guild – a forerunner of the trade union – by which means Goethe hopes the workers will take up arms against the negative effects of industrialization. The proposal is one of several points of contact with the British social reformer Robert Owen. The measures put forward, chiefly in the Pedagogic Province (*cw*, X, 199–207; 267–77) and in the rules for workers, aim to instil an attitude to labour based on respect, by which to counter alienation and forestall unrest. Instead of rights (a demand on others) Goethe calls for reverence (a duty to self and others). He likewise rebuts Adam Smith's idea of the citizen as defined by the pursuit of financial profit,[67] symbolized by the haggard, prematurely aged figure of Werner in *Wilhelm Meister's Apprenticeship*, and again sides with Owen.[68] Goethe favours the individual who seeks cultural gain. This emphasis on culture greatly contributed to Germany's spiritual avocation, a national decision which shaped its history, whereby Germany chose to solve its political questions in the sphere of individual cultivation.[69] This is precisely what Pierre Bourdieu (1930–2002) more rigorously describes as the preference for 'cultural' over 'commercial' capital.[70]

In contrast to Marx, Goethe does not treat the value of labour but the value of the labourer. The humanity of the individual should be increased by his/her exertions; labour should not serve to add value to raw materials and to goods, but to increase the value of the personality. This is what Goethe means by *Bildung*. Hence Goethe does not stress the degradation of society in modernity as highlighted by Marx, but the necessity for improvement. The key for this is specialization (*cw*, X, 118) – to be achieved by what the novel's subtitle calls 'renunciation'.[71] Modern man/woman must submit to specialism. The same contraction of worldly ambition occurs in *Faust II*. This means the end of Goethe's encyclopaedic project – as far as his readers go. Industrialization severs the ties

Goethe, drawing in a commonplace book for Princess Caroline of Saxon Weimar, 1807.

to the Renaissance, with its ideal of the universal human being, and replaces it with the modern specialist. Goethe's vision was, once again, to prove foundational for sociology. As seems to have escaped attention, the English sociologist Herbert Spencer borrowed Goethe's concept of an organic society (in which the individual grows to full perfection) and of social 'metamorphosis'.[72] Via Spencer, Goethe's vision entered English social thought.

Goethe's utopia has one serious limitation. It excludes the Jewish people: 'we tolerate no Jews among us' (*CW*, x, 378). This must be relativized, as it is not an authorial comment, but the prejudice is consistent with his views.[73] When Carl August to a large extent lifted Weimar's racial laws in 1823 to permit Jews to marry non-Jews, this elicited Goethe's violent protest. He foresaw 'the worst and crassest results': 'do we want to be the first everywhere in absurdities and the grotesque?'[74] His reaction displays the characteristic anxiety over a breach of the moral order associated with Jew-hatred. The exclusion from utopia in his novel represents an act of social closure in Weber's sense – the excision of a group on pretexts such as race or descent – which undermines the irenic ambition.[75] Given that G. E. Lessing had long since set the gold standard for tolerance among Christians, Muslims and Jews in German literature with his play *Nathan the Wise*, Goethe can only be regarded as a recidivist. His wish to maintain the racial laws in Weimar may be seen as a sorry foreshadowing of the Nuremberg laws.[76] This legislation prohibiting sexual and marital relations between Germans and Jews founded the German racial state and formed the legal prelude to the Final Solution. Had this persecutory moment appeared in a lesser book than *Wilhelm Meister's Travels*, it might have been less problematic, but the lapse indicates a weakness in the project. His titanic ambition, encompassing literature, science, criticism and the rest, exceeds any human bounds. Such totality is only attainable at the price of moral imperfection. If that does not diminish Goethe's achievement, it certainly qualifies it: the reader sees that even the author cannot match his own maxim to 'reform ourselves daily' (*cw*, x, 424). Yet it should be recalled that this is an aesthetic artefact, and in its dicta Goethe has found a way to project a scale of values by which to assess and correct its ideas. In his various ethical dicta, *Wilhelm Meister's Travels* provides the reader with the criteria by which to judge its author: and once again, Goethe stands condemned by his own creation. But it does well to keep Goethe's attitude in perspective. The historian Peter Pulzer hits the right note in calling his views 'unkind', but not evil.[77] They are indeed relatively insignificant in the wider context of his work, albeit the passage in *Wilhelm Meister* was often quoted in anti-Semitic discourse. In sum, however, Goethe's humanism was far more influential. Indeed, as even the far from generous philosopher Hannah Arendt argues, his cosmopolitanism was pivotal for the emancipation of the Jews.[78]

Goethe was granted one last great romance – and it almost killed him. For all his sobriety, the ageing poet continued to flout convention. The affair began in 1821 in Marienbad, Bohemia, when the poet, then aged 72, fell in love with the seventeen-year-old Ulrike von Levetzow (1804–1899). The following year matters grew more intense. Carl August, not without a hint of roguishness, played the broker and communicated Goethe's marriage proposal.[79] Ulrike's

Ulrike von Levetzow, 1821, pastel.

mother refused: 'No, my child, you are too young.'[80] The affair led to
outrage. The news reached Weimar. Everyone took sides. Goethe's
daughter-in-law did not wish to be usurped. Schiller's widow
pruriently hoped that the old chap would not be 'exposed'. Caroline
von Humboldt believed that the wedding had already occurred.
Goethe's son August threatened to decamp to Berlin. The affair
ended in perhaps his most moving and tragic poem, 'Trilogy of
Passion' ('Trilogie der Leidenschaft'; 1827). As ever it was his creativity
which furnished him with a moral compass. Yet nowhere else did he
come so close to cynicism as here, when addressing Werther:

Zum Bleiben ich, zum Scheiden du erkoren,
Gingst du voran – und hast nicht viel verloren. (*FA*, II, 416)

This is perhaps the most pessimistic couplet that Goethe ever wrote; but though joy is largely his muse, it is as well to remember his capacity for tragedy – a point too often neglected:

I stayed, you left, our fate was not our choosing,
You went before – how little you were losing. (*sp*, 135)

Thanks to the combination of biblical and erotic imagery, the rejection resembles the banishment of Adam and Eve from Paradise – though in this instance, it is only the man who is expelled:

Der Kuß der letzte, grausam süß, zerschneidend
Ein herrliches Geflecht verschlungener Minnen.
Nun eilt, nun stockt der Fuß die Schwelle meidend,
Als trieb ein Cherub flammend ihn von hinnen;
Das Auge starrt auf düstrem Pfad verdrossen,
Es blickt zurück, die Pforte steht verschlossen. (*FA*, II, 458)

Once again, John Whaley excels himself in the translation, the result of a lifetime of unflagging dedication to Goethe. Like all the best translators, Whaley seems to capture not just the sense, but the spirit of the poet's meaning:

The kiss, the last one, sweet and anguished, shearing
A weave of love so marvellously connected,
Foot runs, holds back, never the threshold nearing,
As though by Cherubim in flames ejected;
Eye stares on sombre path as torments blind it,
Looks back one more, the gate stays close behind it. (*sp*, 137)

The poet's perspective overpowers the reader by his fusion of reminiscence with immediacy. He seems to torture himself with his memories in the very act of trying to annul their effect. The result is a lyrical threnody. One also has the sense of a fugue unfolding, until the finale does indeed attain transcendence: 'Then vibrant music soars on wings supernal,/ A million weaves of tones round tones creating together.' (*sp*, 145) This ardent musicality may well have been inspired by the Polish pianist and composer Maria Szymanowska (1789–1831),[81] who played music by Beethoven to him to assuage his grief. Via such art he finally attains his accustomed affirmation: 'The double bliss of tones and love.' (*sp*, 145) Even in agony, life – for Goethe – must be celebrated.

In *Faust II* Goethe continues the task, begun in *Wilhelm Meister's Travels*, of explaining the mechanisms of the great social transformation.[82] Money is key.[83] Goethe recognizes, with Simmel, that money is the 'breeding ground' of 'economic individualism' and 'subjectivity': it is an expression of the Faustian self.[84] Goethe has two main economic premises: one is that defined by Weber as 'the monetary constitution of the state',[85] apparent from the emperor's role in *Faust*; and the other is that stated by Marx in his early notes, 'The Power of Money' With a Commentary on *Faust*,[86] – namely the identity of 'money' and 'self'. This latter position can be seen, for example, in the behaviour of courtiers in *Faust II* (*cw*, ii, 137, ll. 6,142–54). Marx borrows Goethe's concept of 'transformation' for his economics. Indeed, *Faust* anticipates Marx's theory by explicating a transformative economic process: man extracts ore from mines, both 'coined and un-coined gold' (*cw*, ii, 128, ll. 4,890ff.), by which means 'all other things are obtainable' (*cw*, ii, 129, ll. 4,965ff.). This is what Marx, using Goethe's terminology, calls the '*metamorphosis of the commodity*'.[87] Since gold is a natural product, and man is a creature of nature, money itself must be seen as a natural arbiter of value – an essentially organic quantity.[88] Thus Goethe's analysis of value sets in at the very process critiqued in *Capital*. Indeed, Goethe, like Marx, treats money as the product of 'universal alienation'. This becomes apparent in *Faust*'s satire on the invention of paper money to avert a financial crisis.[89] The epochal 'transformation' that takes place here is that from mercantilism (to which Goethe subscribed) to capitalism (which brought woe to the investors in the mine he directed). At a time when 'currency had become the pivot of national politics', great wealth could arise from paper money which, as Adam Smith expounds, generates new riches.[90] Yet this very money as advocated by Smith, the founder of modern capitalism,[91] forms the butt of Goethe's ridicule. When a courtier in *Faust II* gleefully proclaims that the national debt will be repaid thanks to its invention, the emperor gives in: 'Much as I find it strange, I see I must accept it.' (*CW*, II, 156, l. 6,085) But Faust recognizes the disturbing truth: the wealth buried in a mine, which it is hoped will underwrite the money's value, is only a fantasy: 'imagination in its loftiest flight may strain/ but cannot ever do them feeble justice.' (*CW*, II, 157, ll. 6,115f.) Thus the play reveals the instability, not to say the illusory nature of modern reality.

Here Goethe tackles a much debated problem in eighteenth-century economics. In the Enlightenment, proponents of paper money argued that it could be used as a public policy instrument to increase inflation and thereby to promote happiness. Hume attacked this position, and Goethe likewise disposes of it by demonstrating the superficiality of such joys. Nonetheless, Goethe does accept that paper may serve as an instrument to pay off debt (*CW*, II, 157, ll. 6,145–9).[92] The emperor in *Faust II* has the last word: it makes no difference (*CW*, II, 157f., ll. 6,150–53). Paper money is merely so much hot air. The argument is taken up in Simmel's *Philosophy of Money* (*Philosophie des Geldes*; 1900). As Simmel observes, money and ethics are linked: monetary dreams are nothing but moral fantasies.[93] A collapse in monetary value will necessarily entail a political crash – as became all-too apparent in the twentieth century.

At the origin of modern economics, Goethe's critique, though simpler, is as shrewd as Marx's and Simmel's inasmuch as he recognizes how capitalism – which had only just taken shape as the dominant economic form – may implode. As elsewhere Goethe attacks mathematical science, he uses *Faust II* as a vehicle with which to attack the newest economic system. Both the mathematics and the empiricism that underwrite modern culture lack any true value: 'What you can't count, you don't believe is true.' (*cw*, II, 128, l. 4,920) Against the standard, materialistic ideology, Goethe places life itself as the ultimate value.

Goethe suffuses the drama with myth. Scenes like Classical Walpurgisnacht (*cw*, II, 180–215, ll. 7,005–8,487) bring together creatures such as the sphinxes with Nereids and Tritons and Goethe, like Schelling, lends ancient myth the same validity as scientific truth. It represents what the latter calls 'the primal consciousness' of humanity.[94] Like Schelling and the other Romantics, too, Goethe goes beyond the ancient Greeks, and includes Egyptian and Hindu elements in his new mythology. The most moving moment of this kind, however, is Faust's affair with Helen of Troy in Part II, Act 3 (*cw*, II, 216–53, ll. 8,488–10,038). From being a spectacle, as in Marlowe's play, Goethe turns the motif into a moving passion, symbolizing the sacred union of modernity with antiquity. Here is Schiller's 'aesthetic education' in action. When Faust teaches Helen to rhyme, they unite: nothing could more touchingly effect the marriage of love and art. In this way *Faust* proves to be a lesson in the civilizing process. Literature itself is seen to be of incalculable value.

The play extends its treatment of 'Faustian man' to what the German philosopher of history Spengler calls 'the Faustian age': modernity itself.[95] Apart from economics it also includes science within its purview. All of Spengler's themes are found in the play: power and knowledge, science and myth, natural forces and God. Faust is driven by the same quest for knowledge that science pursues: the desire to know what holds the world together (*cw*, II, 13, ll. 379ff.).

Yet his strivings take him further, until he actually creates artificial life – Homunculus. Faust's creation of a tiny man in a retort affords a vibrant and visionary, but ultimately fateful, symbol of human inventiveness. The likely inspiration was Friedrich Wöhler's (1800–1882) urea synthesis *in vitro* in February 1828, the founding moment of organic chemistry.[96] The news probably reached Goethe that summer via his friend J. J. Berzelius (1779–1848), the foremost chemist of the day, with whom Goethe enjoyed excellent relations.[97] Berzelius, though an empiricist himself, saw that the finding might validate Schelling's (and hence Goethe's) *Naturphilosophie* as it appeared to prove the identity of inorganic and organic matter.[98] Goethe lost no time in exploiting the results in his play. The link is confirmed by the textual echo (*CW*, II, 176, l. 6,860) of Wöhler's process of 'crystallisation': the unity of nature is not just a Romantic dream, but an experimental fact.[99] In presenting Faust as a chemist capable of creating life, Goethe expands the play's paradigm from magic – as exemplified in the opening scenes, and presented in Marlowe's *Doctor Faustus* – to natural science. In this way, he creates a myth of the omnipotent scientist as the epitome of modernity. Yet science and technology prove Faust's moral undoing.

At the end of the play, in its most tragic episode (*CW*, II, 279–87, ll. 11,042–383), to enable Faust's land reclamation project his workers (the 'Mighty Men') brutally cause the death of two aged innocents, Philemon and Baucis, who stand in the way of the plan. Faust becomes a god.[100] He achieves a new creation of 'paradisiacal land' (*CW*, II, 293, l. 11,569). The convulsion echoes the Industrial Revolution and its vast technologies. It specifically recalls grandiose schemes like the Bremen Harbour extension of 1827 (*FA*, I, VII/2, 707f.) – built by a workforce of nine hundred men – and the plans, which Goethe knew, for the Panama, Suez and Rhein–Danube canals (*CE*, 10 February 1829, 363). The mighty feats of the new technologiy rival natural forces in their power. Unlike the engineers, however, the play counts the human cost of progress. The heart-rending episode, a fearful prolepsis, evokes modernity's disgrace, rebutting the myth of progress almost before it begins. Yet despite his guilt, Faust is saved. This is a scandalous reversal of the legend. The Angels declare:

This worthy member of the spirit world
Is rescued from the devil:
For him whose striving never ceases
We can provide redemption; (*CW*, II, 301, ll. 11,934–7)

The very quality that in previous versions led to Faust's damnation becomes the key to his deliverance. This volte-face turns evil from a radical fact into a problem. Since Mephistopheles' rule is subordinate to the Lord, goodness remains supreme. Although it uses a Christian framework, the play ironizes the ritual and specifics of faith and instead provides a worldly scheme based on humanism.[101] This leads to a subtle interfusion of spirituality with secularism. Hence, imperfection is inscribed into this new reality. As the Lord says at the start: 'men err as long as they strive' (cw, II, 10, l. 317). The absolute is unattainable and cannot be used to judge mankind. The mere fact of striving, despite error, validates salvation.[102] Everything hinges on Faust's undoubted 'effort' (*Mühe*; HA, I, 18) suggested by the verb *bemühen*. This is a biblical term which signifies human 'labour' or 'travail':[103] in Goethe's play, it suggests that by his endeavours Faust is fulfilling his earthly lot in a quasi-religious way. That is reason enough for the Lord to save him. Aspirational work attains a redemptive quality. Marx adopts but desacralizes this idea of a labour that 'transforms' nature and 'realizes' man's 'purpose' in the world.[104] Faust's redemption underwrites the great fourfold alliance – science and capital, progress and individualism – that defines modernity.

The conclusion of the play validates the Lord's words in the 'Prologue in Heaven': 'Ein guter Mensch in seinem dunklen Drang / Ist seines Weges wohl bewußt' (HA, I, 18): being in essence a 'good man', although his 'impulse' may be 'obscure', Faust is in some way 'conscious of his way.' Not for Goethe the antithesis between good and evil: the soul contains both. He remains a child of the Enlightenment, and upholds Leibniz's theodicy, according to which, despite human imperfection, the world exhibits a harmony between God's will and human action.[105] Of all the many interpretations of Goethe's play, only the setting of the final scene in the conclusion of Mahler's Eighth Symphony does justice to this vision. If, however, there is a transcendental absolute, it does not

Manuscript of
the conclusion of
Faust II.

impose standards on mankind. As Simmel has demonstrated,
by introducing 'psychological relativism', Goethe offsets relativism
against an absolute world-view.[106] He thereby balances two
opposite orders. Values are relative. From being irrefutable facts,
as in the past, at the end they become negotiable. The world is
'only a symbol' (*CW*, II, 305, ll. 12, 105). Goethe rejects the allegorical
medieval world-view in favour of a symbolic universe (*HA*, XII,
470–71). Such a sphere is open-ended – in terms of both astronomy
and ethics. This means that hope can never be obliterated by
despair. Thus Goethe dispels Dante's anxious, ramified, riven
universe of cruelty, in which the saintly and the damned remain
eternally divided, and replaces it by a unitary cosmos in which even
for a sinner, true bliss can be attained – in a form of reincarnation
– when the individual is 'reborn for Heaven' (*CW*, II, 305, l. 12,099).
Here, Goethe returns once again to the Hinduism that had
animated his early poem, 'Wanderer's Night Song', to create his
own, polytheistic universe.

Faust took Goethe sixty years to complete. In a very real sense, it
was his life's work. The congruence of life and art intimates that his
life itself was a work of art – planned and polished. On finishing the
play, in the summer of 1831, he sealed up the manuscript and put it
away, to be published after his death. 'My remaining days', he said
to Eckermann, 'I may now consider a gift; and it is now, in fact, of
little consequence what I now do, or if I do anything.' (*CE*, 401) Less

Friedrich Preller the Elder, 'Goethe on his Deathbed on the Day of his Funeral', drawing.

than one year later, on 22 March 1832, he died peacefully. His last words were 'More light'; or perhaps, 'One is abed' (*Mehr licht / Man liegt* – in Frankfurt dialect). It was a typical ambiguity – to the end. Later that year his masterpiece was published, like a phoenix rising from the grave – his lien on immortality. In no small part thanks to this example, the Faust theme established itself as the most popular in the West.[107] Countless versions in drama and fiction, music and opera, film and television, testify to its impact. From Franz Liszt's (1811–1886) symphony to Charles Gounod's (1818–1893) opera, and from Mikhail Bulgakov's fiction *The Master and Margarita* (1928–40) to Thomas Mann's novel *Doctor Faustus* (1947), or to the dramas by Fernando Pessoa (1888–1935) and Paul Valéry (1871–1945), the theme has established itself in every culture. Through *Faust* the West learned to understand itself. In his valedictory letter, written to Wilhelm von Humboldt on 15 March 1832, seven days before his death, Goethe continues to expound his philosophy of striving (*HA*, Briefe, IV, 480). He notes the fragmentary character of his Faust. He accepts that his project is a 'shipwreck'. He laments the sway of 'confusing doctrines and confusing commerce'. And he refines his ideal of *Bildung*: a process that enhances the 'organs' of a human being until he or she becomes a 'unity'.

At the centre of Goethe's manifold achievements lies his humanity. The word *humanitas* is first used by Cicero in the sense of civilization, human nature and kindness; Petrarch, the father of Humanism, revived the concept; and from thence it travelled into the German Enlightenment, to Lessing and Herder, to Goethe and Schiller, who jointly stressed the ethical dimension of the classical idea by recentring it on 'goodness'. Goethe applied it to friends, of course, but also to strangers, as a cosmopolitan ideal. It appears in poems such as 'The Divine'; in plays such as *Iphigenie on Tauris*; in the novel *Wilhelm Meister's Apprenticeship*; and in the epic *Hermann and Dorothea*. Goethe retains a trust in this lofty norm to the very end: in a wide-ranging testimonial written for Carlyle in 1828, Goethe explicitly praises 'beauty and humanity, goodness and greatness' (*HA*, Briefe, IV, 273): the human task is to compensate for weakness and suffering by 'striving and activity', and then, thanks to an 'innate goodness', to help others to attain enlightenment. This vision completes the view of man in *Faust*, which presents a humanity as fallible as it is noble. From Goethe and his kind the idea travelled to the twentieth century, when it helped to inspire the programme of the Weimar Republic; and leading writers like Thomas Mann and Hermann Hesse invoked it in defiance of the Third Reich. The credo resurfaced after the Second World War in the attempt to re-ground civilization, notably in the existential philosophy of Karl Jaspers and the political aspirations of Carlo Schmid. It was Goethe's supreme ideal. As he writes in a masque co-authored with Herder (*WA*, I, 16, 271): 'Let Humanity be our eternal goal.'

References

Introduction

1 Harold Bloom, *Shakespeare: The Invention of the Human* (New York, 1998).

2 Marcel Proust, *Contre Sainte-Beuve* (Paris, 1971), p. 480; Friedrich Nietzsche, *Kritische Studienausgabe*, ed. Giorgio Colli and Mazzino Montinari, 15 vols (Berlin and New York, 1980), vol. XI, p. 13, vol. II, p. 7.

3 Gustav Seibt, *Goethe und Napoleon. Eine Historische Begegnung* (Munich, 2010).

4 Hans Eichner, 'Thomas Mann and Goethe', *Publications of the English Goethe Society*, XXVI (1957), pp. 81–98.

5 Ernst Robert Curtius, *Deutscher Geist in Gefahr* (Stuttgart and Berlin, 1932).

6 Thomas Mann, *Goethe als Repräsentant des Bürgerlichen Zeitalters. Rede zum 100. Todestags Goethes am 18. Marz 1932 in der Preussischen Akademie der Künste in Berlin* (Berlin, 1932).

7 Petra Weber, 'Goethe und der Geist von Weimar. Die Rede Werner Thormanns bei der Verfassungsfeier in der Paulskirche am 11. August 1932', *Vierteljahresheftet für Zeitgeschichte*, XLVI (1998), p. 126.

8 W. Daniel Wilson, 'Goethe and the Nazis', *Times Literary Supplement* (12 March 2014).

9 Karl Jaspers, *Unsere Zukunft und Goethe* (Bremen, 1949).

10 Carlo Schmid, 'Gemessen an Goethe', *Die Zeit* (1 September 1967), www.zeit.de, accessed 20 April 2019.

11 Jeremy Adler, 'The Importance of Goethe's Concept of Human Dignity for the Universal Declaration of Human Rights and German Basic Law', *Publications of the English Goethe Society*, in press.

12 Giorgio Vasari, *The Lives of the Painters, Sculptors and Architects*, trans. A. B. Hinds (London, 1900), vol. VIII, p. 3.

13 Michael Hamburger, 'A Perilous Multiplicity', in *Goethe Revisited: A Collection of Essays*, ed. E. M. Wilkinson (London, 1984), pp. 11–30.

14 Matthew Arnold, 'A French Critic on Goethe', in *Mixed Essays* (London, 1879), p. 311.

15 Arthur Schopenhauer, *Gespräche. Neue, stark erweiterte Ausgabe*, ed. Arthur Hübscher (Bad Canstatt, 1971), p. 33.

16 David Hume, *Treatise of Human Nature*, ed. A. A. Selby-Bigge (Oxford, 1960), vol. I, IV, VI, p. 252.

17 Immanuel Kant, 'What is Enlightenment?' [1784], available at www.indiana.edu, accessed 12 April 2018.

18 Giambattista Vico, *On Humanistic Education: Six Inaugural Orations, 1699–1707*, with an introduction by Donald Phillip Verene (Ithaca, NY, and London, 1993), pp. 2–3.

19 Charles D. Wright, 'Matthew Arnold on Heine as a "Continuator of Goethe"', *Studies in Philology*, LXV (1968), pp. 693–701; see p. 697.

20 Franz Kafka, *Tagebücher. Kritische Ausgabe*, ed. Hans-Gerd Koch et al. (Frankfurt, 1990), 13 January 1912, p. 367.

21 Bernard Levin, 'A Self-made Superman', *Sunday Times* (19 May 1991).

22 Ferdinand Mount, 'Super Goethe', *New York Review of Books* (21 December 2017).

23 Jacob Burckhard, *The Civilization of the Renaissance in Europe*, part II: 'The Development of the Individual', trans. S.G.C. Middlemore (London, 1878), pp. 53–5.

24 Ibid., p. 54.

25 Barker Fairley, 'The Chameleon Image: Goethe's Animula Vagula', *Monatshefte für Deutschen Unterricht*, XXXVII/4/5 (1945), pp. 25–30.

26 Siegbert Prawer, 'A Change of Direction? Sigmund Freud between Goethe and Darwin', *Publications of the English Goethe Society*, LXXVI (2007), pp. 103–17.

27 Gerald Holton, 'Einstein and the Cultural Roots of Modern Science', *Daedalus*, CXXVII (1998), pp. 1–44.

28 Philippe Boudes, 'Morphologie sociale et sociologie de l'environment: l'apport de Halbwachs à l'étude des relations entre les sociétés et leur milieu naturel', *L'Année sociologique*, LXI (2001), pp. 201–24.

29 Ernst Cassirer, *Philosophy of Symbolic Forms*, 4 vols (New Haven, CT, 1953–7).

30 Siegbert Prawer, 'Mephisto and Old Nick: Refractions of Goethe in the Writings of Karl Marx', *Publications of the English Goethe Society*, xlv (1975), pp. 23–63.

31 August Schleicher, 'Zur Morphologie der Sprache', *Mémoires de l'Académie Imperiale des Sciences de St Pétersbourg*, vii/7 (1859), p. 35. Anna Morpurgo Davies, *History of Linguistics*, vol. iv: *Nineteenth Century Linguistics* (London and New York, 1998), pp. 196–201.

32 Jonas Maatch, ed., *Morphologie und Moderne. Goethes "Anschauliches Denken" in den Geistes- und Kulturwissenschaften* (Berlin and New York, 2014). Ernst-Jürgen Dreyer, *Versuch einer Morphologie der Musik zu begründen. Mit einer Einleitung über Goethes Tonlehre* (Bonn, 1976).

33 Vladimir Propp, *Morphology of the Folktale*, trans. Laurence Scott (Austin, tx, 1968).

1 The Birth of a Poet

1 Nicholas Boyle, *Goethe: The Poet and the Age*, vol. i: *The Poetry of Desire* (Oxford, 1991), p. 43.

2 T.C.W. Blanning, *The Culture of Power and the Power of Culture: Old Regime Europe, 1660–1789* (Oxford, 2002); T. J. Reed, *Light in Germany: Scenes from an Unknown Enlightenment* (Chicago, il, and London, 2015).

3 C. D. Broad, *Leibniz: An Introduction* (Cambridge, 1975); G. MacDonald Ross, *Leibniz* (Oxford, 1984); Maria Rosa Antognazza, *Leibniz: An Intellectual Biography* (Cambridge, 2009).

4 Michael J. Murray and Sean Greenberg, 'Leibniz on the Problem of Evil', *Stanford Encyclopedia of Philosophy* (Winter 2016), https://plato. stanford.edu, accessed 27 February 2017.

5 Alexander Pope, *Poetical Works*, ed. Herbert Davies (Oxford, 1966), Epistle i, pp. 246ff.

6 G. H. Lewes, *The Life and Works of Goethe* [1855] (London, 1908), p. 33.

7 *Mozart: Briefe und Aufzeichnungen. Gesamtausgabe. Band 1: 1755–1766*, ed. Wilhelm A. Bauer and Otto Erich Deutsch (Basel, 1962), p. 89.

8 Robert H. Brown, 'The "Demonic" Earthquake: Goethe's Myth of the Lisbon Earthquake and Fear of Modern Change', *German Studies Review*, xv (1992), pp. 475–91.

9 T. D. Kendrick, *The Lisbon Earthquake* (London, 1956); Edward Paice, *Wrath of God: The Great Lisbon Earthquake of 1755* (London, 2008).

10 Voltaire, 'Poem on the Lisbon Disaster', trans. Antony Lyon, available at www.antonylyon.com, accessed 24 February 2017.

11 Jean-Jacques Rousseau, Letter to Voltaire, 18 August 1756.

12 Voltaire, *Candide; or, Optimism* [1759], trans. Theo Cuffe (London, 2005), pp. 13–15.

13 Walter Benjamin, 'The Lisbon Earthquake', in *Selected Writings*, vol. II: *1927–1934*, ed. M. W. Jennings et al., trans. Rodney Livingstone et al. (Cambridge, MA, 1969), pp. 536–40.

14 Theodor W. Adorno, *Negative Dialectics*, trans. E. B. Ashton (London and New York, 1973), pp. 361f.

15 G. W. Leibniz, *Protogaea*, trans. Claudine Cohen and Andre Wakefield (Chicago, IL, and London, 2008).

16 Ibid., p. xxii.

17 Arthur O. Lovejoy, *The Great Chain of Being: A Study of the History of an Idea* (Cambridge, MA, 1936).

18 Giambattista Vico, *On Humanistic Education: Six Inaugural Lectures, 1699–1707*, trans. Giorgio A. Pinton and Arthur W. Shippe (Ithaca, NY, and London, 1993), p. 73.

19 Thomas Hobbes, *Leviathan*, Everyman's Library (London and New York, 1947), p. 2.

20 See Johann Joachim Winckelmann, *On Art, Architecture and Archaeology* (Rochester, NY, and Woodbridge, 2013); Alex Potts, *Flesh and the Ideal: Winckelmann and the Origins of Art History* (New Haven, CT, and London, 1994); Katherine Harloe, *Winckelmann and the Invention of Antiquity: History and Aesthetics in the Age of Altertumswissenschaft* (Oxford, 2013).

21 Goethe, 'Winckelmann und sein Jahrhundert', *HA*, XII, pp. 96–129 (pp. 96f.); *CW*, III, pp. 99f.

22 Peter Boerner, *Johann Wolfgang von Goethe in Selbstzeugnissen und Bilddokumenten* (Reinbek, 1965), pp. 15f.

23 Aristotle, *Metaphysics*, trans. W. D. Ross (Oxford, 1924), B2: 980a; Hobbes, *Leviathan*, p. 26.

24 Mark Zuss, *The Practice of Theoretical Curiosity* (Dordrecht, 2012), p. 4.

25 Galileo Galilei, *Dialogues Concerning Two New Sciences*, trans. Henry Crewe and Alfonso de Salvio (New York, 1954), p. 1.

26   Steven Nadler, 'Baruch Spinoza', in *The Stanford Encyclopedia of Philosophy*, ed. Edward N. Zalta (Spring 2019 Edition), available at https://plato.stanford.edu, accessed 25 May 2019.

27   Richard Mason, *The God of Spinoza: A Philosophical Study* (Cambridge, 1997), pp. 143f.

28   Frederick Amrine, 'Goethean Science', in *Goethe's Way of Science: A Phenomenology of Nature*, ed. David Seamon and Arthur Zajno (New York, 1998), p. 47.

29   Friedrich Gottlieb Klopstock, *Ausgewählte Werke*, ed. Karl August Schleiden (Munich, 1962), p. 197.

30   Boyle, *Goethe: The Poet and the Age*, vol. I, pp. 78f.

31   Erwin Panofsky, *The Life and Art of Albrecht Dürer* (Princeton, NJ, 1955), pp. 156–71; Erwin Panofsky, Raymond Klibansky and Fritz Saxl, *Saturn and Melancholy* (New York, 1964).

32   Wolf Lepenies, *Melancholy and Society*, trans. Jeremy Gaines and Doris Jones (Cambridge, MA, 1992).

33   Matthew Bell, *Melancholia: The Western Malady* (Cambridge, 2014).

34   See T. J. Reed, 'Goethe and Happiness', in *Goethe Revisited*, ed. E. M. Wilkinson (London, 1984), pp. 111–31.

35   A. Potts, *Flesh and the Ideal: Winckelmann and the Origins of Art History* (New Haven, CT, and London, 2000); Harloe, *Winckelmann and the Invention of Antiquity*.

36   Winckelmann, *History of Ancient Art*, cited after Potts, *Flesh and the Ideal*, p. 156.

37   Johann Joachim Winckelmann, *Gedanken über die Nachahmung der griechischen Werke in der Malerei und Bildhauerkunst* (Berlin, 2016), p. 40.

38   Astrid Seele, *Frauen um Goethe* (Reinbek, 2000), p. 16.

39   J. A. Lewis, *Zinzendorf, The Ecumenical Pioneer: A Study in the Moravian Contribution to Christian Mission and Unity* (London, 1962); Arthur J. Freeman, *An Ecumenical Theology of the Heart: The Theology of Count Nicholas Ludwig von Zinzendorf* (Bethlehem, PA, 1998).

40   Ronald Gray, *Goethe the Alchemist: A Study of Alchemical Symbolism in Goethe's Literary and Scientific Works* (Cambridge, 1952).

2 *Sturm und Drang*

1 See Roy Pascal, *The German Sturm und Drang* (Manchester, 1953).

2 Carl Hammer, *Goethe and Rousseau: Resonances of the Mind* (Lexington, KY, 1973).

3 Jean-Jacques Rousseau, *The Social Contract*, trans. Maurice Cranston (Harmondsworth, 1968), pp. 49f.

4 Friedrich Schiller, 'Die Worte des Glaubens', 1797, available at http://gutenberg.spiegel.de, accessed 22 October 2018.

5 The Declaration of Independence, available at www.archives.gov/founding-docs, accessed 5 March 2017.

6 Goethe, 'America, You Are Better Off', available at www.theiramerica.org, accessed 5 March 2017.

7 Hans Adler and Wulf Küpke, eds, *A Companion to the Works of Johann Gottfried Herder* (Rochester, NY, 2001); Isaiah Berlin, *Vico and Herder* (London, 1976).

8 On the complex subject of Kant's philosophy, see these helpful introductions: C. D. Broad, *Kant: An Introduction* (Cambridge, 1978); Otfried Höffe, *Immanuel Kant* (Albany, NY, 1994); Henry Allison, *Kant's Transcendental Idealism* (New Haven, CT, 1983).

9 Michael Rohlf, 'Immanuel Kant', *Stanford Encyclopedia of Philosophy* (Spring 2016 Edition), https://plato.stanford.edu, accessed 8 March 2017.

10 Michael Forster, 'Johann Gottfried von Herder', *Stanford Encyclopedia of Philosophy* (Summer 2015 Edition), https://plato.stanford.edu, accessed 6 March 2017.

11 Johann Gottfried Herder, *Werke in Fünf Bänden*, ed. Regine Otto (Berlin and Weimar, 1978), vol. II, p. 182 and vol. I, pp. 22, 53.

12 Ibid., vol. I, pp. 45ff.

13 Ibid., p. 281.

14 Immanuel Kant, *Werke*, ed. Wilhelm Weischedel, 6 vols (Wiesbaden, 1960), vol. IV, p. 788.

15 See *MA*, I/1, pp. 165–84.

16 Herder, 'Auszug aus einem Briefwechsels über Ossian und die Lieder alter Völkes', in *Werke in Fünf Bänden*, vol. II, pp. 226–75, see p. 251.

17 Johann Gottfried Herder, *Stimmen der Völker in Liedern* (Leipzig, 1978), p. 149.

18 Sir Philip Sidney, *Poems*, The Muses Library, ed. John Drinkwater (London, 1922), p. 66.

19 Herder, *Werke in Fünf Bänden*, vol. II, p. 91f.

20 William Wordsworth, *The Poetical Works*, ed. Thomas Hutchinson and Ernest de Selincourt (Oxford, 1951), p. 62.

21 William Wordsworth, 'Preface', in William Wordsworth and Samuel Taylor Coleridge, *Lyrical Ballads* (Oxford, 2013), p. 111.

22 Johann Georg Hamann, *Aesthetica in Nuce*, in Hamann, *Ausgewählte Schriften*, ed. Hans Eichner (Berlin, 1994), p. 7.

23 Ibid.

24 Jeremy Adler, 'Goethe's *Gedankenlyrik*', in *Goethe at 250*, ed. T. J. Reed et al. (Munich, 2000), pp. 247–64.

25 On magical sympathy see Sir Kenelm Digby, *A Late Discourse . . .* (London, 1658); Anon., *Theatrum Sympatheticum* (Nuremburg, 1660); Aggripa von Nettesheim, *Die magischen Werke* (Wiesbaden, 1982).

26 J. J. Stoudt, *Sunrise to Eternity: A Study in Jacob Boehme's Life and Thought* (Philadelphia, PA, 1957); Andrew Weeks, *Boehme: An Intellectual Biography* (Albany, NY, 1991).

27 Ronald Gray, *Goethe the Alchemist: A Study of Alchemical Symbolism in Goethe's Literary and Scientific Works* (Cambridge, 1952), pp. 37ff.

28 Jakob Böhme, *Six Theosophical Points and Other Writings*, trans. John Rolleston Earle (New York, 1920).

29 *The Golden Chain of Homer: A Work of Alchemy*, trans. Sigismund Bacstrom [1891] (Lexington, KY, 2016), p. 4.

30 For the earliest study of Kant and Goethe see Georg Simmel, *Kant und Goethe. Zur Geschichte der modernen Weltanschauung* (Leipzig, 1916).

31 John D. Glenn Jr, 'Kant's Theory of Symbolism', *Tulane Studies in Philosophy*, XXI (1972), pp. 13–21; Heiner Bielefeldt, *Symbolic Representation in Kant's Practical Philosophy* (Cambridge, 2003).

32 Ernst Cassirer, *The Philosophy of Symbolic Forms*, 2 vols (Newhaven, CT, 1955).

33 Hennig Brinkmann, ed., *Liebeslyrik der deutschen Frühe* (Düsseldorf, 1952), p. 100.

34 Ezra Pound, *Personae: Collected Shorter Poems* (London, 1952), pp. 18ff.

35 Max Wehrli, 'Zur Geschichte der Manesse-Philologie', in *Codex Manesse*, ed. Walter Koschorrek and Wilfried Werner (Kassel, 1981), pp. 145ff.

36 Leonard Forster, *The Icy Fire: Five Studies in European Petrarchism* (Cambridge, 1969), pp. 1–61.

37 J. W. Goethe et al., *Von deutscher Art und Kunst*, ed. Edna Purdie (Oxford, 1924).

38 Preserved Smith, *Revival: A History of Modern Culture*, vol. II: *The Enlightenment* (London, 1934), p. 255; W. D. Robson-Scott, *The Literary Background to the Gothic Revival in Germany* (Oxford, 1965).

39 See Penelope Hunter-Stiebel, *Of Knights and Spires: Gothic Revival in France and Germany* (New York, 1989); Megan Aldrich, *Gothic Revival* (London, 1994).

40 George D. Painter, *Marcel Proust: A Biography*, vol. I (London, 1959), pp. 256–87; On Goethe: Marcel Proust, *Correspondence*, 21 vols, ed. Philip Kolb (Paris, 1970–93), vol. V, pp. 256f; *Contre St.-Beuve*, ibid., p. 479; Marcel Proust, 'La mort des cathédrales', in *Pastiches et mélanges*, ed. Pierre Clarac (Paris, 1971), pp. 141–9.

41 Elizabeth Emery, *Romancing the Cathedral* (Albany, NY, 2001), p. 141; Proust, *Pastiches et mélanges*, p. 89.

42 Martha Winburn England, 'Garrick's Stratford Jubilee: Reactions in France and Germany', *Shakespeare Survey*, IX (1956), pp. 90–100; Roger Paulin, *The Critical Reception of Shakespeare in Germany, 1682–1914* (Hildesheim, 2003).

43 George Winchester Slone Jr and George M. Kahrl, *David Garrick: A Critical Biography* (London and Amsterdam, 1979), p. 582; Paulin, *The Critical Reception of Shakespeare in Germany*, pp. 160f.

44 *MA*, I/1, pp. 916ff; *HA*, Briefe, I, p. 133.

45 Herder, *Werke in Fünf Bänden*, vol. II, pp. 225–6.

46 J. G. Herder, *Sämmtliche Werke*, ed. Bernhard Suphan (Berlin, 1877–1913), vol. III, pp. 470–71.

47 Hanna Fischer-Lamberg, ed., *Der junge Goethe*, 2nd edn (Berlin, 1999), vol. II, p. 27.

48 Friedrich Engels, *The Peasant War in Germany*, Marx and Engels Collected Works (New York, 1975–2005), p. 10. Karl Marx, *Capital: A Critique of Political Economy* [1867] (Harmondsworth, 1976), vol. I, pp. 725–913, esp. p. 741.

49 Henrik Ibsen, *The Master Builder*, in *Four Major Plays*, trans. James McFarlane and Jens Arup (Oxford, 1998), p. 353.

50 Proust, *Pastiches et mélanges*, p. 500.

51 Hans Reiss, *Goethe's Novels* (London, 1969), pp. 10–67; Martin Swales and Erika Swales, *Reading Goethe: A Critical Introduction to the Literary Work* (Rochester, NY, 2002), pp. 64–70.

52 R. D. Miller, *The Beautiful Soul: A Study of Eighteenth-century Idealism as Exemplified by Rousseau's 'La Nouvelle Héloïse' and Goethe's 'Die Leiden des jungen Werthers'* (Harrowgate, 1981); A. O. Tantillo, 'A New Reading of *Werther* as a Critique of Rousseau', *Orbis Literarium*, LVI/6 (2001), pp. 443–65.

53 Ernst Rober Curtius, *European Literature and the Latin Middle Ages*, trans. Willard Trask (New York, 1956).

54 Jane Campbell, *Albrecht Dürer: A Biography* (Princeton, NJ, 1990), pp. 67–9.

55 Curtius, *European Literature and the Latin Middle Ages*, 10. 6.

56 T. S. Eliot, 'Tradition and the Individual Talent' [1919], in *Perspecta* (1982), vol. XIX, pp. 36–42.

57 William Makepeace Thackeray, 'Werther', in *A Nonsense Anthology*, ed. Carolyn Wells (New York, 1915), p. 242.

58 Jan Thorson and Per-Ame Öberg, 'Was There a Suicide Epidemic After Goethe's *Werther*?', *Archives of Suicide Research*, VII/1 (2003), pp. 69–72.

59 See also Søren Kierkegaard, *The Present Age*, trans. Alexander Dru (New York, 1962), p. 3; for its original in Goethe's work see *CW*, XI, p. 34, where the term is translated as a 'mortal disease'.

60 Peter Salm, 'Werther and the Sensibility of Estrangement', *German Quarterly*, XLVI (1973), pp. 47–55.

61 Irina Paperno, *Suicide as a Cultural Institution in Dostoyevsky's Russia* (Ithaca, NY, and London, 1997), pp. 13f. A link has also been made to *The Brothers Karamazov*; see Victor Terras, 'Problems of Human Existence in the Works of the Young Dostoyevsky', *Slavic Review*, XXIII/1 (1964), p. 79, note 4.

62 See Leo Tolstoy, *Anna Karenina* [1877], trans. Rosemary Edmonds (Harmondsworth, 1954) vol. II, pp. 191; Albert Camus, *The Myth of Sisyphus* [1942], trans. Justin O'Brien (New York, 1955), p. 3.

63 Gustave Flaubert, *Sentimental Education* [1869], trans. Robert Baldick (Harmondsworth, 1981), vol. I, p. 27; vol. III, p. 413.

64 Annelies Schulte Nordholt, 'Proust and Subjectivity', in *Subjectivity*, ed. Willem van Reijen and Willem G. Westersteijn (Amsterdam, 2000), pp. 81–106; Marcel Proust, *Remembrance of Things Past* [1913–27], trans. C. K. Scott Moncrieff, Terence Kilmartin and Andreas Mayor (London, 1983), vol. III, p. 1106.

3 First Years in Weimar

1 For excellent brief introductions to the history of the Holy Roman
   Empire see Barbara Stollberg-Rilinger, *The Holy Roman Empire: A Short
   History* (Princeton, NJ, 2018) and Joachim Whaley, *The Holy Roman
   Empire: A Very Short Introduction* (Oxford, 2018).

2 Madame de Staël, *D'Allemagne* (Paris, 1874), p. 79; on Weimar
   see H. Bruford, *Culture and Society in Classical Weimar, 1775–1806*
   (Cambridge, 1962); Nicholas Boyle, *Goethe: The Poet and the Age*,
   vol. I: *The Poetry of Desire* (Oxford, 1991), pp. 233ff.; W. Daniel
   Wilson, 'Goethe and the Political World,' in *The Cambridge
   Companion to Goethe*, ed. Lesley Sharpe (Cambridge, 2002),
   pp. 207–18.

3 MA, II/2, pp. 653–9 (student clubs); 663–4 (laboratory); pp. 673–80
   (military); pp. 681–703 (taxation); pp. 704–15 (factories).

4 C.A.H. Burckhardt, ed., *Goethes Unterhaltungen mit dem Kanzler
   Friedrich von Müller* [1870] (Paderborn, 2015), 16 March 1824, p. 83.

5 G. A. Wells, *Goethe and the Development of Science, 1750–1900* (Alphen
   aan den Rijn, 1978); W. Scott Baldridge, 'The Geological Writings of
   Goethe', *American Scientist*, LXXII/2 (1984), pp. 163–7.

6 H. Prescher, ed., *Goethes Sammlungen zur Mineralogie, Geologie und
   Paläontologie* (Berlin, 1978).

7 See Rachel Laudan, *From Mineralogy to Geology: The Foundations of a
   Science, 1650–1830* (Chicago, IL, and London, 1987).

8 On Thales, see G. S. Kirk and J. E. Raven, *The Presocratic Philosophers*
   (Cambridge, 1981), pp. 87ff; on Anaxagoras, see Patricia Curd,
   Anaxagoras of Clazomenae: Fragments and Testimonia (Toronto, 2007),
   pp. 149ff.

9 Boyle, *Goethe: The Poet and the Age*, vol. I, p. 298.

10 Ernest Hatch Wilkins, *Life of Petrarch* (Chicago, IL, and London, 1961),
    p. 12.

11 Francesco Petrarca, *Opera* (Basle, 1581), pp. 624–7.

12 *Corpus der Goethe Zeichnungen*, ed. Gerhard Femmel, 7 vols in 10
    (Leipzig, 1972–9), vol. I, p. 190.

13 Wordsworth, 'Preface', *Lyrical Ballads* (1798), p. 111.

14 Edgar Zilsel, 'The Genesis of the Concept of Scientific Law',
    Philosophical Review, I/1 (1942), pp. 245–79.

15 Jonathan Israel, *The Radical Enlightenment: Philosophy and the Making of Modernity, 1650–1750* (Oxford, 2001), pp. 159–74.

16 Spinoza, *The Chief Works*, trans. R.H.M. Elwes (New York, 1951), vol. II, p. 55.

17 Ibid., p. 188.

18 GHB, IV/2, p. 1001.

19 Theobald Ziegler, *Goethes Welt-und Lebensanschauung* (Berlin, 1914), p. 30; *CW*, XII, p. 8.

20 Baron de Montesquieu, *The Spirit of the Laws*, trans. Thomas Nugent [1752] (Kitchener, Ontario, 2001), pp. 246–60.

21 Ann ℧. Shteir, 'Albrecht von Haller's Botany and "Die Alpen"', *Eighteenth-century Studies*, XX/2 (1976–7), pp. 169–84; Otto Sonntag, 'Albrecht von Haller and the Future of Science', *Journal of the History of Ideas*, XXXV/2 (1974), pp. 313–22, see 318f.

22 Wells, *Goethe and the Development of Science*, pp. 12ff.; John M. Opitz, 'Goethe's Bone and the Beginnings of Morphology', *American Journal of Medical Genetics*, Part A, 1126A, Issue 1 (2004), pp. 1–8; Aaron G. Filler, *The Upright Ape: A New Origin of the Species* (Franklin Lakes, NJ, 2007), pp. 43–60.

23 Charles Darwin, *On the Origin of Species* [1859] (London, 1968), pp. 54f.

24 H. B. Nisbet, 'Lucretius in Eighteenth-century Germany: With a Commentary on Goethe's "Metamorphose der Tiere"', *Modern Language Review*, 100 (2005), Supplement, pp. 115–33.

25 Immanuel Kant, *Natural Science*, ed. Eric Watkins (Cambridge, 2012), pp. 182–308.

26 See *Rigveda*, in Jan Gonda, *Visnuism and Sivaism: A Comparison* (London, 1970), pp. 71–2; Nicol Macnicol, ed., *Hindu Scriptures* (London and New York, 1938), p. 12; Klaus K. Klostermaier, *Hinduism: A Short History* (Albany, NY, 2007), pp. 83–4; S. Giora Shoham, *To Test the Limits of Our Endurance* (Cambridge, 2010), p. 116.

27 Adolf Schöll, ed., *Goethes Briefe an Frau von Stein*, 2 vols (Frankfurt, 1883).

28 Ibid., vol. II, pp. 85, 90, 324, 329.

29 Ibid., pp. 80, 96, 28, 339, 97, 129.

30 Iris Murdoch, *The Sovereignty of Good* (London, 1970).

31 Plato, *The Republic*, trans. Benjamin Jowett, in *The Dialogues of Plato*, 5 vols (London, 1970), vol. IV, p. 291, 308.e.

32 Cicero, *De finibus bonorum et malorum* (London, 1914), p. 467.

33 Michael Allen Gillespie, *The Theological Origins of Modernity* (Chicago, IL, 2008), p. 67.

34 Bruford, *Culture and Society in Classical Weimar*, pp. 184–253; Hans Adler, 'Johann Gottfried Herder's Concept of Humanität', in *A Companion to the Works of Johann Gottfried Herder*, ed. Hans Adler and Wulf Koepke (Woodbridge, 2009), pp. 93–116.

35 Schöll, *Goethes Briefe an Frau von Stein*, vol. I, p. 87.

36 CW, I, pp. 60ff; see also Ilse Graham, 'Transmigrations: Some Thoughts on Goethe's "Warum gabst du uns die tiefen Blicke"', *German Life and Letters*, XXIV (1970), pp. 42–53; Edward Timms, 'The Matrix of Love: "Warum gabst du uns die tiefen Blicke"', *German Life and Letters*, XXXVI (1982–3), pp. 49–63.

37 Jonas Fränkel, ed., *Goethes Briefe an Frau von Stein*, 3 vols (Jena, 1908), vol. I, p. 43.

38 G. H. Lewes, *The Life and Works of Goethe* [1855] (London, 1908), p. 311.

39 Boyle, *Goethe: The Poet and the Age*, vol. I, p. 359.

40 Benedict de Spinoza, *Theological-political Treatise*, ed. Jonathan Israel, trans. Michael Silverthorne and Jonathan Israel (Cambridge, 2007), pp. 202, 252.

41 *HA*, IV, p. 430; Spinoza, *Complete Works*, ed. Michael Morgan (Indianapolis, IN, 2002), p. 557.

42 Petra Maisak, 'Zwischen Gefühl und Verstand: Goethes Blick auf Rembrandt', *Goethe und 'Rembrandt der Denker'* (Frankfurt, 2014), pp. 1–37; *Der junge Goethe*, ed. Hanna Fischer-Lamberg (Berlin, 1963–74), vol. IV, p. 252; Bob Cornelis van den Boogert, *Goethe and Rembrandt: tekeningen uit Weimar*, exh. cat., Rembrandt House Museum (Amsterdam, 1999).

43 Maisak, 'Zwischen Gefühl und Verstand', pp. 30–36.

44 Oswald Spengler, *The Decline of the West*, trans. C. F. Atkinson, 2 vols (New York, 1927), vol. I, pp. 316, 290.

45 Spinoza, *Theological-political Treatise*, p. 202.

46 E. M. Wilkinson, 'The Relation of Form and Meaning in *Egmont*', in E. M. Wilkinson and L. A. Willoughby, eds, *Goethe: Poet and Thinker* (London, 1962), pp. 55–74.

47 F. J. Lamport, 'The Charismatic Hero: Goethe, Schiller and the Tragedy of Character', *Publications of the English Goethe Society*, LVIII (1988), pp. 62–83.

48 Max Weber, *Economy and Society: An Outline of Interpretive Sociology*, ed. Guenther Roth and Claus Wittich, 2 vols (Berkeley, CA, 1978), vol. I, pp. 1111–57.

49 Angus Nicholls, *Goethe's Concept of the Demonic: After the Ancients* (New York, 2006).

50 For a more sanguine account, see Ritchie Robertson, *Goethe: A Very Short Introduction* (Oxford, 2016), pp. 75f.

51 Spinoza, *Theological-political Treatise*, p. 252.

4 The Italian Turn

1 Joachim Whaley, *Germany and the Holy Roman Empire*, 2 vols (Oxford, 2012), vol. II, chap. 8.

2 E. P. Thompson, *The Making of the English Working Class* (London, 1991), p. 43.

3 Geoffrey Trease, *The Grand Tour* (London, 1967); Jeremy Black, *Italy and the Grand Tour* (New Haven, CT, and London, 2003).

4 Ibid., pp. 27ff.

5 Goethe, *Diary of the Italian Journey* (*Tagebuch der Italienischen Reise*), *FA*, XV/1, p. 660.

6 Nicholas Boyle, *Goethe: The Poet and the Age*, vol. I: *The Poetry of Desire* (Oxford, 1991), p. 418.

7 Giambattista Vico, 14 July 1720; see Vico, *Universal Rights*, trans. Giorgio Pinton and Margaret Diehl (Amsterdam. 2000), p. xlvi.

8 W. H. Auden and Elisabeth Mayer, 'Introduction', Goethe, *Italian Journey* (Harmondsworth, 1962), p. 11.

9 See for example John Ruskin, *The Stones of Venice*, 3 vols (London, 1851–3).

10 Lewis Mumford, *The City in History* (Harmondsworth, 1961), pp. 368, 373–6.

11 Lord Byron, *Childe Harolde's Pilgrimage*, Book IV: *Byron's Poetical Works* (Oxford, 1945), p. 227.

12 Salvador Giner, *Mass Society* (London, 1976), p. 29.

13 Descartes, *Rules for the Direction of the Mind*, Rule IX, in *The Essential Descartes*, ed. Margaret D. Wilson (New York, 1969), pp. 65ff.

14 Vicenzo Ferrone, *The Politics of Enlightenment: Constitutionalism,*

Republicanism, and the Rights of Man in Gaetano Filangieri, trans. Sophus A. Reinert (London, 2014), p. 40.

15 Ibid., p. 90.

16 Jean-Jacques Rousseau, *A Discourse on Inequality*, trans. Maurice Cranston (Harmondsworth, 1984); Jean-Jacques Rousseau, *The Social Contract*, trans. Maurice Cranston (Harmondsworth, 1966); Jeremy Bentham, *An Introduction to the Principles of Morals and Legislation* [1789] (Oxford, 1996), p. 13.

17 Letter to Carl August, 14 October 1786 (*HA*, Briefe, II, p. 15).

18 Letter to Charlotte von Stein, 14 December 1786 (*HA*, Briefe, II, p. 28f.).

19 Cited after the keynote article, Theodore E. Mommsen, 'Petrarch and the Conception of the "Dark Ages"', *Spaeculum*, XVII (1942), p. 232.

20 John Keats, Letter to Hobhouse, 27 October 1818.

21 E. M. Butler, *The Tyranny of Greece Over Germany* (Cambridge, 1935).

22 Vico, *Universal Rights*, p. 110.

23 For an essay on Heine and Goethe and for further reading, see *GHB*, II, 479–81.

24 Günter Häntzschel, 'Das Ende der Kunstperiode. Heinrich Heine und Goethe', in *Goethes Kritiker*, ed. Karl Eibel and Bernd Scheffer (Paderborn, 2001), pp. 57–70.

25 Plutarch, *De Exilio*, trans. Phillip H. De Lacy and Benedict Einarson, ed. W. P. Goodwin (Boston, MA, 1959), p. 14.

26 A. A. Long, 'The Concept of the Cosmopolitan in Greek and Roman Thought', *Daedalus*, CXXXVII (2008), p. 56.

27 Immanuel Kant, *Anthropology from a Pragmatic Point of View*, ed. Robert C. Louden (Cambridge, 2000), p. 236.

28 Moses Hadas, 'From Nationalism to Cosmopolitanism in the Greco-Roman World', *Journal of the History of Ideas*, IV (1943), p. 110.

29 James S. Ackerman, *Palladio* (Harmondsworth, 1966); Bruce Boucher, *Andrea Palladio: The Architect in His Time* (New York, 1994).

30 The edition Goethe bought was the noted facsimile published by Joseph Smith, the former consul in Venice: *I Quattro libri del'architettura di Andrea Palladio* (Venice, *c.* 1770); see *CW*, VI, p. 52.

31 Palladio, *I Quattro libri*, I/1.

32 Boucher, *Andrea Palladio*, pp. 290–98; Andrea Palladio, *The Complete Illustrated Works*, ed. Guido Beltramini and Antonio Padoan (New York, 2001), pp. 64–7; Boucher, *Andrea Palladio*, p. 291.

33 Ackerman, *Palladio*, p. 160.

34 David Lowe and Simon Sharp, *Goethe and Palladio* (Great Barrington, 2005).

35 Rudolf Wittkower, *Architectural Principles in the Age of Humanism* (London, 1962), pp. 52–62.

36 Ibid., pp. iii–iv.

37 Ackerman, *Palladio*, p. 164.

38 Erich Heller, 'Goethe and the Avoidance of Tragedy', in *The Disinherited Mind: Essays in Modern German Literature and Thought* (Harmondsworth, 1961), pp. 37ff; Euripides, *Three Plays: Hippolytus; Iphigenia in Tauris; Alcestis*, trans. Philip Vellacott (Harmondsworth, 1974), pp. 176ff.

39 T. J. Reed, *Light in Germany: Scenes from an Unknown Enlightenment* (Chicago, IL, and London, 2015).

40 Immanuel Kant, *Kritik der reinen Vernunft* [1787], Bände, XVI–XVII, in *Werke*, ed. Wilhelm Weischedel (Frankfurt, 1964), vol. II, p. 25; on the Copernican analogy, see S. Morris Engel, 'Kant's Copernican Analogy: A Re-examination', *Kant-studien*, LIV (1963), pp. 63–80, and Ermanno Bencivenga, *Kant's Copernican Revolution* (Oxford, 1987); on Goethe and Kant, see Ernst Cassirer, *Rousseau, Kant, Goethe*, trans. James Gutman et al. (Princeton, NJ, 1970); Nicholas Boyle, *Goethe: The Poet and the Age*, vol. II: *Revolution and Renunciation, 1790–1803* (Oxford, 2000), passim.

41 Ilse Graham, *Goethe, Portrait of the Artist* (Berlin and New York, 1977), pp. 171–81.

42 Michel de Montaigne, 'On the Cannibals', in *The Complete Essays* [1580], trans. M. A. Screech (London, 1991), pp. 228–41.

43 On the impact of Montaigne on Montesquieu in general, see John M. Bomer, *The Presence of Montaigne in the Lettres Persanes* (Birmingham, AL, 1988), see esp. pp.75f; Montesquieu, *Persian Letters* [1721], trans. J. C. Betts (Harmondsworth, 1973).

44 See Max Horkheimer and Theodor W. Adorno, *Dialectic of Enlightenment* [1944] (Stanford, 2002); on Foucault's analysis of enlightenment, see his 'What is Enlightenment?', in *The Foucault Reader*, ed. Paul Rainbow (New York, 1984), pp. 32–50; on the dark side of the enlightenment, see his *Discipline and Punish: The Birth of the Prison* (New York, 1977).

45 See Tomaz Mastnak, ed., *Hobbes's Behomoth: Religion and Democracy* (Exeter, 2012); Étienne de la Boétie, *The Politics of Obedience: The Discourse of Voluntary Servitude*, ed. Murray N. Rothbard (Auburn, AL, 2015); Immanuel Kant, 'What is Enlightenment?', in *What is Enlightenment? Eighteenth-century Answers and Twentieth-century Questions* (Berkeley, CA, 1996), pp. 58–64.

46 Norbert Elias, *The Civilizing Process* [1939], revd edn (Oxford, 1994).

47 Reed, *Light in Germany*, p. 73.

48 Mary Wollstonecraft, *A Vindication of the Rights of Woman* (London, 1792), p. 135.

49 Ibid., p. 177.

50 Emer de Vattel, *The Law of Nations* (Indianapolis, IN, 2008), p. 267.

51 Jeremy Adler, '"die Epoche der Welt-Literatur ist an der Zeit". Goethe und die Erfindung der modernen Dichtung', *Goethe Jahrbuch*, CXXXIV (2017), pp. 27–38, here pp. 31–2.

52 Bruce Broomhall, *International Justice and the International Criminal Court: Sovereignty and the Rule of Law* (Oxford, 2003), p. 22.

53 Michel Foucault, *The Order of Things: An Archaeology of the Human Sciences* (New York, 1970).

54 James L. Larson, 'Goethe and Linnaeus', *Journal of the History of Ideas*, XXVIII/4 (1967), pp. 590f.

55 Wolf Lepenies, *Das Ende der Naturgeschichte. Wandel kultureller Selbstverständlichkeiten in den Wissenschaften des 18. und 19. Jahrhunderts* (Munich, 1976); Larson, 'Goethe and Linnaeus', p. 593.

56 H. B. Nisbet, 'Lucretius in Eighteenth-century Germany, with a Commentary on Goethe's "Metamorphose der Tiere"', *Modern Language Review*, LXXXI (1986), pp. 97–115.

57 This field, opened up by Ann Shteir and Londa Schiebinger, is examined in Sam George, *Botany, Sexuality, and Women's Writing, 1760–1830: From Modest Shoot to Forward Plant* (Manchester, 2007).

58 Rudolf Magnus, *Goethe as a Scientist*, trans. Heinz Norden (New York, 1961), p. 63.

59 Agnes Arber, *Goethe's Botany: The Metamorphosis of Plants (1790)*, *Chronica Botanica*, X (1946); Agnes Arber, *The Natural Philosophy of Plant Form* (Cambridge, 1950), pp. 40–47, 56–64.

60 Charles Darwin, *On the Origin of Species* [1859], ed. J. W. Burrow (Harmondsworth, 1985), p. 415.

61 Sander Gliboff, 'Gregor Mendel and the Laws of Evolution', *History of Science*, XXXVII (1999), pp. 217–35. Peter Schilperoord, 'Goethe's Metamorphosis of Plants and Modern Plant Genetics', http://natureinstitute.org, accessed 24 May 2019. John M. Opitz and Diana W. Bianchi, 'MENDEL: Morphologist and Mathematician Founder of Genetics . . .', *Molecular Genetics and Genomic Medicine*, III/1 (January 2015), pp. 1–7, www.ncbi.nlm.nih.gov, accessed 24 May 2019.

62 Henry Gee, 'Goethe und das Genom', *Die Zeit*, 18 May 2000, https://www.zeit.de.

63 D'Arcy Wentworth Thompson, *On Growth and Form* [1917] (Cambridge, 1942), pp. 1026–93; Stephen Jay Gould, 'D'Arcy Thompson and the Science of Form', *New Literary History*, II (1971), pp. 229–58; Wallace Arthur, 'D'Arcy Thompson and the Theory of Transformations', *Nature Review Genetics*, VII (2006), pp. 401–6; Margaret A. Boden, 'D'Arcy Thompson: A Grandfather of A-life', in *The Mechanical Mind in History*, ed. Philip Husbands, Owen Holland and Michael Wheeler (Cambridge, MA, 2008), pp. 41–60; see esp. pp. 46–9.

64 A. M. Turing, 'The Chemical Basis of Morphogenesis', *Philosophical Transactions of the Royal Society of London*, Series B, Biological Sciences, CCXXXVII/641 (14 August 1952), pp. 37–72; Miguel A. Herrero, 'Alan Turing's Work on Morphogenesis', *Arbor*, 189 (764): a081, p. 181; Boden, 'D'Arcy Thompson'. pp. 46–50.

5 The Classical Centre

1 I borrow the chapter title from the masterly study by T. J. Reed, *The Classical Centre: Goethe and Weimar, 1775–1832* (Oxford, 1986).

2 Frédéric Soret, *Zehn Jahre bei Goethe* (Leipzig, 1926), p. 630.

3 Walt Whitman, 'Song of Myself', in *Complete Poetry and Selected Prose and Letters*, ed. Emory Holloway (London, 1971), p. 84.

4 Walt Whitman Archive, annotations to Goethe's *Complete Works*, duk.00184, undated, available at http://whitmanarchive.org, accessed 15 October 2017; Walt Whitman Archive, annotations on Goethe from

circa 1750, duk.00178, undated, available at http://whitmanarchive. org, accessed 16 October 2017.

5 Walt Whitman Archive, annotations to Goethe's *Complete Works*, duk.00184, undated, available at http://whitmanarchive.org, accessed 15 October 2017.

6 H. B. Nisbet, *Goethe and the Scientific Tradition* (London, 1972), pp. 115–33.

7 H. Baron, 'The *Querelle* of the Ancients and the Moderns as a Problem for Renaissance Scholarship', *Journal for the History of Ideas*, XX (1959), pp. 3–22.

8 Goethe, 'Response to a Literary Rabble-rouser' ('Literarischer Sansculottismus'; 1795), *CW*, III, p. 189.

9 Elizabeth M. Wilkinson and L. A. Willoughby, *Models of Wholeness: Some Attitudes to Language, Art and Life in the Age of Goethe*, ed. Jeremy Adler, Martin Swales and Ann Weaver (Oxford, 2002).

10 Karoline Jagemann, *Die Erinnerungen*, ed. Eduard von Bamberg (Dresden, 1926), p. 97.

11 Nicholas Boyle, 'What Really Hapens in *Die Wahlverwandtschaften*', *German Quarterly*, LXXXIX (2016), pp. 398–412.

12 Rosemary Ashton, 'Coleridge and Faust', *Review of English Studies*, XXVIII (1977), pp. 156–67; Frederick Burwick, 'Coleridge's Critique of Goethe's *Faust*', in *Goethe's Faust and Cultural Memory: Comparatist Interfaces*, ed. Lora Fitzsimmons (Bethlehem, PA, 2012), p. 69; Frederick Burwick, *Thomas De Quincey: Knowledge and Power* (London, 2001), pp. 27f.; Walt Whitman Archive, annotations on Goethe from circa 1750, duk.00178, undated, available at http://whitmanarchive.org, accessed 16 October 2017; Julie D. Prandei, *'Dare to be Happy!' A Study of Goethe's Ethics* (Lanham, NY, 1993), p. 39.

13 Goethe, *Works*, ed. Nathan Haskell Dole (London and Boston, MA, 1901–2), vol. IX, pp. 230–32.

14 See Gertrud Herwig-Hager, 'Goethes Properz-Begegnung', in *Synusia. Festgabe für Wolfgang Schadewaldt*, ed. Hellmut Flashar and Konrad Gaiser (Pfullingen, 1965), pp. 429–52.

15 Letter from Goethe's mother to Goethe, 17 April 1807, *HA*, *Briefe an Goethe*, I, p. 468.

16 Wolfgang Frühwald, *Goethes Hochzeit* (Frankfurt, 2007).

17 Letter from Goethe to Sulpiz Boisserée, 24 June 1816, *HA*, *Briefe*, III, p. 358.

18 T. J. Reed, 'Goethe and Happiness', in *Goethe Revisited*, ed. Elizabeth M.

Wilkinson (London and New York, 1984), pp. 111–31.

19 Aristotle, *On the Art of Poetry*, trans. Ingram Bywater (Oxford, 1967), pp. 34ff.; Pierre Corneille, 'Of the Three Unities of Time, Place and Action', in *The Continental Model: Selected French Critical Essays of the Seventeenth Century in English Translation*, ed. Scott Elledge and Donald Schier (Minneapolis, MN, 1960), pp. 117–31.

20 Christoph Martin Wieland, *Werke*, ed. Fritz Martini and Hans Werner Saffert, 5 vols (Munich, 1963), vol. III, p. 474.

21 J. Michelet, *Histoire de France au Seizième Siècle: Renaissance*, 19 vols (Paris, 1833–44), vol. VII, pp. lvii–lxxxvi; Jo Tollebeek, '"Renaissance" and "Fossilization": Michelet, Burckhardt and Huizinga', *Renaissance Studies*, XV (2001), pp. 354–66.

22 Jeremy Adler, 'Modelling the Renaissance: Intertextuality and the Politics of Goethe's *Tasso*', *Publications of the English Goethe Society*, LXIII (1992–3), pp. 1–48.

23 Michelet, *Histoire de France au Seizième Siècle*, p. ii.

24 Theodore E. Mommsen, 'Petrarch's Conception of the Dark Ages', *Speculum*, XXVI (1942), pp. 226–42.

25 Raymond Klibansky, *The Continuity of the Platonic Tradition During the Middle Ages* (Munich, 1981); James Hawkins, *Plato in the Italian Renaissance* (New York, 1990); A. M. Patterson, 'Tasso and Neoplatonism: The Growth of his Epic Theory', *Studies in the Renaissance*, XVI (1971), pp. 105–33.

26 Giorgio Vasari, *Lives of the Artists: A Selection*, trans. George Bull (Harmondsworth, 1971), vol. I, pp. 325–442.

27 Thomas Carlyle, *On Heroes, Hero-worship, and the Heroic in History*, ed. David R. Sorensen and Brent E. Kinser (New Haven, CT, and London, 2013), p. 77.

28 Ibid., p. 53.

29 E. M. Wilkinson, '"Tasso – ein gesteigerter Werther" in the Light of Goethe's Principle of "Steigerung"', in *Goethe: Poet and Thinker*, ed. E. M. Wilkinson and L. A. Willoughby, (London, 1962), pp. 185–213.

30 Goethe to Chancellor von Müller, 23 March 1823, quoted FA, V, p. 1388.

31 E. M. Wilkinson. 'Torquato Tasso: The Tragedy of the Poet', in Wilkinson and Willoughby, *Goethe: Poet and Thinker*, pp. 75–94; Ilse Graham, 'A Poet's No Man's Land', in *Goethe and Lessing: The Wellsprings of Creation* (London, 1973), pp. 137–63.

32 Norbert Elias, *The Civilizing Process*, 2 vols (Oxford, 1969 and 1982).

33 On Hegel's theory of tragedy see Peter Szondi, *An Essay on the Tragic*, trans. Paul Fleming (Stanford, CA, 2002), pp. 15–22, esp. pp. 17f.

34 Sophocles, *Oedipus*, trans. Lewis Campbell, in *The Seven Verse Plays in English* (Oxford, 1906), pp. 122, 123.

35 William Shakespeare, *King Lear*, ed. Russell Fraser (New York, 1963), p. 178.

36 Owen Connelly, *The Wars of the French Revolution and Napoleon, 1792–1815* (London, 2006), pp. 18–39.

37 Voltaire, *De la paix perpetuelle* [1769], in *Ouevres complètes* (Paris, 1785), vol. XXIX, pp. 35ff.

38 Samuel Taylor Coleridge, *The Poems*, ed. Sir A. T. Quiller-Couch (London, 1930), p. 377.

39 Friedrich Schiller, *On the Aesthetic Education of Man in a Series of Letters*, ed. and trans. E. M. Wilkinson and L. A. Willoughby (Oxford, 1967).

40 Ibid., Letter VI, pp. 35, 37.

41 On Marx, see S. S. Prawer, 'What Did Marx Think of Schiller?', *German Life and Letters*, XXIX (1975), p. 123; Leonard P. Wessell, 'The Aesthetics of Living Form in Schiller and Marx', *Journal of Aesthetics and Art Criticism*, XXXVII (1978), p. 191; on Marcuse, see Herbert Marcuse, *One Dimensional Man* (New York, 1962).

42 E. M. Wilkinson and L.A. Willoughby, 'The "Whole" Man in Schiller's Theory of Culture and Society', in Wilkinson and Willoughby, *Models of Wholeness*, pp. 233–68; Joseph Addison, *The Spectator* (7 March 1710).

43 Friedrich Schiller, *On the Aesthetic Education of Man in a Series of Letters*, Letter XXVII, p. 41.

44 Hans Reiss, *Goethe's Novels* (London, 1969), pp. 68–144.

45 Friedrich Schlegel, *Philosophische Fragmente. Erste Epoche. II*, Nr. 662, in *Kritische Friedrich Schlegel Ausgabe* (Paderborn, 1958–), vol. XXIV, p. 208.

46 Roger Stephenson, *Goethe's Wisdom Literature: A Study in Aesthetic Transmutation* (Bern, 1983).

47 Celeste Friend, 'Social Contract Theory', *Internet Encyclopaedia of Philosophy*, www.iep.utm.edu/soc-cont, accessed 22 November 2017.

48 W. H. Bruford, *The German Tradition of Self-cultivation: 'Bildung' from Humboldt to Thomas Mann* (Cambridge, 1975).

49 Jean-Jacques Rousseau, *Émile* [1762], trans. Barbara Foxley (London, 1974), p. 5.

50 Jane K. Brown, *Goethe's Allegory of Identity* (Philadelphia, PA, 2014), pp. 39–42; Joel Schwarz, *The Sexual Politics of Jean-Jacques Rousseau* (Chicago, IL, 1984), p. 76.

51 George Eliot, *Selected Critical Writings*, ed. Rosemary Ashton (Oxford and New York, 1992), p. 131.

52 F. R. Leavis, *The Great Tradition* (Harmondsworth, 1962), p. 10.

53 George Mosse, *German Jews Beyond Judaism* (Bloomington, IN, 1985).

54 Thomas Hobbes, *Leviathan* [1651], Everyman (London, 1965), pp. 90ff.

55 Jean-Jacques Rousseau, *The Social Contract* [1762], trans. Maurice Cranston (Harmondsworth, 1968), pp. 49, 61.

56 T. J. Reed, *Light in Germany: Scenes from an Unknown Enlightenment* (Chicago, IL, and London, 2015), pp. 5–12.

57 Martin Swales, *The German Bildungsroman from Wieland to Hesse* (Princeton, NJ, 2015); Michael Beddow, *The Fiction of Humanity: Studies in the Bildungsroman from Wieland to Thomas Mann* (Cambridge, 1982); Thomas L. Jeffers, *Apprenticeships: The Bildungsroman from Goethe to Santayana* (London, 2004); Franco Moretti, *The Way of the World: The Bildungsroman in European Culture* (London, 1987).

58 Franco Moretti, *The Way of the World: The Bildungsroman in European Culture* (London, 1987).

6 The Intellectual Capital of the World

1 Tom Rockmore calls Jena 'the intellectual capital of Germany'. See 'Hegel', in *The World's Great Philosophers*, ed. Robert J. Arlington (Oxford, 2003), pp. 92–104; esp. p. 92. Nicholas Boyle calls it 'the most exciting place in the world'; see Nicholas Boyle, *Goethe: The Poet and the Age*, vol. II: *Revolution and Renunciation, 1790–1803* (Oxford, 2000), p. 465.

2 Hans J. Morgenthau, *Politics and Nations: The Struggle for Power and Peace* (New York, 1993), pp. 91ff.

3 On the development of Romanticism, see Susan Bernofsky, 'Infinite Imagination: Early Romanticism in Germany', in *A Companion to European Romanticism*, ed. Michael Ferber (Oxford, 2005), pp. 86–100; on the philosophy of idealism, see Frederick Beiser, *German Idealism: The Struggle against Subjectivism* (Cambridge, MA, 2002).

4   Maren Meinhardt, *A Longing for Wide and Unknown Things: The Life of Alexander von Humboldt* (London, 2018).

5   Nicholas Boyle and Liz Dirley, eds, *The Impact of Idealism: The Legacy of Post-Kantian German Thought*, 4 vols (Cambridge, 2013).

6   Friedrich Schlegel, *116th Athenaeum Fragment* (1798), trans. John Skolnik, available at http://ghdi.ghi-dc.org, accessed 18 February 2018.

7   Allen Speight, 'Friedrich Schlegel', *Stanford Encyclopaedia of Philosophy* (Winter 2016 Edition), https://plato.stanford.edu, accessed 18 February 2018.

8   Andrew Cunningham and Nicholas Jardine, eds, *Romanticism and the Sciences* (Cambridge, 1990); Robert J. Richards, *The Romantic Conception of Life: Science and Philosophy in the Age of Goethe* (Chicago, IL, 2002); E. P. Hamm, 'Romantic Life and Science', *Annals of Science*, LXII (2005), pp. 377–85; Jocelyn Holland, *German Romanticism and Science: The Procreative Poetics of Goethe, Novalis, and Ritter* (London, 2009).

9   Novalis, *Notes for a Scientific Encyclopaedia*, trans. David W. Wood (Albany, NY, 2007).

10 Wordsworth, 'Preface', *Lyrical Ballads*, p. 107.

11 Eckermann, *Conversations with Goethe*, trans. John Oxenford, 2 vols (London, 1850), vol. I, p. 149.

12 Hannah Arendt, *Rahel Varnhagen: The Life of a Jewess*, trans. Richard and Clara Winston (Baltimore, MD, 1997).

13 David Veit to Rahel Varnhagen, in *Rahel Varnhagen im Umgang mit ihren Freunden (Briefe 1795–1833)*, ed. Friedhelm Kemp (Munich, 1967), p. 12.

14 *Rahel Varnhagen im Umgang mit ihren Freunden*, pp. 58–60.

15 Judith E. Martin, *Germaine de Staël in Germany: Gender and Literary Authority, 1800–1850* (Plymouth, 2011), pp. 62f.

16 Madame de Staël, *De L'Allemagne*, English edn, 3 vols (London, 1913), vol. I, pp. 265f.

17 Dennis L. Sepper, *Goethe Contra Newton: Polemics and the Project for a New Science of Color* (Cambridge, 1988).

18 Boyle, *Goethe: The Poet and the Age*, vol. II, p. 102.

19 Rudolf Magnus, *Goethe as Scientist*, trans. Heinz Norden (New York, 1961), pp. 100ff.

20 Jeffrey Barnouw, 'Goethe and Helmholtz: Science and Sensation', in *Goethe and the Sciences: A Reappraisal*, ed. Frederick Amrine et al. (Dordrecht, 1987), p. 46.

21 Albrecht Schöne, *Goethes Farbentheologie* (Munich, 1983).

22 Wilhelm Dilthey, *Der Aufbau der geschichtlichen Welt in den Wissenschaften*, ed. Manfred Riedel (Frankfurt am Main, 1981), pp. 89–232.

23 Joseph Agassi, *Towards an Historiography of Science* (The Hague, 1963); Imre Lakatos, ed., *Criticism and the Growth of Knowledge* (Cambridge, 1970). For other views see Robert K. Merton, *The Sociology of Science: Theoretical and Empirical Investigations* (Chicago, IL, 1973); Alexander Bird, *The Philosophy of Science* (London, 1990), pp. 261f.; Nancy Cartwright, *The Dappled World* (Cambridge, 2001); James Bogen, 'Empiricism and After', in Paul Humphreys, ed., *The Oxford Handbook of the Philosophy of Science* (Oxford, 2015), pp. 780–93.

24 Alexandre Koyré, *The Astronomical Revolution Copernicus – Kepler – Borelli* (Paris, 1973), pp. 18–116; J. V. Field, *Kepler's Geometrical Cosmology* (London, 1988); Edward Slowik, 'Descartes' Physics', in *The Stanford Encyclopedia of Philosophy*, ed. Edward N. Zalta, Fall 2017 edition, https://plato.stanford.edu, accessed 23 May 2019; Betty Jo Teeter Dobbs, *The Foundations of Newton's Alchemy* (Cambridge, 1983).

25 Alexandre Koyré, *Newtonian Studies* (London, 1965), pp. 139–63.

26 Eric Schliesser, 'Hume's Newtonianism and Anti-Newtonianism', *The Stanford Encyclopedia of Philosophy*, ed. Edward N. Zalta, Winter 2008, https://plato.stanford.edu, accessed 23 May 2019.

27 James Gleick, *Chaos: Making a New Science* (Harmondsworth, 1988), p. 197.

28 Ludwig Wittgenstein, *Remarks on Colour*, ed. G.E.M. Anscombe (Oxford, 1977), pp. 11–11e.

29 Sir Isaac Newton, *Opticks; or, A Treatise of the Reflections, Refractions, Inflections and Colours of Light*, Based on the Fourth Edition London, 1930, with a Foreword by Albert Einstein (New York, 1952), p. 1; Goethe, *Beyträge zur Optik* [1791] (Hildesheim, 1964), p. 1.

30 Denis L. Sepper, 'Goethe Against Newton: Towards Saving the Phenomena', in *Goethe and the Sciences*, p. 175.

31 Ibid., p. 177.

32 Stanley Plumly, *The Immortal Evening: A Legendary Dinner with Keats, Wordsworth, and Lamb* (New York, 2016); Alexander P. D. Penrose, ed., *The Autobiography and Memoirs of Benjamin Robert Haydon, 1786–1846: Compiled from his 'Autobiography and Journals' and 'Correspondence and Table-talk'* (New York, 1926), p. 231.

33 Goethe, *Theory of Colours*, trans. Charles Locke Eastlake (Cambridge, MA, 1982), pp. 130–51.

34 Werner Heisenberg, 'Goethe and Modern Science', in *Goethe and the Sciences*, pp. 115–32.

35 Arthur O. Lovejoy, *The Great Chain of Being: A Study of the History of an Idea* (New York, 1960), pp. 61–6.

36 Doron Schultzinger, 'A Jewish Conception of Human Dignity: Philosophy and its Ethical Implications for Israeli Supreme Court Decisions', *Journal of Religious Ethics*, XXXIV (2006), pp. 667f.

37 Wolf Lepenies, *The Seduction of Culture in German History* (Princeton, NJ, 2006).

38 For Goethe on Kant, see his *Campagne in Frankreich 1792*, WA, XXXIII, p. 196; on Schelling, see Jeremy Adler, 'The Aesthetics of Magnetism: Science, Philosophy and Poetry in the Dialogue Between Goethe and Schelling', in *The Third Culture: Literature and Science*, ed. E. S. Shaffer (Berlin and New York, 1998), pp.75f.

39 William Gilbert, *On the Loadstone*, trans. T. F. Mottelay (Baltimore, MD, 1941); Alexandre Koyré, *Galileo Studies*, trans. John Mepham (Tonbridge, 1978), pp. 187f.; Rod Noel Malcolm, 'Hobbes's Science of Politics and his Theory of Science', in *Aspects of Hobbes* (New York, 2002), pp. 146–55.

40 Gilbert, *On the Loadstone*, pp. 107, 190.

41 Newton, *Opticks*, Query 30, p. 374.

42 Ibid., Query 31, pp. 389, 397.

43 I here follow Eric Schliesser, 'Hume's Newtonianism and Anti-Newtonianism', *Stanford Encylopaedia of Philosophy* (2008), https://plato.stanford.edu, accessed 6 February 2018.

44 Isaiah Berlin, 'Hume and the Sources of German Anti-rationalism', in *Against the Current: Essays in the History of Ideas*, ed. Henry Hardy (Princeton, NJ, 2013), pp. 204–35.

45 David Hume, *A Treatise of Human Nature*, ed. D. F. Norton and M. J. Norton (Oxford, 2000), para 1.2.5.25.

46 Ibid., para 1.2.5.26n.12.

47 Schliesser, 'Hume's Newtonianism and Anti-Newtonianism', para 3.

48 E. A. Burtt, *The Metaphysical Foundations of Modern Physical Science* (London, 1932); A. N. Whitehead, *Science and the Modern World* (London, 1925); Ernst Cassirer, *The Philosophy of Symbolic Forms*, trans. Ralph Manheim, 2 vols (New Haven, CT, 1955).

49 Gleick, *Chaos*, pp. 163–5, 197. Gleick tells me that this information is based on an interview with Feigenbaum; personal communication, 16 December 2017.

50 Edwin H. Land, 'Experiments in Color Vision', *Scientific American*, CC (1959), pp. 286–98.

51 Ibid., p. 289.

52 Ibid., p. 298.

53 Neil Ribe and Friedrich Steinle, 'Exploratory Experimentation: Goethe, Land, and Colour Theory', *Physics Today*, LV/7 (2002), pp. 43–9; Dennis Sepper notes the parallel to Land, but without recognizing its significance, in Sepper, *Goethe contra Newton*, pp. 14–15.

54 Will David, 'You Won't Look Back', The London Library Blog, 29 June 2012, www.londonlibrary.co.uk, accessed 13 February 2018.

55 Arthur Schopenhauer, *Ueber das Sehen und die Farbe* (Leipzig, 1854).

56 Wittgenstein, *Remarks on Colour*, pp. 28e, 33e, 45e, 33e, 42e, 47e.

57 M. W. Rowe, 'Goethe and Wittgenstein', *Philosophy*, LXVI (1991), pp. 283–303.

58 F.W.J. Schelling, *Von der Weltseele* [1798], in *Sämmtliche Werke*, ed. K.F.A. Schelling (Stuttgart, 1857), Part I, vol. II, pp. [345]–583.

59 Patrick J. Boner, *Kepler's Cosmological Synthesis: Astrology, Mechanism and the Soul* (Leiden, 2013).

7 The Faustian Age

1 Dr Eckartt Ullrich, 'Franz Grillparzer besucht Goethe in Weimar', www.eckhard-ullrich.de, accessed 27 May 2019.

2 Goethe to Chancellor von Müller, 29 December 1825, in *Goethes Unterhaltungen mit dem Kanzler Friedrich von Müller*, ed. C.A.H. Burckhardt (Paderborn, 2015), p. 104.

3 There is a nice summary of Goethe's career by Dieter Borchmeyer online at *Goethezeitportal*, www.goethezeitportal.de, accessed 2 November 2018.

4 Hannah Arendt, *Rahel Varnhagen: The Life of a Jewess*, trans. Richard and Clara Winston (Baltimore, MD, 1997).

5 Hans J. Morgenthau, *Politics Among Nations: The Struggle for Power and Peace* (New York, 1993), pp. 91ff.

6 Friedrich Nietzsche, 'The Wanderer and his Shadow', in *Human, All Too Human: A Book for Free Spirits*, trans. R. J. Hollingdale (Cambridge, 1986), p. 336.

7 Hayden White, *Metahistory: The Historical Imagination in Nineteenth-century Europe* (Baltimore, MD, 1972), pp. 73–4.

8 Ibid., p. 73.

9 Katharina Mommsen, ed., *Die Entstehung von Goethes Werken*, vol. V: *Fastnachtspiel – Faust* (Berlin, 2017).

10 Swane L. Hardy, *Goethe, Calderon und die romantische Theorie des Dramas* (Heidelberg, 1965).

11 Eudo C. Mason, *Goethe's Faust: Its Genesis and Purport* (Berkeley, CA, 1967), p. 59.

12 Mikhail Bakhtin, *Rabelais and his World*, trans. Hélène Iswolsky (Bloomington, IN, 1965), pp. 244–56.

13 Christopher Marlowe, *Doctor Faustus*, ed. Roma Gill (London, 1963), p. 9, l. 78; *The Historie of the Damnable Life and Deserved Death of Doctor Iohn Faustus*, in *The Sources of the Faust Tradition*, ed. P. M. Palmer and R. P. More (New York, 1966), p. 137.

14 Susanne Kord, *Murderesses in German Writing, 1720–1860: Heroines of Horror* (Cambridge, 2009).

15 Michel Foucault, ed., *Moi, Pierre Rivière, ayant égorgé ma mère, ma soeur et mon frère . . . Un cas de parricide au XIXe siècle* (Paris, 2007).

16 Kord, *Murderesses in German Writing*, p. 139.

17 Ruth Benedict, *The Chrysanthemum and the Sword: Patterns of Japanese Culture* (New York, 1946).

18 Kord, *Murderesses in German Writing*, p. 122.

19 Mommsen, *Die Entstehung von Goethes Werken*, p. 107.

20 Goethe to Knebel, 21 November 1782, *HA, Briefe*, I, p. 416.

21 Goethe to Eckermann, 14 March 1830, *CE*, p. 456.

22 Rüdiger Scholz, *Das kurze Leben der Johanna Catharina Höhn* (Würzburg, 2004), pp. 27ff.

23 Volker Wahl, ed., *Das Kind in meinem Leib* (Vienna, 2004), p. 93.

24 Ibid., p. 345.

25 John H. Hayes and Carl A. Holladay, *Biblical Exegesis: A Beginner's Handbook*, 3rd edn (Louisville, KY, and London, 2007), p. 43.

26 Martha Nussbaum, *Poetic Justice: The Literary Imagination and Public Life* (Boston, MA, 1995), pp. 79–121.

27 T. J. Reed, 'Der Behauste Mensch: On Being at Home in the Universe. Kant, Goethe, and Others', *Publications of the English Goethe Society*, LXXXIII (2014), p. 137f.

28 'A Meeting of Genius: Beethoven and Goethe, July 1812', available at www.gramophone.co.uk, accessed 22 February 2018; Scott Godard, 'Beethoven and Goethe', *Music and Letters*, VIII (1927), pp. 165–71.

29 Goethe to Zelter, 2 September 1812, *HA*, Briefe, III, p. 200; Beethoven to his publisher Härtel, 9 November 1812, available at www.zeit. de/2012/28/Beethoven-Goethe/seite-3, accessed 2 November 2018.

30 Roger H. Stephenson, *Goethe's Wisdom Literature: A Study in Aesthetic Transmutation* (Bern, 1983).

31 H.L.A. Hart. *The Concept of Law*, 2nd edn (Oxford, 1997), pp. 203–4.

32 Goethe to Jacobi, 13 January 1813, *HA*, Briefe, III, p. 220.

33 Alexandre Koyré, *From the Closed World to the Infinite Universe* (Baltimore, MD, 1957), p. 42.

34 Blaise Pascal, *Pensées*, in *Oeuvres complètes*, ed., Michel Le Guern (Paris, 2000), vol. II, p. 615.

35 Hans Blumenberg, *Paradigms for a Metaphorology*, trans. Robert Savage (Ithaca, NY, 2010), p. 29.

36 Martin Schonfeld, 'Kant's Early Cosmology', in *A Companion to Kant*, ed. Graham Bird (Oxford, 2006), p. 55; Helghe Krag, 'Big Bang Cosmology', in *Cosmology*, ed. N. S. Hetherington (New York, 1993), pp. 371–89.

37 Maurice Benn, 'Goethe and T. S. Eliot', *German Life and Letters*, V (1952), pp. 151–61.

38 Astrida Orle Tantillo, *Goethe's Elective Affinities and the Critics* (Rochester, NY, 2001), p. 47.

39 Heinz Härtl, *Die Wahlverwandtschaften. Eine Dokumentation der Wirkung von Goethes Roman 1808–1832* (Berlin, 1983).

40 Jeremy Adler, 'Goethe's Use of Chemical Theory in his *Elective Affinities*', in *Romanticism and the Sciences*, ed. Andrew Cunningham and Nicholas Jardine (Cambridge, 1990), pp. 263–79.

41 P. Casini, 'Newton's Principia and the Philosophy of the Enlightenment', *Notes and Records of the Royal Society of London*, XLII (1988), pp. 45f.

42 E. J. Dijksterhuis, *The Mechanization of the World Picture*, trans. C. Dikshoorn (Oxford, 1961).

43 H. B. Nisbet, *Goethe and the Scientific Tradition* (London, 1972), p. 69.

44 Nicholas Boyle, 'What Really Happens in *Die Wahlverwandtschaften*', *Germanic Quarterly*, LXXXIX/3 (2016), pp. 298–312. See pp. 307–11.

45 H. G. Barnes, 'Ambiguity in *Die Wahlverwandtschaften*', in *The Era of Goethe: Studies Presented to James Boyd* (Oxford, 1956), pp. 1–16.

46 F.W.J. Schelling, *Ideen*, in *Werke*, vol. I: *Zur Naturphilosophie*, ed. Manfred Schröter (Munich, 1962), p. 706.

47 Andrew Bowie, 'Freidrich Wilhelm Joseph von Schelling', *Stanford Encyclopedia of Philosophy*, https://plato.stanford.edu, accessed 28 September 2018.

48 Martin Swales and Erika Swales, *Reading Goethe: A Critical Introduction to the Literary Work* (Rochester, NY, 2002), p. 76.

49 Michel Löwy, 'Le concept d'affinité elective chez Max Weber', *Archives de sciences sociales des religions*, XLIX (2004), pp. 93–103; Richard Herbert Howe, 'Max Weber's Elective Affinities: Sociology Within the Bounds of Pure Reason', *American Journal of Sociology*, LXXXIV (1978), pp. 366–85.

50 Rosemary Ashton, *Four English Writers and their Reception of German Thought, 1800–1860* (Cambridge, 1980), pp. 155–77; E. S. Shaffer, 'George Eliot and Goethe: "Hearing the Grass Grow"', *Publications of the English Goethe Society*, LXVI (1996), pp. 3–22.

51 Jeremy Adler, '"A Vast Intellectual Fusion . . . of the Various National Tendencies": Goethe and Henry James', *Publications of the English Goethe Society*, LXXXIII (2014), pp. 53–72.

52 Hans Reiss, *Goethe's Novels* (London, 1969), p. 200.

53 A. C. Bradley, *Shakespearean Tragedy: Lectures on Hamlet, Othello, King Lear, Macbeth* (London, 1905), p. 23.

54 Maurice Crosland, 'Lavoisier, the Two French Revolutions and "The Imperial Despotism of Oxygen"', *Ambix*, XLII (1955), pp. 101–18.

55 Goethe to Uwarow, 18 May 1818, available at www.zeno.org, accessed 2 November 2018.

56 John Pizer, 'Goethe's "World Literature" Paradigm and Contemporary Globalization', *Comparative Literature*, LII (2000), pp. 213–27.

57 Émile Durkheim, *The Rules of Sociological Method and Selected Texts on Sociology and its Method*, ed. Steven Lukes and trans. W. D. Halls (London, 1982), pp. 191–2; Maurice Halbwachs, *Morphologie Sociale* (Paris, 1938), pp. 7–18.

58 Katharina Mommsen, *Goethe and the Poets of Arabia*, trans. Michael M. Metzger (Rochester, NY, 2014).

59 Navid Kermani, *Zwischen Kafka und Koran. West-östliche Erkundungen* (Munich, 2016).

60 Fiona MacCarthy, *William Morris: A Life for Our Time* (London, 1994), p. 236.

61 Georg Simmel, *Soziologie* (Leipzig and Munich, 1923).

62 Ibid., p. 311.

63 Max Wundt, *Goethes Wilhelm Meister und die Entstehung des modernen Lebensideals* (Leipzig, 1932), pp. 367–89.

64 Karl Polanyi, *The Great Transformation: The Political and Economic Origins of our Time* (Boston, MA, 2001), p. 39.

65 Brian Bailey, *The Luddite Rebellion* (Thrup, 1998), p. 143.

66 Polanyi, *The Great Transformation*, pp. xxiiif.

67 Spencer J. Pack, *Capitalism as a Moral System: Adam Smith's Critique of the Free Market Economy* (Aldershot, 1991), p. 166.

68 Robert Owen, 'Observations on the Effects of the Manufacturing System', in *A New View of Society and Other Writings* (London, 1927), p. 124.

69 Wolf Lepenies, *The Seduction of Culture in German History* (Princeton, NJ 2006), p. 205.

70 Robert Moore, 'Capital', in *Pierre Bourdieu: Key Concepts*, ed. Michael Grenfell (Durham, 2008), pp. 101–17.

71 Karl Marx, *Capital: A Critique of Political Economy*, trans. Ben Fowkes, 3 vols (London, 1976), vol. I, p. 391; Wundt, *Goethes Wilhelm Meister*, pp. 389–401.

72 Herbert Spencer, *Principles of Sociology* [1876–96], ed. Stanislav Andreski (London, 1969), pp. 136–45.

73 Klaus L. Berghahn and Jost Hermand, ed., *Goethe in German-Jewish Culture* (Rochester, NY, 2001).

74 W. Daniel Wilson, 'Goethe's Distaste for Jewish Emancipation', ibid., pp. 152f.

75 Raymond Murphy, *Social Closure: The Theory of Monopolization and Exclusion* (Oxford, 1988), pp. 3–4, 8–14.

76 See Hans-Christian Jasch (with a contribution by Rüdiger Ernst), 'Die Rassengesetzgebung im Dritten Reich', in *Die Nürnberger Gesetze – 80 Jahre danach. Vorgeschichte – Entstehung – Auswirkungen*, ed. Magnus Brechtkhen et al. (Göttingen, 2017), pp. 165–204.

77 Peter Pulzer, *The Rise of Political Anti-Semitism in Germany and Austria*, revd edn (London, 1988), p. 54.

78 Hannah Arendt-Stern and Haun Saussy, 'Rahel Varnhagen and Goethe', *Critical Inquiry*, XL (2013), pp. 15–24.

79 Astrid Seele, *Frauen um Goethe* (Reinbek bei Hamburg, 2000), p. 148.

80 Ibid., p. 149f.

81 Norbert Miller, *Die ungeheure Gewalt der Musik: Goethe und seine Komponisten* (Munich, 2009), p. 11.

82 Polanyi, *The Great Transformation*, p. 195.

83 Heinz Schlaffer, *Faust Zweiter Teil. Die Allegorie des 19. Jahrhunderts* (Stuttgart, 1981), pp. 79ff.

84 Georg Simmel, *Philosophie des Geldes* (Munich and Leipzig, 1920), p. 490.

85 Max Weber, *Economy and Society: A Study in Interpretative Sociology*, trans. Guenther Roth and Claus Wittich, 2 vols (Berkeley, CA, 1978), vol. I, pp. 166–73.

86 Karl Marx, 'The Power of Money' (1844), available at www.marxists. org/archive/marx, accessed 20 February 2018.

87 Marx, *Capital*, vol. I, pp. 198ff.

88 Georg Simmel, *Philosophie des Geldes* (Munich and Leipzig, 1920), p. 93.

89 Marx, *Capital*, vol. I, p. 205; Anne Bohnenkamp-Renken, '"Der Zettel ist tausend Kronen Wert". Zur Papiergeldszene in Goethes Faust', *Forschung Frankfurt*, II (2012), pp. 106–9.

90 Polanyi, *The Great Transformation*, p. 25; Adam Smith, *An Inquiry into the Nature and Causes of the Wealth of Nations* (Ware, 2012), pp. 34–58.

91 Patricia H. Werhane, *Adam Smith and His Legacy for Modern Capitalism* (Oxford, 1991).

92 Maria Pia Paganelli, 'Vanity and the Daedalian Wings of Paper Money in Adam Smith', in *New Voices on Adam Smith*, ed. L. Montes and E. Schliesser (London, 2006), p. 273; Andrew S. Skinner, 'Hume's Principles of Political Economy', in *The Cambridge Companion to Hume*, ed. David Norton Fate and Jacqueline Taylor, 2nd edn (Cambridge, 2009), p. 407.

93 Simmel, *Philosophie des Geldes*, pp. 13–29.

94 Friedrich Schelling, *Philosophie der Mythologie, Werke*, part II, volume II (Stuttgart and Augsburg, 1857), pp. 142, 152 and 154.

95 Osman Durrani, *Faust: Icon of Modern Culture* (London, 2004), pp. 164–6; Oswald Spengler, *The Decline of the West: Form and Actuality*, trans. C. F. Atkinson, 2 vols (New York, 1916), vol. I, pp. 375ff.

96 Peter J. Ramberg, 'The Death of Vitalism and the Birth of Organic Chemistry: Wöhler's Urea Synthesis and the Disciplinary Identity of Modern Chemistry', *Ambix*, XLVII (2000), pp. 170–95.

97 Hans Gerhard Gräf, 'Goethe und Schweden. Ein Versuch', in *Goethe. Skizzen zu des Dichters Leben und Werken* (Leipzig, 1924), p. 65.

98 Ramberg, 'The Death of Vitalism and the Birth of Organic Chemistry', p. 172.

99 Friedrich Wöhler, 'On the Artificial Production of Urea', in *The Origins and Growth of Physical Science*, ed. D. L. Hurd and J. J. Kipling, 2 vols (Harmondsworth, 1964), vol. II, p. 108.

100 J. M. van der Laan, *Seeking Meaning for Goethe's Faust* (London, 2007), p. 120.

101 Swales and Swales, *Reading Goethe*, p. 146.

102 T. J. Reed, *Goethe* (Oxford, 1984), p. 78.

103 'Mühe', *Grimms Worterbuch*, 33 vols (1854–1961), http://woerterbuchnetz.de, accessed 26 May 2019.

104 Marx, *Capital*, vol. I, p. 284.

105 Leibniz, *Die Theodicee*, trans. Artur Buchenau (Leipzig, 1925), III, paragraph 344, p. 357.

106 Georg Simmel, *Goethe* (Leipzig, 1920), pp. 165–9.

107 Durrani, *Faust, passim*.

Select Bibliography

Translations

The most useful resource to find versions of an individual work, whether a poem, play, novel or other writings, is Derek Glass, *Goethe in English: A Bibliography of the Translations in the Twentieth Century* (London, 2005). The best available English edition is that listed under 'Abbreviations'. What follows is a selection of some fine texts of individual works and two generous collections.

Colour Theory, ed. Rupprecht Matthaei, trans. Herb Aach (London, 1971)

Conversations of Goethe, trans. John Oxenford (London, 1898; New York, 1998)

Elective Affinities, trans. David Constantine (Oxford, 1994)

Elective Affinities, trans. R. J. Hollingdale (Harmondsworth, 1971)

Erotic Verse, trans. David Luke (Oxford, 1998)

The Essential Goethe, ed. Matthew Bell (Princeton, NJ, 2016)

Faust, trans. David Constantine (London, 2005 and 2009)

Faust, trans. David Luke (Oxford, 1987 and 1998)

Faust: A Tragedy In Two Parts and The Urfaust, trans. John Williams (London, 2007)

Goethe on Art, ed. John Gage (Berkeley, CA, 1980)

'Goethe's Botany: The Metamorphosis of Plants' [1790], trans. Agnes Arber, *Chronica Botanica*, x/2 (1946)

Italian Journey, trans. W. H. Auden and Elizabeth Mayer (Harmondsworth, 1970)

Maxims and Reflections, trans. Elizabeth Stopp (London, 1998)

The Metamorphosis of Plants, ed. Gordon L. Miller, trans. Douglas Miller (Cambridge, MA, 2009)

Poems of the West and the East, trans. John Whaley (Oxford, 1998)

Selected Poems, trans. John Whaley (London, 1998)
Selected Verse, trans. David Luke (London, 1981)
Selected Works, ed. Nicholas Boyle (London, 2000)
Theory of Colours, trans. Charles Lock Eastlake (New York, 2006)
The Sorrows of Young Werther, trans. David Constantine (Oxford, 2012)
The Sorrows of Young Werther, trans. Michael Hulse (London, 1989)
West-Eastern Divan, trans. Martin Bidney (Binghampton, 2010)
Wilhelm Meister [parts I and II], trans. H. M. Waidson (Richmond, n.d.)

Biographies

Boyle, Nicholas, *Goethe: The Poet and the Age*, vol. I: *The Poetry of Desire,
    1749–1790*; vol. II, *Revolution and Renunciation, 1790–1803* (Oxford,
    1991–2000)
Friedenthal, Richard, *Goethe: His Life and Times* (London, 1965)
Lewes, G. H., *The Life and Works of Goethe* [1875] (London, 1949)
Safranski, Rüdiger, *Goethe: Life as a Work of Art*, trans. David Dollenmayer
    (New York, 2017)
Williams, John R., *The Life of Goethe: A Critical Biography* (Oxford, 1998)

Selected Criticism

Amrine, Frederick, et al., eds, *Goethe and the Sciences: A Reappraisal*
    (Dordrecht, 1987)
Bell, Matthew, *Goethe's Naturalistic Anthropology: Man and Other Plants*
    (Oxford, 1994)
Bishop, Paul, ed., *A Companion to Goethe's Faust: Parts I and II* (Rochester,
    NY, 2001)
Blackall, Eric, *Goethe and the Novel* (Ithaca, NY, and New York, 1976)
Bruford, W. H., *Culture and Society in Classical Weimar, 1775–1806*
    (Cambridge, 1962)
Durrani, Osman, *Faust: Icon of Modern Culture* (London, 2004)
Fairley, Barker, *Goethe as Revealed in his Poetry* (London, 1932)
—, *A Study of Goethe* (Oxford, 1950)
Graham, Ilse, *Goethe, Portrait of the Artist* (Berlin and New York, 1977)

Magnus, Rudolf, *Goethe as a Scientist*, trans. Heinz Norden (New York, 1961)

Mason, Eudo C., *Goethe's Faust: Its Genesis and Purport* (Berkeley, CA, 1967)

Nisbet, H. B., *Goethe and the Scientific Tradition* (London, 1972)

Peacock, Ronald, *Goethe's Major Plays* (Manchester, 1959)

Reed, T. J., *The Classical Centre: Goethe's Weimar, 1775–1832* (Oxford, 1986)

—, *Goethe*, Past Masters (Oxford, 1984)

Reiss, Hans, *Goethe's Novels* (London, 1969)

Robertson, Ritchie, *Goethe: A Very Short Introduction* (Oxford, 2016)

Sharpe, Lesley, ed., *The Cambridge Companion to Goethe* (Cambridge, 2002)

Stephenson, Roger, *Goethe's Conception and Knowledge of Science*
    (Edinburgh, 1995)

Swales, Martin, *Goethe: The Sorrows of Young Werther* (Cambridge, 1987)

—, and Erika Swales, *Reading Goethe: A Critical Introduction to the Literary
    Work* (Rochester, NY, 2002)

Wagner, Irmgard, *Critical Approaches to Goethe's Classical Dramas: Iphgenie,
    Torquato Tasso, and Die Natürliche Tochter* (Columbia, NY, 1995)

Wilkinson, E. M., and L. A. Willoughby, *Goethe, Poet and Thinker*
    (London, 1962)

Williams, John R., *Goethe's Faust* (London, 1987)

Acknowledgements

This book is the result of a lifetime's preoccupation. I have incurred many debts. To the late Claus Victor Bock, who always harboured the intention to produce a major Goethe study, I owe my first introduction to Goethe scholarship. The late Elizabeth Mary Wilkinson, the doyenne of British Goethe scholars, taught me to understand the power of Goethe's ideas. Jim Reed has been a constant companion: like no other, he is a guide to Goethe's joy. Martin Swales, likewise a long-standing friend, has helped me grapple with Goethe as a writer. And I particularly treasure my friendship with Nicholas Boyle, greatest of all Goethe biographers. My special thanks are due to Joachim Whaley, the historian of the Holy Roman Empire, for his kind permission to quote liberally from his late father's versions of Goethe's poems: it is a privilege to be able to print at such length from John Whaley's superlative translations. A warm word of gratitude also goes to Katharina Mommsen and Werner Keller for their encouragement. My dear friend, the late Dorothea Hölscher-Lohmeyer, offered an example of what scholarship can achieve. A group of scholars who attended the first British conference on science and literature in Edinburgh around 1970, including the late Roy Porter, worked jointly on a methodology that links science, criticism and intellectual history. This created the interdisciplinary frame for my work. I have also profited greatly from my colleagues in the English Goethe Society (UK) and the International Goethe Society (Weimar). I thank James Gleick for responding to my questions about Goethe and chaos theory. For their thoughts on the current state of the history and philosophy of science I am grateful to my long-standing colleagues David Papineau and Myles Jackson. For various pieces of assistance and advice I am grateful to my colleagues Matthew Bell, Anne Bohnenkamp-Renken, Angus Nicholls and W. Daniel Wilson. In the writing of this book, I have relied heavily on the two finest editions of our time: the *Frankfurter Ausgabe* and the *Münchener Ausgabe*. I also wish to acknowledge my debt to the *Goethe Handbuch* (1996–8); this work marks the gold standard and has always been my first port of call. Everyone at Reaktion Books has been unfailingly helpful throughout the production of this book: Michael Leaman, the publisher, who has been a model of encouragement; Aimee Selby, who corrected my text with an eagle eye; Amy Salter, who unfailingly edited the manuscript; and Susannah Jayes, who generously sourced the illustrations. Finally, I extend my particular thanks to the librarians of the London Library for their constant support and for making so many essential texts available.

Photo Acknowledgements

The author and the publishers wish to thanks to the below sources of illustrative material and/or permission to reproduce it:

Alamy: pp. 52 (Chronicle), 71 (Granger Historical Picture Archive), 161, 194, 209 (The Picture Art Collection), 191 (Lebrecht Music & Arts); © DACS 2019: p. 214; Getty Images: p. 122 (ullstein bild); Science Photo Library: p. 180 (Royal Astronomical Society).